Social History of Africa

GENDERS AND GENERATIONS APART

GENDERS AND GENERATIONS APART

LABOR TENANTS AND CUSTOMARY LAW IN SEGREGATION-ERA SOUTH AFRICA, 1920s TO 1940s

Thomas V. McClendon

HEINEMANN
Portsmouth, NH

JAMES CURREY
Oxford

DAVID PHILIP
Cape Town

Heinemann
A division of Reed Elsevier Inc.
361 Hanover Street
Portsmouth, NH 03801-3912
USA
www.heinemann.com

James Currey Ltd.
73 Botley Road
Oxford OX2 0BS
United Kingdom

David Philip Publishers (Pty) Ltd.
208 Werdmuller Centre
Claremont 7708
Cape Town, South Africa

Offices and agents throughout the world

ISBN 0–325–07088–1 (Heinemann cloth)
ISBN 0–325–07110–1 (Heinemann paper)
ISBN 0–85255–956–9 (James Currey cloth)
ISBN 0–85255–955–0 (James Currey paper)

British Library Cataloguing in Publication Data

McClendon, Thomas V.
  Genders and generations apart : labor tenants and customary law in segregation-era South Africa, 1920s to 1940s—(Social history of Africa)
  1. Agricultural laborers—Legal status, laws, etc.—South Africa—Kwazulu Natal—History—20th century 2. Land tenure—Law and legislation—South Africa—Kwazulu Natal—History—20th century 3. Customary law—South Africa—Kwazulu Natal—History—20th century 4. South Africa—Politics and government—1909–1948
  I. Title
  333.3'3553'09684'09041

ISBN 0–85255–956–9 (James Currey cloth)
ISBN 0–85255–955–0 (James Currey paper)

Library of Congress Cataloging-in-Publication Data

McClendon, Thomas V., 1954–.
  Genders and generations apart : labor tenants and customary law in segregation-era South Africa, 1920s to 1940s / Thomas V. McClendon.
    p. cm.—(Social history of Africa, ISSN 1099–8098)
  Includes bibliographical references and index.
  ISBN 0–325–07088–1 (alk. paper)—ISBN 0–325–07110–1 (pbk. : alk. paper)
  1. Agricultural laborers—Legal status, laws, etc.—South Africa—KwaZulu-Natal—History—20th century. 2. Land tenure—Law and legislation—South Africa—KwaZulu-Natal—History—20th century. 3. Customary law—South Africa—KwaZulu-Natal—History—20th century. 4. South Africa—Politics and government—1909–1948. I. Title. II. Series.
  KTL6531.6.A37 M39 2002
  333.33'553'0968409041—dc21   2002017331

Paperback cover photo: Married woman, wearing *ibhayi*, weaving *icansi*, seated in front of traditional-style grass hut. (Photograph by L. Accutt. Supplied and reproduced by kind permission of the Campbell Collections of the University of Natal [D10.067].)

Printed in the United States of America on acid-free paper.

06 05 04 03 02 SB 1 2 3 4 5 6 7 8 9

Copyright Acknowledgments

The author and publisher gratefully acknowledge permission to reprint the following material:

Excerpts from Thomas McClendon, "Tradition and Domestic Struggle in the Courtroom: Customary Law and the Control of Women in Segregation-Era Natal," *International Journal of African Historical Studies* 28, 3 (1995): 527–61 are reprinted by permission of the editors.

Excerpts from Thomas McClendon, "A Dangerous Doctrine: Twins, Ethnography, and Inheritance in Colonial Africa," *Journal of Legal Pluralism* 39 (1997): 121–40 are reprinted by permission of the editor-in-chief.

To the memory of my father,
James W. McClendon, Jr.,
who taught me to write.

CONTENTS

ILLUSTRATIONS

MAPS

PHOTOGRAPHS

FIGURES

TABLE

PREFACE

As I sit in the comfort of my friends' house on the outskirts of Pietermaritzburg on a warm winter's day, the landscape of apartheid stretches before me. Looking down and southward from suburban heights, I see first the lushness of a KwaZulu-Natal garden. Beyond it, my eyes follow the slopes down through the forest plantations that ring the northern edge of the city. Next, I notice a small pocket of middle- and lower-middle-class suburbia near the city center (itself obscured by a hill), formerly a white "group area," now gaining black residents. Just over the ridge from that relatively comfortable pocket lie the densely packed "township" (black suburb) areas in the Edendale valley. That area is one of many sites in this province of a decade-long war in the late 1980s and early 1990s involving a complex mix of struggles over political allegiance, culture, gender, generation, wages, and state repression.

Edendale has deeper layers of history, as well, although these are less visible than the bands I am describing. After centuries of settlement by African cultivators and herders, a Dutch-speaking emigrant from the Cape Colony (Andries Pretorius, for whom Pretoria is named) staked out Edendale valley as his farm in the late 1830s. The 1843 British annexation of the nascent trekker republic, south of the heartland of the Zulu kingdom, sparked his renewed trek to the north. Later, the area was the site of a mission reserve settlement, initiated by Methodist missionary James Allison and his Swazi congregants. The mission spawned a successful community of westernized African peasants and professionals who rose on the tide of Victorian liberalism, many of whose descendants were left high and dry by the development of segregation, the precursor of apartheid, at the turn of the twentieth

century. Under apartheid, the Edendale valley came from midcentury
to house the remnants of the black professional classes as well as a
burgeoning population of working-class Africans. The new residents
were refugees from the overcrowded rural reserves and mechanizing
white farmlands, hoping for a job or some kind of living in the provincial capital, small city, and farming supply and market center that
nearby Pietermaritzburg had become.

The haze generated by the dust of South Africa's dry winter and a Berg
wind coming off the Drakensberg mountains, combined with the smoke
from thousands of township stoves and fires, obscures the view beyond
Edendale. Nevertheless, I see the outlines of the peri-urban areas formerly
consigned to the KwaZulu "homeland" under apartheid, and beyond them
white farms, the former homes of many township residents or their fore-
bears, stretching into the distance. The intrafamilial struggles of farm tenants, in the context of industrialization and the state's attempt to control
the resultant social forces through a policy of traditionalism, form the
main subject of this book.

My current visit to South Africa shows apartheid's traces in a mul-
titude of other ways, related to differential access to wealth and power
in the new South Africa. South Africa's political settlement, cemented
by a new Constitution in 1996 and the overwhelming victory of the
African National Congress (ANC) in the country's second democratic
election in 1999, generates a new sense of optimism and pride here.
However, the past refuses to depart. Tomorrow a handyman and gardener will arrive early at my friends' house, both from over the hill in
Edendale valley. One is an aspiring young athlete who bicycles the
eight uphill miles to work and recently ran the double marathon held
annually in KwaZulu-Natal under the unintentionally ironic name
"Comrades," his running shoes supplied by my friends, his part-time
employers. The other is a man who worked for the previous owner of
the house, who asked my friends to keep him on. A stroll through
town or a glance at the news reveals that there is a powerful rising
black middle class, although one can still easily predict race in many
social and work settings by reference to status and wealth. At the
Pietermaritzburg Archives Repository, for instance, the director is
white, at least one midlevel staff person is Indian, and the reception-
ist, cleaning staff, and document retrievers are black. More and more,
in fact, I am struck by how similar South Africa is becoming to the
United States. The rich get richer, their number grows, and the spec-
trum of their colors widens, but the poor are left mainly to their own
devices. The major difference, of course, is that in South Africa the
poor are the majority.

The struggles of gender and generation over land, labor, and law that I describe in this book remain central to the issues facing the new South Africa. The Constitution adopted in 1996, by all accounts one of the most progressive anywhere in the world, contains a strong Bill of Rights, including guarantees of equality on the basis of gender as well as a long list of other categories. On the other hand, the politics of violence and resultant atmosphere of tension surrounding the negotiations leading to South Africa's first democratic elections in 1994 meant that many issues were left unresolved. Despite the guarantees of equality, therefore, the Constitution continues to recognize traditional authorities (i.e., chiefs and headmen) and customary law (i.e., the system of civil law that pertained to Africans from colonial times onward). The Constitution gives supremacy to the rights clauses, but potential conflicts loom, as customary law and the regime of traditional authorities are in many ways predicated on hierarchies of birth, gender, and generation. More broadly, the country is caught between its liberal constitutional order and the nationalist sentiments that intersect to some degree with the notion of a traditional social order, despite the ways in which that order was compromised by white rule. In this province, recently emerged from a bloody war that was partly over these issues, the contrast is stark. Here the state, acting under the authority of the Zulu king in the form of the Ingonyama Trust, continues to hold nearly half the land. Meanwhile, the young men and women who sacrificed their education to fight apartheid in the 1980s lack the skills needed in the neoliberal world economy of the dawning millennium. In addition, the government's promises of land reform face many difficult obstacles, including the recognition of existing property rights in the Constitution, meaning that the government is limited to acquiring land for redistribution at market rates. While this is a work of history designed to illuminate the past, then, it is important precisely because of the way in which these issues continue to play themselves out in the present, albeit in new forms.

ACKNOWLEDGMENTS

Over the course of more than a decade, many people and institutions helped me to develop this project and bring it to completion. I am indebted to several institutions for their financial support, to numerous colleagues for their intellectual challenge and collegiality, and to dozens of other people for their help and friendship.

The research was assisted by generous funding from a Fulbright-Hays Doctoral Research Abroad Fellowship, a Social Science Research Council (SSRC) International Doctoral Research Fellowship, Title VI Foreign Language Area Studies Fellowships, a grant from the Stanford Center on Conflict and Negotiation, and a National Endowment for the Humanities (NEH) Summer grant. The SSRC, Stanford University's Weter Award, and a Stanford Department of History fellowship enabled me to write the dissertation on which this book is based. More recently, the generous support of Southwestern University (in the form of Cullen Faculty Development grants and a Brown Research Fellowship) has enabled me to complete the book, while my colleagues in the Department of History have provided important encouragement and logistical support. My parents, Marie Gammie and Jim McClendon, also offered financial support at critical junctures.

Many people have helped me through the intellectual journey that has resulted in this book. Most important is my graduate adviser, Richard Roberts, who coaxed this former lawyer into the field of law and colonialism and who has been a superb mentor throughout the process. I thank him for what he has taught me and for his friendship and support. Donald S. Moore, who was my fellow graduate student at Stanford, has also been an important mentor and friend from the inception of this project, helping to broaden my intellectual horizons while also keeping me firmly grounded in the soil of southern Africa. John Wright helped me to see the importance of precolonial and nineteenth century struggles over identity to my project, and underscored the necessity of a close engagement with sources. I have also received crucial advice, encouragement, and criticism along the way from Ben Carton, Clifton Crais, Gill Hart, Jim Lance, Meredith McKittrick, Emery Roe, Pamela Scully, and Bill Worger. The editors of this series, Allen Isaacman and Jean Allman, together with the anonymous readers of the manuscript, offered very valuable advice, and Jean Hay gave important encouragement at an earlier stage. I have also benefited from the comments of editors and anonymous readers of the *International Journal of African Historical Studies*, *African Economic History*, and the *Journal of Legal Pluralism*, as well as questions and comments of discussants and audience members at numerous paper presentations. My students at UCLA, Berkeley, and Southwestern have pushed me both to clarify and to broaden my analysis.

I am very grateful to Greg Herriman, who created the maps, and Dan Yoxall, who copyedited the manuscript, and to the Greenwood production staff for putting the work into its perfected form.

I deeply appreciate the institutional support and friendly surroundings provided by the staff of the University of Natal's former Department of Historical Studies during my initial research, and I wish to thank its successive heads of department at that time, John Benyon and Bill Guest. Tim Nuttall and Margie Shaw helped to orient my wife and myself to the university and Pietermaritzburg. I am also indebted to the staff of the university's library, especially Thuli Radebe, and the staffs of the computer center and the language lab.

My most constant companions during the day-to-day work of research were the personnel of the Pietermaritzburg Archives Repository, who have been enormously helpful. I wish especially to thank Chief Archivist Judith Hawley and her staff, including Pieter Nel, Nisha Gokool, Edgar Ince, Unay Narrine, Hussein Solomon, Thami Ntuli, Patrick Dlamini, and Pius Mabi. I also enjoyed the support and advice of fellow researchers there and at other archives in South Africa, including Keith Breckinridge, Catherine Burns, John Lambert, Stephan Schirmer, and Jabulani Sithole. John Morrisson and fellow staff members at the Natal Society Library were also most helpful, as were the staffs of the Killie Campbell African Library, especially Nellie Somers, and the Natal Museum Library, especially Sharynne Hearne. I have also benefited from the assistance of the staffs of The Association for Rural Advancement, (AFRA); the library of the University of Natal, Durban; the National Archives; and the Historical Documents Archive and the Institute for Advanced Social Research, both at the University of the Witwatersrand (Wits). In addition, I received much helpful advice and encouragement from Phil Bonner, Carolyn Hamilton, Tom Lodge, and Paul La Hausse at Wits, and Bill Freund, Jeff Guy, Robert Morrell, and Cherryl Walker at the University of Natal, Durban.

Many people and organizations helped me to conduct interviews with elderly labor tenants and former labor tenants in the Natal countryside, the subjects of this study, to whom I am most indebted. Mantombi Hlongwane, Duduzile Moerane, and Thandi Puoane did their best to instruct me in *isiZulu* at Stanford, while Adrian Koopman, Nelson Ntshangase, and others helped me in South Africa. For help with interviewing, I wish to thank Rauri Alcock, Natty Duma, Bheki Mbata, Antony Ntuli, Siyazi Zulu, T.J. Zungu and Nhlanhla Zungu for interpreting, and Sifiso Ndlovu for translating and transcribing the interview tapes. Afra's Peter Brown and Richard Clacey, and CAPFarm Trust's (CAP) Rauri Alcock and Natty Duma helped me to locate informants; Rauri Alcock and other CAP employees in many cases transported me to informants' homes. I am especially grateful to the many women and men who were willing to tell me about their experiences and perceptions. Without their words and insights, this story would be a dry shell.

So many people have provided hospitality in southern Africa over the last ten years that it is impossible to list them all. However, I wish especially to thank Paul Forsyth and Shelagh McLoughlin, who have provided extraordinary material and moral support in the form of bed, board, bottle, and banter. In addition, I have been a lucky and grateful guest at the households of Creina Alcock, Mashiya Dladla and family, Angela Impey, Barbara and John Lambert, the Mawoko family, Louise Meintjes, Francois and Jane Meintjes, Kotayi Mkhize and family, Donald Moore, and Siyazi Zulu and family, among others.

My family and friends, many of whom are not academics and have no direct involvement with Africa, have kept me going throughout this project. My brother Will and sister-in-law Dosh have been enthusiastic supporters and have provided enjoyable respites from African history, as have my parents and in-laws. My wife, Nancy Schmechel McClendon, was my companion in the field and has endured the trials and enjoyed the successes of this project for more than ten years. I am deeply grateful for her love and support.

GLOSSARY

abathakathi	Witches, sorcerers.
amabutho	Regiments.
amaZulu	Zulu people.
baas	Boss.
bhokide	Yellow maize meal.
draai	Full-time work. See also *idilayi*.
eGoli	In or to Johannesburg.
hlonipha	Physical and linguistic deference (that a married woman must give to her husband, or a junior must give to a senior).
ibhayi (**pl.** *amabhayi*)	Cloth cape(s) worn by married women.
ibheshu (**pl.** *amabheshu*)	Goat skin(s) worn by men.
icansi (**pl.** *amacansi*)	Mat(s).
idilayi	Full-time work. See also *draai*.
igosa (**pl.** *amagosa*)	Dance company leader(s).
induna (**pl.** *izinduma*)	Headman, foreman.
inkosi (**pl.** *amakhosi*)	Chief.
inyanga (**pl.** *izinyanga*)	Herbalist(s).
inzindlubu	Black beans.
isangoma (**pl.** *izangoma*)	Diviner(s).
isibalo	Forced labor.
isibongo	Praise name, surname.

isidwaba (**pl.** *izidwaba*)	Leather skirt(s) worn by wife (wives).
isigodi (**pl.** *izigodi*)	District(s).
isithupa	Six; six-month (period of labor tenant service).
isiZulu	Zulu language.
izinene	A covering of fur strips worn by men.
kaffir	African (derogatory).
kholwa (**pl.** *amakholwa*)	Christian(s); believer(s).
khonza	Submission (As a verb: to submit to).
kraal	Homestead. See also *umuzi*.
kufanele	"It is necessary."
lobola (**also** *ilobola* [**noun**], *ukulobola* [**infinitive**])	Bridewealth.
Nobamba	Weenen.
nquthu	Portion of bridewealth given to bride's mother.
sangoma	Diviner.
sisa	Cattle loan.
sjambok	Ox-hide whip.
togt	Casual labor.
ubuthakathi	Witchcraft.
ukungena	To enter; levirate marriage.
ukusebenza	To work.
umakoti	Bride.
umnumzane (**pl.** *abanumzane*)	Homestead (or *kraal*) head(s).
umthandazi	Prophetess.
umuntu munsundi	Brown man.
umuthi (**pl.** *imithi*)	Medicine(s).
umuzi (**pl.** *imizi*)	Homestead(s). See also *kraal*.

1

INTRODUCTION

In proto-apartheid South Africa, the regime of customary law and the institution of labor tenancy each revolved around hierarchies of gender and generation. Both systems depended on and attempted to reinforce those hierarchies, but both left crucial openings for subalterns that threatened to undermine the authority of African fathers and white settler farmers, exposing weaknesses in wider structures of social control. This book explores intersections of labor tenancy and customary law with tensions of gender and generation, focusing on the province then known as Natal (now KwaZulu-Natal) from the late 1920s to the early 1940s, the peak era of segregation. My aim is to shed light on each of these areas in order to contribute to the historiographical conversations concerning land, labor, and law, as well as contributing to the growing understanding of the importance of gender and generation in modern African history.

Labor tenancy was a system of organizing agricultural labor on white-owned farms, but it both rested on and deeply affected relations within African homesteads on those farms; "white" production and "black" reproduction were intimately connected. The expansion of white commercial agriculture in Natal brought most rural Africans outside the reserves into relations of labor tenancy in the early twentieth century.[1] In the 1920s and 1930s, however, the system began to be threatened by a crisis of control as young men and women left South Africa's farms for the greater wages and independence of the rapidly industrializing cities. In response to this problem, as well as to an upsurge in rural radicalism in the late 1920s, the South African state attempted to ensure control of Africans through further elaboration of the broad set of policies known as segregation, the precursor of apartheid. An important facet of segregation policy was the drive to shore up chiefly and patriarchal authority in rural areas through a customary law regime, building on the indirect rule system that Theophilus Shepstone had established in nineteenth-century colonial

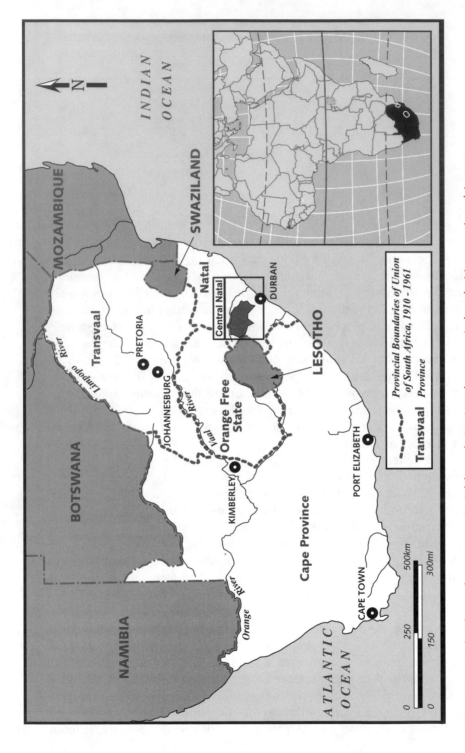

Map 1.1 South Africa, showing provincial boundaries in relevant period and cities mentioned in text.

Natal. The customary law regime attempted to reinforce hierarchies of gender and generation in the countryside—and to harness those hierarchies to reproducing social order in the midst of strains caused by industrialization—while clothing itself in the legitimacy of tradition. The administration of customary law at the level of white-staffed Native Commissioner (NC) Courts, however, ironically provided opportunities for women and youths to challenge patriarchal authority and the unitary, unchanging conception of tradition expressed in the customary law regime. The records of litigation in those courts provide windows onto domestic struggle and contests over tradition among labor tenants and other rural Africans in the segregation era.

This book examines these parallel processes of change and draws connections among them in order to provide a deeper understanding of labor tenancy, social change, and the formation of settler-colonial states in twentieth-century Africa. It examines gender and generation conflict within African labor tenant households in Natal through the lens of the colonial state's system of customary law. As a study of labor tenancy, it is part of the ongoing study of rural dispossession and social change in southern Africa that began to be written in the 1970s and 1980s. It is also a study within the somewhat newer field of law and African social history; it uses litigation under the Natal Code of Native Law in the NC Courts to look at conflicts within labor tenant households. It thereby departs from most previous studies of rural and agricultural history in South Africa by focusing on relations within African communities rather than on conflict between Africans and the state or between Africans and whites. The study addresses the relationship of customary law and economic change to conflicts of gender and generation among Africans, and it explores the social history of South African labor tenancy in a time and place that has received surprisingly little attention: rural Natal from the 1920s to the 1940s.

LABOR TENANCY, DOMESTIC STRUGGLE, AND LAW IN SOUTH AFRICAN HISTORY

This book draws on three strands of historiography concerning colonial and settler-dominated Africa. First, it draws on and expands the analysis of law and social history, an area that has been underexplored in the South African context. Second, it adds to the accelerating drive to understand the social and cultural histories of Africa in terms of dynamics of gender and generation. Third, it attempts to revive and contribute to the study of rural dispossession and social change. Each of these concerns has considerable importance in the rebuilding and transformation taking place in post-apartheid South Africa, as well as being fascinating in its own historical right. Though these strands have separate historiographies and grew out of distinct concerns, this study brings them together in a way that I hope will contribute to each strand but also, by weaving a new pattern, strengthen African and colonial studies in general. I will proceed by discussing each of the strands separately, in the order of their appearance in southern African historiography, in order to show the development of the conversation in which I see myself involved. I will then discuss how this book attempts to weave the strands together before going on to describe the setting, sources, and methods of the study.

Rural Social History

A new school of rural social history, in concert with the broad revisionist attack on liberal historiography, appeared in southern African studies in the 1970s, as apartheid peaked and neo-Marxist and Africanist groups of historians began to challenge liberal orthodoxies. Colin Bundy's article, "The Emergence and Decline of a South African Peasantry," set a new agenda for agrarian research.[2] His work provided a new understanding of the changes wrought in the countryside by the mineral revolution and state action on behalf of white farming and in opposition to the aspirations of a black peasantry. Robin Palmer and Neil Parsons widened this agenda into a regional focus in *The Roots of Rural Poverty in Central and Southern Africa*.[3] The new agrarian historians worked largely from the perspective of world systems and dependency theory, which held that underdevelopment in the Third World was not coincidental, but flowed inexorably from capitalist development. This approach saw labor reserves as functional to mining and industrial economies.[4] In this early phase of the new agrarian studies in southern Africa, African peasants were active agents who sought to make their own histories, but who, as the titles suggested, were doomed to fail.

Later scholars in this field were influenced by the theory of "articulation of the modes of production," which looked more closely at political economies of the periphery, examining how they worked in tandem with those of the core rather than being wholly separate. In the early 1980s, scholars of rural social history poured their efforts into detailed local studies that produced a more nuanced view of agrarian history. This methodology emphasized resistance, African agency, and the inability of the state or "capital" (the structuralists' personification of capitalists and capital-

ism) to unambiguously achieve their ends.[5] Both William Beinart's study
of Pondoland and Timothy Keegan's examination of sharecropping on the
Highveld exemplified this richly detailed, complex, and ironic approach
to the story of rural transformations.[6] They and those who joined them
looked at dynamic processes within African societies and homesteads that
both affected and were transformed by wider social and economic processes.[7]

The promise of rural social history in South Africa seemed especially exciting in the late 1980s, when I first traveled to the region as
a backpacker and picked up a discounted hardback copy of Colin
Bundy's *Rise and Fall of the South African Peasantry* in the university bookshop in Lusaka. By then, many scholars had begun to write
a more nuanced social history focused on 1920s rural social movements, implicitly seeing them as precursors of the rural revolutions
that had toppled settler regimes across southern Africa in the 1970s,
and hinting at the radical potential of a seemingly resigned rural South
Africa under apartheid. It was this material that engaged me most
when I first began to articulate a research agenda as a graduate student, during what turned out to be apartheid's dying days at the end
of the 1980s. Helen Bradford provided an exhaustive treatment of the
widespread fluorescence of rural protest around the Industrial and
Commercial Workers Union (ICU), while Bundy and Beinart explored
detailed dimensions of "hidden struggles" over land, labor, and politics in the Transkei and Eastern Cape.[8] These studies emphasized both
everyday resistance and the potential radicalism of rural communities,
and they began to engage with Gramsci's theories about the effects of
culture and consciousness on historical processes.[9] With the mid-1980s
explosion of the urban revolt that led to apartheid's collapse in the
early 1990s, however, less new work appeared on South African rural
social history, as scholars there increasingly turned their attention to
urban political and social landscapes.[10] Meanwhile, southern African
historiography was belatedly coming to terms with the importance of
gender in history.

Engendering Rural Social History

The studies of South African rural social history in the 1970s and
1980s, beginning from a Marxist perspective, saw conflict in rural communities primarily in terms of class. In the southern African context of
white settler colonies, race was also an inescapable line of division, but
the emphasis on nonracialism in the antiapartheid struggle led to emphasizing class over race. Gender was rarely discussed or analyzed in any

serious way, except in the context of bridewealth.[11] In 1983, however, Belinda Bozzoli's influential piece on Marxism and feminism argued persuasively for the indispensability of gendered analysis.[12] Bradford, whose 1980s work reflected the times by failing to incorporate gender analysis, has in recent years launched a strong attack on the gender-blind nature of southern African historiography.[13] She has demonstrated the ways in which lack of attention to gender necessarily distorts historical understanding of southern Africa.

In the past, the gender-myopia of contemporary officials and modern historians has meant that labor tenancy was usually understood as an ungendered but implicitly male institution. Statutes defined labor tenants as patriarchs who contracted with a white farmer, leaving the other members of the tenant *umuzi* (homestead) as assumed, silent, and unproblematic appendages. However, as in precolonial southern African agricultural communities, women were the linchpin of the system of labor tenancy on white-owned farms.[14] In order to secure a place on a farm, a man had to have labor to supply: his own or that of his sons, daughters, and wives. This, of course, required women's reproductive labor, in the sense of both giving birth to and raising children and raising crops (primarily defined as female labor) to feed them. Furthermore, it was often women who looked after the homestead while the men were away working, either on the farm or *eGoli* (in Johannesburg). In response to such understandings of the ways in which peasant communities operate, scholars of development and social change have thoroughly deconstructed the concept of the undifferentiated household.[15] Their work has focused attention on the conflicting interests and contested terrain within households, forcing us to notice that "households" do not make decisions, offer labor, or engage in strategies: *people* do.[16] Following this analysis, a labor tenant household includes the *umnumzane* (homestead head), other adult men, wives of one or more generations, and unmarried sons and daughters—all having divergent but overlapping positional as well as personal interests.

Compared to the question of gender, less attention has been focused on generational divides within the household, especially in the context of farm labor in South Africa.[17] Yet the differing interests and actions of fathers and sons are absolutely crucial for understanding the operation of the labor tenant system in Natal, as Carton's recent study shows for peasant communities in general in the context of accelerated change under settler rule in the region.[18] Beinart's Pondoland study anticipated the move away from a purely class analysis by examining the tensions between youths and elders and between chiefs and commoners that arose in the context of migrant labor.[19] Keegan examined conflicts within labor tenant households on early twentieth century Highveld farms. He noted, as I do, that the labor tenant contract revolved around the control of household labor by the patriarch, and that this resulted in tensions between fathers and sons and between husbands and wives, especially at times of expansion of production.[20] Both Beinart's and Keegan's books were important advances in the study of rural dispossession in that they consciously focused attention on the dynamics of household production and the consequences for relations within the household. Although they pioneered the study of generation in South African rural social history, neither sufficiently addressed gender.[21] In the mid-1990s, Charles Van Onselen's biography of sharecropper Kas Maine provided fascinating evidence of gendered and generational divides in rural southern Africa, but his narrative approach shied away from theorizing these tensions.[22] New work on peasantries and colonial change in the region by authors such as Ben Carton and Meredith McKittrick, however, has emphasized the importance of indigenous conceptions of generation, showing these to be inherently gendered constructions.[23]

Bozzoli's 1983 piece emphasized gender as a central principle of social organization through a "patchwork quilt of patriarchies" in southern Africa.[24] In the article, Bozzoli raised the issue of tension between men and women in the household, characterizing it as "domestic struggle." Like generational conflict, domestic struggle between men and women was both transformed by and influential in the region's modernizing political economy. The cheap labor thesis claimed that men migrated to work while women were left behind to reproduce the labor force in the reserves because this pattern enabled capital to avoid paying the costs of reproduction.[25] According to Bozzoli, however, this form of migrant labor resulted partly from the subordination of women's labor in what she called precapitalist societies of southern Africa.[26] Migrancy was therefore an outcome of domestic struggle, but it also altered the terms of that struggle by adding to the burden of women in rural areas while also increasing their independence, as Cherryl Walker argued.[27] This insight showed that scholars needed to come to terms with the nature of gender relations to examine the role of domestic struggle—a concept that I expand to incorporate generational struggles—in shaping southern African history. In other words, to understand labor tenancy we need to look at the forces shaping labor tenant households, including gender and generational struggles.

Feminist scholars emphasized that patriarchy was a common element in the articulation of social worlds under colonialism. In the 1980s, some scholars began to be concerned with this issue from another angle: that of the creation of customary law regimes in the colonial era. These writers had a particular concern with the place and actions of women with regard to customary law.

Customary Law and Domestic Struggle

Detailed attention to the practice of customary law offers important avenues toward understanding the many dimensions of domestic struggle and its complex relationship to the structures of segregation and economic expansion in southern Africa. Since the early 1980s, law has emerged as an important site for analysis of social struggles in the colonial and postcolonial eras.[28] Law in colonial Africa has come to be seen as one of the tools of indirect rule through which states and subjects shaped a corpus of invented traditions.[29] Terence Ranger's groundbreaking piece on the "invention of tradition" argued that the period of transition to colonial rule in Africa was a time of upheaval and social fluidity. He found that African rulers and elites shaped the content of tradition in alliance with colonial officials in order to reassert control over women and youth. In the process, the powers of chiefs expanded and the concept of tradition hardened. Soon after the appearance of Ranger's piece, Martin Chanock published his case study of the invention of customary law in Central Africa.[30] Chanock agreed that tradition, as understood by colonial states, was an invention of the colonial era, and he applied the concept specifically to the invention of customary law. He contended that the early colonial era offered new opportunities, especially for women, and that the colonial courts were initially receptive to their claims.[31] As colonial rule was consolidated, however, officials and African elders became concerned to reestablish control over women and youth. In this era, customary law as we know it was invented, institutionalized, and hardened.[32] Sally Falk Moore countered that customary law had its origins in precolonial practices concerning marriage and rights to land, but she agreed that its shape was significantly altered in the colonial and postcolonial eras as a result of changes in political economies, including the intervention of the state into legal spheres.[33]

Chanock's thesis provocatively asserted the nonidentity of precolonial indigenous dispute resolution with the colonial practice of customary law. Although Chanock's early work concentrated rather exclusively on these anomalies, it is important to see (as Moore did, for instance) that customary law also had clear elements of continuity with the precolonial past. The effort to establish "native" law was successful in part because the invented traditions of customary law were grounded to some degree in the social realities of precolonial Africa.[34] This was certainly so in Natal. The way in which customary law is linked to precolonial realities, however, is a vexed question. To a large degree the difficulty arises from the absence of any comprehensive understanding of basic issues such as the role of women and the nature of gender relations in precolonial times. Some attempts have been made to answer these questions, but they are only beginnings, and they are riddled with difficulties.[35]

Scholars of southern Africa have turned increasing attention to legal systems and records in the last dozen years or so, but that attention remains partial and inadequate. Studies in the late 1980s looked at legislation concerning control of workers and court records documenting African resistance to dispossession.[36] None of these studies, however, considered the system of "native" law as an instrument of colonial power that shaped conflict within African communities in the process of industrial transformation. More recent research has begun to mine records of customary law cases for aspects of southern African social history.[37] In 1989, Chanock previewed a large project looking at the construction of the South African legal system, but he restricted his view to appellate cases and to the shaping of law rather than to the interstices of social history.[38] Mahmood Mamdani's influential work brought renewed attention to the creation of customary law and indirect rule systems in South Africa, arguing that they were the basis of apartheid and the model for colonial systems throughout Africa. The book offered a valuable view of the broad features of these systems and their genesis and successfully made the case (with which I agree) that apartheid grew from the same roots as indirect rule, leaving similar distorted legacies. Mamdani's sweeping view, however, showed little appreciation for the nuances of customary law on the ground or for the way in which it influenced and was used by ordinary people in their daily struggles.[39]

Three important pieces in the last decade used litigation records from nineteenth-century South Africa to examine African agency, foreground African voices, and consider the role of law in social change.[40] Sandra Burman looked at civil litigation under a customary law regime to examine gender and the construction of patriarchy in the context of the brief Cape Colony rule of Basutoland. John Mason provided a compelling account of one slave's use of the office of Protector of Slaves in the period just before abolition to examine ideologies and actions of slaves and

masters in the face of legal and ideological change. Pamela Scully exca-
vated constructions of race, class, and gender in rape and infanticide pros-
ecutions in the Western Cape at the end of slavery. These writers
demonstrated the ways in which the study of law and legal records can
be used to examine conflicts and debates within states as well as within
social groups.

Weaving the Strands Together

How can these strands of historiography be woven together in a way
that will strengthen the fabric of African history as a whole? In the present
work, I bring both gender and legal social history to bear on rural social
history. Thus, my study is not only of labor tenancy or only of law; it is
an attempt to integrate both of these with issues of gender and generation, which are central to a nuanced understanding of each of the other
strands. In combining legal and rural social history with gendered analysis, I also take seriously Bozzoli's notion of domestic struggle by adding
to it the element of generational conflict.

Generational struggle has formed an important backdrop to the discussion of gender in southern African social history. Beinart, Diana
Jeater, and Elizabeth Schmidt all analyzed debates about bridewealth
among African fathers and sons, white employers, and the colonial
state.[41] Yet Beinart neglected a specific examination of gender and
patriarchal alliance, whereas Jeater and Schmidt ignored the potential
of generational struggle as an important issue in itself. Indeed, conflict and negotiation between rural fathers and sons is inevitable where
marriage is predicated on bridewealth. Like relations between men and
women, relations between fathers and sons were deeply affected by
the colonial situation. The increase in wage labor and in urban jobs
gave sons geographic independence and independent access to
bridewealth. The deteriorating conditions in the countryside, particularly the farms, made young men less able to rely on their fathers for
the accumulation of bridewealth and encouraged them to spend longer
periods in the cities or to relocate permanently. All these factors were
thrown into sharp relief under labor tenancy in Natal in the second
quarter of the twentieth century.

In the early 1990s, two social histories of the colonial era in Zimbabwe were especially concerned with gender issues and used legal
records to advance their arguments.[42] Schmidt, in particular, built on
Chanock's paradigm concerning the role of law in colonial rule. She
offered a richly textured account of colonial attempts to manipulate
African marriage practices in the early colonial era, elaborating the

construction of patriarchal alliances between colonizers and African male elders seeking to control the movements and sexuality of women in the 1930s.[43] In her work and in Jeater's, however, women and gender took precedence over other issues. Furthermore, both seemed to rather uncritically adopt the model of colonial customary law developed by Chanock. Although I agree with the view that there was a hardening of customary law in the 1920s and 1930s, it is important to see that women and juniors continued to use courts and law for their own ends, even in the heyday of indirect rule.[44]

Making law and court records a central focus of this study not only gives access to the voices of ordinary Africans (discussed below) but also brings continuing constructions of rural and migrant African cultures to the fore.[45] As Africans—men women, elders and youths, farm tenants and reserve dwellers, locals and immigrants—contested specific legal issues in the courts, they debated and reported on competing practices and the meanings of such categories. What did it mean to be a father, a son, a wife, a follower of Zulu tradition, a *kholwa* (Christian), a migrant? These identities competed and coexisted in the world of Natal's labor tenants. I hope to shed light on these identities by showing the context in which they operated and by zeroing in on the debates among Africans over customary law in the era of segregation.

NATAL'S CUSTOMARY LAW REGIME

By the dawn of the segregation era in the early twentieth century, the province of Natal already had a long history of rigid traditionalism sanctioned and shaped by the colonial state. The British colony of Natal, annexed in 1843, occupied the colonial space created by the brief occupation of the trekkers from the Eastern Cape. British colonial officials in Natal quickly abandoned any pretense of the type of liberal egalitarianism they had espoused in the Cape Colony during the first half of the nineteenth century.[46] The colony of Natal presented the British colonial effort with a new situation. In 1838–1839, the Dutch Emigrant farmers (later known as Voortrekkers) had carved out a space of colonial domination through a series of military contests and alliances between themselves and forces from the Zulu kingdom. Despite British efforts to encourage them to stay, most of the Emigrants departed from Natal, leaving the new colonizers to rule an area dominated by African homesteads with a thin sprinkling of white settlers and an imaginary overlay of colonial land claims. Officials' immediate preoccupations were to establish effective authority in the territory and to make the colony pay its way, ever an overriding concern of the Colonial Office in London.[47]

It fell mainly to Theophilus Shepstone, Natal's Secretary for Native Affairs in the colony's formative decades, to resolve these competing demands on the state. The "Shepstone system" grew out of the sort of contingency identified by Sara Berry in reference to twentieth-century colonial Africa: the need to establish authority despite severe constraints of resources.[48] Shepstone's solution to the creation of "hegemony on a shoestring," as Berry phrased it, was therefore quite similar to the model of indirect rule that became the normal model throughout the British African colonies in the 1920s and 1930s after a brief period of more direct, interventionist rule.[49] The colonial government would rule Africans as a separate category of subjects through the agency of African chiefs (some with hereditary claims to chieftainship, but all subject to the continuing favor of the colonial government) and through the medium of a curious mix of colonial law and ideology and "native" social structures, a mix later denominated customary law.

The recognition of chiefs and the definition and legalization of custom ensured that the Shepstone system would be, as Jeff Guy has suggested, an "accommodation of the patriarchs."[50] Historians and anthropologists have portrayed precolonial southern African societies as sharply patriarchal. The gender division of labor put most of the burden of agricultural production on women while limiting their opportunities for independence; bridewealth-based marriage systems ensured the dependence of junior males on their elders.[51] Although the general picture of these societies as patriarchal and gerontocratic is no doubt correct, the picture as it is usually presented tends to shield from view the opportunities of which women and juniors took advantage to challenge and limit the power of senior males. The image of an unchallenged and unchallengeable patriarchy therefore denies any possibility of change in precolonial Africa. The picture also ignores the individual perspective, which involved movement within the hierarchical order over a lifetime. The individual passed through stages and levels of the ideal hierarchy as a result of the attainment of adult status through initiation and marriage, becoming a parent, and becoming an elder, to say nothing of gradations of power and wealth that crossed gender and generational lines.[52]

In order to illuminate the problem of the uncertain relationship between precolonial realities and customary law, I want to briefly return to a discussion of writing on gender issues in precolonial southern Africa. Two basic problems are common to existing treatments of the

position of women in precolonial, precapitalist southern Africa, especially Natal. First, scholars have argued at quite a general level, with
only a smattering of empirical support. For instance, John Wright, who
must be given a great deal of credit for asserting the importance of
gender issues in the region's history, relied on the early twentieth-
century work of the missionary A.T. Bryant and on anthropologist
Eileen Krige's compendium of published accounts (including Bryant's)
on Zulu life.[53] Both Bryant and Krige purported to present Zulu social
structure as it was "before the white man came," but they did so only
haphazardly. Bryant, whose work was based on observations made in
Zululand from 1883 to 1935, stated that "the daily life of the Zulu
people had continued practically unaltered (in its fundamental aspects)
since the days of Shaka."[54] Such a statement blithely ignored the widespread effects of conquest, demilitarization, trade, taxation, migrant
labor, and crowding into reserves. These processes, which had begun
in Natal in the 1830s, intensified in both Natal and Zululand from the
late 1880s.[55] Krige, for her part, did an admirable job of compiling a
coherent account from a wide array of travelers' accounts, Bryant's
work, and information garnered from contemporary informants. She
made no attempt, however, to sort out her information on the basis of
period or location, presenting it as a unified and ahistorical whole,
located in the ethnographic present. These problems in the accounts
by Bryant and Krige could not but affect the attempts of Wright, and
later Guy, to use their work.[56]

The other basic problem in the accounts given by Wright and Guy
of women's subordination is the apparent absence of female agency.
Guy, for instance, argued that southern Africa's precolonial modes of
production were based on the oppression of women. Working from a
Meillassouxian model that stressed a link between modes of production and reproduction, he postulated that the precapitalist societies of
southern Africa were "based on the appropriation of women's labour
by men."[57] Because production took place in the homestead and
women's labor was central to both production and reproduction, control of women's fertility was essential. Guy elaborated his model as
follows:

> It is this cycle of production and reproduction which lies at the heart
> of southern Africa's precapitalist societies: the productive capacity of
> women in the domestic and agricultural sphere, together with their re-
> productive potential, being exchanged by their fathers for cattle, which
> allowed this value-creating cycle of production and reproduction to con-
> tinue into the next generation.[58]

According to Guy, the social controls surrounding fertility were therefore central to the organization of these societies. But this model,
while based on plausible interpretations of the gender division of labor and the role of cattle in marriage in the precolonial era, was over-
drawn and therefore distorted in much the same way as colonial
constructions of customary law. The first codification of customary
law in Natal, for instance, listed "subjection of the female sex to the
male" as a basic principle.[59] Although the available material makes it
clear that precolonial gender relations were unequal and that elder men
were dominant, women were by no means passive victims of male
dominance. It is valuable to realize the importance of women's agricultural labor to precolonial as well as colonial economies, but it is a
misstep to assume that this means that women were powerless in
households or in the process of marriage.[60] Guy's initial model, like
the codified customary law of Natal, confused ideology with uniform
practice. The model drew largely on material from the colonial era,
when gender practices changed under the impact of migrant labor,
changes in land tenure, and colonial support for patriarchal norms.

However, both Guy and Wright turned at the end of their pieces to
reconsider the rather one-sided picture of gender relations they presented
initially.[61] Guy argued, "We have still to understand . . . how women
both participated in and resisted their exploitation."[62] He acknowledged
that the role of women in production and ideology gave them forms of
power and status:

> On marriage [women] were given access to productive land, which they
> worked themselves. They were in control of the process of agricultural
> production and retained for their own use a substantial proportion of
> the product of that land and their labour. Work was heavy but it took
> place in a community which provided substantial security. The value
> attached to fertility gave the possessors of that fertility social standing
> and social integrity.[63]

This is a valuable corrective. Nevertheless, they and other scholars
made the important basic point that women were generally subordi-
nate to men in precolonial Natal, and that subordination had both ideological and material elements.[64] The system of production depended
on the labor of women as producers and as social and biological re-
producers. Married women were obliged to practice *hlonipha* (physical and linguistic deference) in their husband's homesteads until they
were beyond childbearing.[65] They were debarred from most interac-
tion with cattle, important as symbolic currency in marriage transac-

tions as well as for milk and for propitiation of ancestors, yet they performed most of the less valued, but often more crucial, agricultural labor.[66] So female subordination and control—especially of fertility and productivity of female bodies—was not invented out of whole cloth in the colonial era as much as it was modified and distorted in the light of new circumstances. We could say that the "cloth" of female subordination was "resewn" in a new social order.

Three very important transformations occurred in southeast Africa in the hundred years beginning in the late eighteenth century; all deeply affected, and were affected by, gender and generational dynamics. The first was the increasing centralization and militarization of southeast African polities in the last decades of the eighteenth century and the first decades of the nineteenth century, a process that resulted in the consolidation of the Zulu kingdom, with a sphere of influence that included at least part of what became Natal.[67] Centralization and warfare meant that while *imizi* (homesteads)—family-based loci of residence and production—remained the basic units of African society, elites made increasing demands on them for labor and tribute. (In return, the state took increased responsibility for security and strengthened the webs of clientage and redistribution.) Homesteads in the Zulu kingdom sent young men to serve at royal capitals in age-set *amabutho* (regiments), which constituted a standing army and provided labor for royal production. Royals also demanded that some young women serve at the garrison capitals, collecting bridewealth when the young women were married to veterans or other clients. Increasing demands on homesteads, now bereft of their young men for long stretches, placed new burdens on the women and girls left behind, as females bore the primary responsibility for producing sustenance and tribute. The increased power of the *inkosi* (chief)-based state, along with the ethos of military prowess, further tended to emphasize male power and dominance.[68] The Zulu state's regulation of marriage also emphasized senior control of juniors, who were not permitted to don the headring denoting majority until their *amabutho* were allowed to marry, at a relatively advanced age.

The second significant transformation in the region was colonization, which brought with it a wide range of institutional and ideological intrusions that affected domestic and chiefly politics. These included land alienation, taxation, *isibalo* (forced labor) and wage labor, increased production for the market, and intense missionary activity, especially on land dedicated as "mission reserves." As always when discussing colonization, we must bear in mind that these processes affected different regions and categories of people unevenly, but nevertheless the impact was broad. In practice, land alienation meant that whereas some Africans retained access to land (albeit relatively poor land) through *khonza* (submission) to a chief (and through him to the colony), others *khonza*'d a farmer as rent or labor tenants, while yet others squatted on the land of speculators or on Crown land. Taxation, *isibalo* for the colonial state, and peasant production all brought about shifts in the dynamics of gender and generation, paradoxically both threatening and strengthening the powers of chiefs and *abanumzane* (homestead heads).[69] These changes again put a greater burden on women's homestead production while also providing new openings to girls and young women to seek "alternative patriarchies" in the mission stations.[70] They also provided young men with new types of independence in the form of wage labor while giving their fathers increased motivation to retain filial wages under the patriarchal thumb.[71]

The third wave of change came with the southern African mineral revolution (ca. 1870 to the end of the century). This was not a revolution in the sense of introducing entirely new processes; many southern Africans had engaged in migrant labor or peasant production since early in the century.[72] However, industrial mineral extraction created such a vast market for labor, crops, and consumer and productive goods that the entire subcontinent began to feel these changes directly through imperial conquest, labor recruitment, and increasing differentiation. In Natal, the acceleration of the market and strengthening of imperial interests coincided with a maturing of settler colonialism. White farmers gained increasing control over the colonial government and began to exploit the land more avidly and successfully, a process that culminated with settler assumption of "responsible government" in the early 1890s. Squatting on white-owned land remained an attractive option to men seeking to establish independent homesteads or to escape the demands of colonial chiefs for *isibalo*. Tenants of the better-capitalized and more "progressive" farmers (those most interested in improvements and production for the market) in central Natal, however, felt the pinch of increased demands for labor at the same time that mines and towns increased opportunities for waged employment. These coinciding factors paradoxically provided cash for taxes, rents, and consumer goods while increasing opportunities for the independence of homestead juniors. Tenant patriarchs struggled to maintain the authority and command of labor on which their access to grazing and farmland depended.[73]

It was during this century of upheaval and change that the accommodating patriarchs, black and white, constructed their vision of a traditional order that would protect the authority of *amakhosi* (chiefs) and *abanumzane* (homestead heads) against recalcitrant or rebellious juniors. That vision was articulated and systematized through the vehicle of customary law. In nineteenth-century Natal, therefore, as in twentieth-century tropical Africa, customary law and indirect rule were "built on a foundation of conflict and change."[74] At a time when young men pursued wage labor, homestead women produced grain for the market, fathers demanded inflated and sometimes monetized bridewealth, and young women sought refuge in mission enclaves from polygynous elderly husbands, the ideology of customary law cast the chiefdom and homestead as timeless, well-ordered bastions of respect, hierarchy, and contentment. The contradictions did not stop there, however. Necessity was the mother of invention of the Shepstone system in the 1850s, but by the late 1860s new demands for revenue, colonial anxiety about polygyny, and the increased confidence of the colonial state led officials to intervene more actively to attempt to reshape homestead dynamics.

Shepstone sought to answer all these demands in one fell swoop by introducing the marriage ordinance of 1869. The law imposed a steep fee for each marriage, required the presence at marriage ceremonies of an "official witness" to ensure the consent of the bride, and established ceilings (variable according to the status of the father of the bride) on *lobola* (bridewealth) transfers.[75] Thus, not surprisingly, the first foray into the codification of customary law in Natal directly concerned regulation of marriage, the principal site of gender and generational dynamics. It was the place where the state's concerns for revenue, order, and hierarchy intersected with the central concern of missionaries seeking to reform what they viewed as African licentiousness and that of settlers seeking to end what they imagined to be indolence. It is ironically fitting that codification of customary law should begin with such an abrupt and self-conscious attempt to alter African practice, although the lawgivers constructed the effort as a counterbalance to "untraditional" behavior on the part of corrupted colonized subjects.[76]

Settler concern over Shepstone's monopolization of knowledge and imperial concern over the maintenance of order and the appearance of justice led to a broader codification of "native law" in 1878, followed by a more thoroughgoing codification in 1891 as the Natal Code of Native Law.[77] While officials continued to insist that custom was subject to evolution and change, customary law was now etched, if not in stone, at least in the black and white of the government gazette. The Code took as its main point of departure the "leading principle" of "the subjection of the female sex to the male and of children to their father."[78] Women were perpetual jural minors, and all "inmates" of a *kraal* (homestead) were obliged to render obedience, respect, and wages to the *umnumzane*, and through him to the chief and ultimately to the colonial governor, cloaked as "Supreme Chief." The Code thus incorporated inflexible notions of homestead hierarchy while it sought to strengthen rule over African subjects by portraying the colonial state as an enlightened heir to Shakan despotism.[79]

Turn-of-the-century traumas, including ecological disasters (drought, locusts, and two major cattle epizootics) and the South African War, engulfed the region and exacerbated tensions within homesteads. Meanwhile, a settler-dominated and revenue-hungry colonial state in Natal aggravated these tensions in 1906 by adding a poll tax on all African males over eighteen, signaling its intention to get blood from impoverished homestead stones and to separate the interests of senior and junior males.[80] The resulting rebellion, ruthlessly crushed by imperial and colonial troops, strengthened the cause of those who argued that the need for a strong state and unified approach to native affairs required the unification of the British colonies and former Boer republics. The 1905 South African Native Affairs Commission (SANAC) placed uniform and thorough control of Africans and their labor at the center of the drive for political unification of the wider region in the wake of the South African War, a goal that was achieved in 1910. SANAC set the emergent settler state on track toward the unification of the principles of labor, social, and political control of African subjects under the banner of segregation, based largely on Shepstonian structures of rule.[81] For state officials and many South African intellectuals, segregation was a paternalistic ideology that promised succor in return for loyalty; liberals as well as some African chiefs and politicians gave various degrees of support to the new policy.[82]

SEGREGATION AND THE UNIFICATION OF NATIVE POLICY

With the coming of Union in 1910, the new government was faced with the need to create a unified native policy from four previously separate political entities.[83] Saul Dubow made a convincing case that segregation was an ambiguous discourse that was politically successful because it appealed, in the 1910s and 1920s, to both liberals and conservatives trying to come to terms with social changes wrought by South Africa's industrialization and urbanization. However, Dubow also noted a significant shift in the tenor of segregation during the

1920s, from what he called an incorporationist view, which still retained traces of Victorian liberalism, to the exclusionary policies established under Nationalist Prime Minister J.B.M. Hertzog.[84] These
changes reflected the more conservative nature of Hertzog's administration, which took power in 1924, and also reflected the growing
white fears of black proletarianization and unrest in both rural and
urban areas that had marked the 1920s.[85]

The first significant measure in the panoply of legislation that became the policy of segregation was the 1913 Natives Land Act. The
Land Act established the framework of territorial segregation, and that
policy in turn laid the basis for political segregation. These policies
were unified with the triumph of Hertzog's Native Bills, extending
the reserves, eliminating the nonracial franchise in the Cape, and establishing separate political institutions for Africans in 1936.[86] Between
the 1913 and 1936 Land Acts, the Union government passed several
other acts that established the administrative and legal framework of
segregation. Concern about African "undesirables" living in disorderly,
uncontrolled conditions in the cities led to passage of a major prong
of segregation legislation, the Natives (Urban Areas) Act of 1923, as
the urban complement of the 1913 Land Act and forerunner of
apartheid's Group Areas Act. The Urban Areas Act provided for segregation and regulation of African locations in the cities under a unified national policy.[87] The Pact government (formed in 1924 from an
electoral alliance between Hertzog's Nationalist Party and the Labour
Party) came to power on a promise to secure the rights of "civilised"
(i.e., white) labor. Prime Minister Hertzog therefore accelerated the
introduction of segregationist legislation, although he was unable to
pass all elements of his program until 1936, after electoral fusion with
Jan Smuts's South African Party. The most important legislation on
native policy passed by the Pact government was the Native Administration Act, discussed more fully in chapter 4.[88] The act essentially
made the Shepstone system national policy, albeit in the context of an
industrializing bureaucratic settler state rather than a nineteenth-century colony. The act gave the Native Affairs Department (NAD) the
right to govern Africans by proclamation, without seeking new legislation. In addition, it created courts under the auspices of white Native Commissioners (NCs) to hear litigation among Africans (a system
already in place in Natal under the Natal Code) and authorized the
courts to follow customary law. Although it was part of the broader
set of policies known as segregation, the act was specifically a response to an upsurge in African radicalism in the 1920s. In the words
of its supporters, it sought to restore "communalism" (i.e., traditional-

ism) in order to stave off "communism." The act therefore put customary law courts, administered by NCs, at the center of struggles
among labor tenants and other rural Africans over the meaning of tradition and the content of hierarchies of gender and generation.

LABOR TENANCY, LAW, AND DOMESTIC STRUGGLE
IN THE 1920s AND 1930s

The system of labor tenancy in Natal depended on a dynamic relationship between white farms and patriarchal African homesteads. African
tenant sons worked on behalf of their fathers to secure a place on a white
farm; they worked "away" (in the cities) to earn cash for the homestead
and for their own bridewealth. Daughters and wives sustained the production and reproduction of tenant homesteads and sometimes worked on
the landlord's farm on behalf of fathers and brothers. *Abanumzane* attempted to control this cycle in order to accumulate wives and cattle, to
maintain authority over dependents, and to escape the indignity of farm
labor.

The resulting fault lines of gender and generation were sharpened
by the growth of commercial agriculture and industrialization after
World War I. Young African men (and, to a lesser extent, young
women) left the farms in increasing numbers, leading to a crisis of
labor and authority by the late 1930s. African fathers, chiefs, and the
South African state all attempted to reassert a version of traditional
patriarchal authority that emphasized the dependence and deference of
women and youth. However, neither traditional patriarchy nor modern
repression-cum-reform was able to stem the flow of youth from the
farms toward the higher industrial wage scales and greater independence offered by South Africa's expanding urban centers. At the same
time, modernizing farmers were beginning to deplore what they saw
as the hoarding of labor by backward and undercapitalized farmer-
landlords. By the 1940s, the increasing dominance of big agriculture
was leading to calls for the abolition of the "inefficient" system of
labor tenancy.[89]

These developments in labor tenancy coincided with important tran-
sitions in South African agriculture. The late 1920s saw a renewed
boom in the export commodities produced in the Natal Midlands, especially wattle bark and wool, but in South Africa, as elsewhere, agricultural prices crashed in the Great Depression of 1929–1932. The
national economy recovered from the Depression after the abolition
of the gold standard in 1932, leading to an unprecedented expansion
of secondary industry. Agricultural prices, however, remained de-

pressed until World War II. The state responded with the introduction of a permanent system of marketing controls to subsidize and regulate the white agricultural economy. The economic problems experienced by agriculture were minor compared to its ecological problems, however, especially in the 1930s and 1940s. Although cattle disease never reached epidemic proportions after East Coast Fever decimated herds in the first decade of the century, drought and locusts caused severe fluctuations in agricultural production and led to periodic famine among rural Africans. These problems were so frequent that references by elderly Africans in KwaZulu-Natal to "the time of the queue" or "the time of bhokide" (yellow mealie-meal provided in famine relief) refer not to a single event but to a series of droughts and famines in the 1930s and 1940s.

The structure of the system exacerbated structural generational tensions revolving around access to bridewealth, marriage, and inheritance. New opportunities for young men and women created by industrial expansion, along with reduced rewards for tenants as commercial farmers sought to rationalize production, further sharpened these tensions in the 1930s. African labor tenant fathers depended on the labor of their sons and daughters to secure their places on the farms, but they also depended on the sons' remittances from seasonal industrial jobs in urban areas to secure cash for taxes, supplemental food, domestic stock for feasting, loans, marriage transactions, and luxury goods. As a system of securing workers, labor tenancy peaked during the interwar period. Contemporaneous industrialization, however, brought about a crisis in labor tenancy around the question of patriarchal control of the younger generation and its labor as young men streamed off the farms and failed to return, or to return on time, to agricultural labor. This resulted in persistent labor shortages and struggles between fathers and sons over generational authority and the obligations surrounding the provenance of bridewealth.

The issue of domestic struggle on gender lines is more hidden and complex, but it is here that the discussion of the customary law regime becomes most important. Examination of litigation surrounding marriage—especially cases involving divorce, domestic violence, and disputes about bridewealth—shows that women were increasingly demonstrating independence in ways that exacerbated patriarchal anxieties (in the state and in rural homesteads) that the men were losing control. I contend that the issue of control—of sexuality and labor—is bound up with the accelerating departure of both men and women from rural areas to the cities and the decreasing security and opportunities for labor tenants on the farms. Litigation in such cases and in those concerned with property rights further shows that women, like the young, were unwilling to accept the customary law regime's definition of tradition. Women and juniors contested the meaning of tradition both through their actions and in the courts. The courts, as an arm of the state, were not neutral in this struggle; they were, instead, arenas for the enactment of state policy as well as for disputation that could either reinforce or undermine aspects of that policy. Though formally neutral, courts were a theater for the reproduction of hierarchies of gender and generation that ironically offered a stage for discordant voices.[90]

Government commissions regularly dissected the "problem" of labor tenancy (a subset of the "native problem") and advocated reforms. By the end of the 1930s, however, a high profile government commission was forced to conclude that no new legislation was needed: control of labor tenants was lacking because of the lack of observance of existing regulations by the very farmers for whose benefit they were written. The system of labor tenancy, with all its inefficiencies and inequities, persisted because of its advantages both to Africans, as a means of access to land and some degree of security, and to settler farmers, who obtained cheap and reliable labor. The fact that the advantages were fewer for those of junior status among the tenants meant that this persistent system was consistently unstable.

SETTING OF THE STUDY

When I began this study, I wanted to look at gender and generational conflict in the Natal Midlands, where commercial agriculture most depended on the labor of African labor tenants and agricultural development had put strains on tenants and their households. I believed, correctly, that records of intra-African litigation in the NC Courts would yield insights into social relations among families and in rural communities. I was constrained, however, by the wanton destruction of court records by the former South African Archives Service (now the National Archives of South Africa) in the 1970s and 1980s.[91] I spent some time working through the remaining records in order to find a set of contiguous magisterial districts, in an area including at least part of the Natal Midlands, whose extant records contained a high proportion of cases involving labor tenants. Cases involving labor tenants were concentrated in several districts of the Midlands, dominated by white farms, as well as a drier contiguous area, the thornveld, an area laced with "labor farms," from which Midlands farms and factories drew much of their labor. My contacts

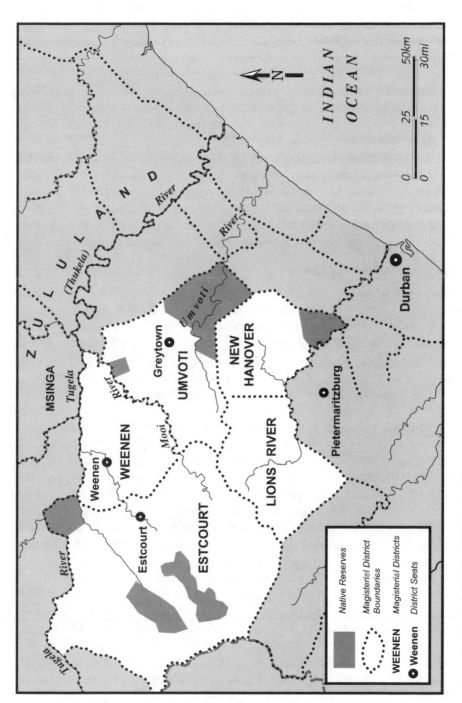

Map 1.2 Central Natal, 1920s to 1940s.

with nongovernmental organizations (NGOs) in the region guided me
to communities of labor tenants in the thornveld and former tenants
now residing in neighboring "reserve" areas.[92] I therefore chose a focus area that included part of the Midlands and thornveld, an area
connected by ties of labor, kinship, and administration. The area as a
whole comprises five contiguous magisterial districts (Estcourt, Lions
River, New Hanover, Umvoti, and Weenen), which I characterize as
Central Natal, depicted in Map 1.2.[93]

The five districts at the heart of this study are in an area of Natal
where labor tenancy was the prevalent system of agricultural labor
through the first half of the twentieth century. The area includes the
heart of the Natal Midlands and the thornveld that arcs around it to
the north and east. The Midlands is a region of rich farmland with
good rainfall and soils.[94] It is especially well suited to dairy farming,
maize cultivation for stock-feed, and wattle growing.[95] The Midlands,
broadly defined, stretches on one axis from Ixopo and Richmond in
the southwest through Pietermaritzburg (the colonial and provincial
capital of Natal) to New Hanover, Umvoti, and Kranskop in the northeast. On the other axis, the Midlands lie between Camperdown in the
southeast through Pietermaritzburg, Lions River, Mooi River, and
Estcourt in the northwest.[96] The altitude of the region ranges from
approximately 2,000 to 4,000 feet; prevalent night and early morning
fog in a large subset of the area led Anglophone settlers to call it the
Mistbelt.[97]

The rich farmland of the Midlands has a close economic and environmental relationship with the regions on which it borders. Most important,
the area is bisected by the road and rail corridor that connects Durban,
South Africa's largest port, with Johannesburg on the Witwatersrand, the
manufacturing, mining, and financial center that is the economic hub of
southern Africa. Since the 1880s, this communications corridor has provided an advantage to white commercial farmers in the agricultural areas
along the line. Midlands farmers took advantage of this transportation
network to market wattle and dairy products as well as sheep and cattle.[98]
Cattle husbandry in the Midlands also connected it closely with two areas that it straddles: (1) the arc above it on the plateau underneath the lip
of the Drakensberg, and (2) the thornveld that lies between the Midlands
and the Thukela River. In the grazing uplands of Mooi River and Estcourt,
transhumance practices sent cattle to graze in the uplands of the
Drakensberg to take advantage of good summer grasses there. In the cold,
dry winter, farmers sent cattle to graze on the good winter grasses of the
thornveld.[99]

Finally, the Midlands were intimately connected to the thornveld region, which served, in effect, as an area of private labor reserves. Many white farmers throughout the Midlands also owned one or more farms in the thornveld. This provided them not only with winter grazing but, equally important, with a secure source of cheap labor. African tenants on the labor farms could be called upon as needed, but their homesteads did not take up valuable space on the commercial farmers' wattle, dairy, or mixed farming land. The labor farm in effect gave the white farmer off-site labor tenants. For the tenants, living on the labor farm was much like living in the reserves except that homesteads secured their tenure by sending varying numbers of inmates for six-month stints on the commercial farm, in effect *khonza*'ing a farmer rather than (or in addition to) a chief.[100]

The study concentrates on the segregation era, especially its peak from the late 1920s to the early 1940s. This era is bracketed by two events consistently mentioned by my informants as markers of time: "the time of the Great Flu"—the worldwide influenza epidemic of 1918 that killed thousands in South Africa—and the 1944 Ngongolo "war," when men of the Chunu and Thembu chiefdoms fought a large-scale battle on a labor farm in Weenen district, an event that lingers more strongly in local memory than does World War II. The main focus is on the 1930s, a period of agricultural crisis in terms of economy (depression) and environment (drought, locusts, and malaria). That decade also saw the beginnings of a labor shortage that farmers and officials blamed on the migration of young men to urban industries. It therefore marked the beginning of attacks on the "inefficiency" of the labor tenancy system by large agricultural interests, foreshadowing the demise of the six-month system in the 1950s and 1960s. These economic and environmental crises coincided with and aggravated the crisis of control that the state attempted to address through segregation, pass controls, and labor repression. At a more local level, African labor tenants demonstrated a heightened anxiety about the meaning of tradition and the inability of male elders to assert control over women and juniors as labor tenancy offered diminishing benefits for those whose labor supported it.

THE SOURCES

This study relies on three types of sources: administrative records, court records, and interviews. The bulk of the chronological narrative is built on the administrative records, supplemented by newspapers and private papers. Although these are official accounts, they do not contain merely official views. The records of evidence presented to official commissions, especially the Native Economic Commission (NEC) and the Native Farm Labour Committee [*sic*] (NFLC), provide extensive accounts of the views of African subjects and white citizens. The local records of magisterial districts also provide a hearing for the voice of rural Africans, especially in the accounts of regular public meetings. The African voices contained in the administrative archives (as well as in newspapers), however, are almost invariably male and are often those of chiefs or prominent *amakholwa* (Christians).[101] The records of disputes among Africans in the NC Courts therefore provide a critical opening to the voice of "ordinary" rural Africans, including women and juniors. The disputes reflected in the court records involve the most important aspects of the economic and social life of rural Africans in Natal: marriage, bridewealth, cattle loans, and inheritance.

The Court Records

The texts of litigation in the NC Courts, like any text, present some problems of interpretation. Historians of nineteenth- and twentieth-century Africa, increasingly drawn to the use of court records, have argued that these previously neglected documents offer a potentially vast set of sources that will shed light on the lives of "ordinary" Africans, exposing their struggles with each other and with colonial and postcolonial states. Those who make use of such sources have also claimed that they can, to various degrees, enable us to hear African voices. Yet the difficulties of these sources require some methodological discussion. I summarize these problems as follows: litigants sometimes lie, rules of evidence often exclude, and translators and transcribers may trammel the truth. How, in the face of such problems, can we make productive use of court records?

Kristin Mann and Richard Roberts argued that the records of colonial courts—from chief's courts to the courts of district commissioners to metropolitan courts of appeal—offered a largely untapped source with considerable potential for gaining insight into the social history of Africa.[102] Their collection exuded optimism about the potential of court records and analysis of legal relations to illuminate the history of nineteenth- and twentieth-century Africa. David Cohen sounded the most pessimistic note in the book in his analysis of colonial litigation in Busoga. He argued that a case could not be adequately understood solely on the basis of the proceedings in court because local disputes tended to have deep histories embedded in long-term relationships and in local institutions (such as competing claims to land use rights) that were not necessarily reflected in the proceedings before the court or in its records.[103] James Clifford, in a piece concerned with competing understandings of indigenous identity in the late-twentieth-century United States, exposed a related problem in the use of court records: the way in which procedural rules and the adversary system conspire to exclude evidence or considerations that an ordinary observer would find relevant. Such evidence is often excluded on the grounds of its provenance (e.g., hearsay) or its prejudicial potential. Clifford was struck by the ways in which these rules created an artificially constrained storytelling ritual in the courtroom.[104] Looking at the problem of using court records for the construction of African social history, Roberts was cautiously optimistic.[105] He agreed with Cohen and Clifford that it will usually be necessary to illuminate the social and political context of disputes with materials from beyond the bounds of what American courts tend to refer to as "the cold record." Roberts continued to insist, however, that court records were rich sources, particularly in their potential to provide windows onto Africans' use of colonial institutions to "shape their own lives" and onto "divergences and disagreements [among Africans] over meanings and over relationships." Roberts concluded that court records could be illuminating, but that using them would require the construction of careful methodologies.[106] Stephan Miescher, working with court records from the Gold Coast colony (modern Ghana), has recently proposed a new methodology for an "enriched" reading of colonial court records through ethnographic study, which is similar to the methods I have attempted to employ here.[107] By using such methods, Miescher argues, scholars can overcome the limitations and distortions of court records.

These cautions and tentative solutions all fail to consider an important fact about court records: beyond being records of adjudicated disputes, they have little in common. There are many types of records, reflecting different intents and resources. The type of record varies with the level of court, the time and place of trial, the archival policies and abilities of the relevant state, and the languages of disputants and judges. At one extreme are bare statistical entries, showing for instance that there were sixty-eight divorce cases filed in a particular district in a particular year and that fifty-three of them were granted. At the other extreme lie the volumes of testimony and reports produced by judicial-style commissions of enquiry, such as South Africa's post-apartheid Truth and Reconciliation Commission (TRC). In between are a considerable variety of types. The records of the *Tribunal de premiere instance* discussed by Roberts, for example, contain quite minimal summaries; they record the nature of the dispute, the names and contentions of the litigants, and the outcome.[108] The records of the *ggombolola* (subcounty) court in Busoga, on the other hand, appear to be quite full transcripts, albeit translated from the language of the witnesses.[109]

This study relies on close readings of records of the NC Courts of Natal. The courts, successors in Natal to the pre-1927 courts of Administrators of Native Law, were charged under the 1927 Native Administration Act with hearing civil cases among Africans. NC Courts also heard appeals from rulings by chiefs (a litigant could begin his case before either the chief or the NC); the chiefs' courts themselves kept no official records until the 1950s. The NC Court records from the segregation era exhibit all the promise and all the problems I have outlined so far. They are indeed a wonderful resource for those of us seeking to understand the social and cultural history of modern South Africa. The records, though not complete transcripts, reflect at great length the words spoken by the litigants and their witnesses in the "native" courts of humble rural towns. They give us at least some access to the words and actions of labor tenants, migrants, widows, prodigal sons, reluctant brides, and would-be heirs, and less expectedly reveal aspects of the lives and views of white farmers and some of the workings of the magistracy. On the other hand, the records exhibit all the difficulties of lying litigants, exclusionary rules of evidence, and problems of transcription and translation. Furthermore, the evidence of court records potentially distorts in another way: such records represent the rare instances in which disputes could not be resolved by other means. Finally, archivists have altered the records through liberal use of the "memory hole."

Let's look at this last problem first. From the 1970s through at least the early 1990s, the former South African Archives Service carried out a policy of decimating the court records in their possession.[110] Archivists "scrutinized" records to determine which should be retained, but the service did not reveal the standards that shaped what would continue to be part of the historical record and what would not. Archivists with whom I discussed this issue, however, suggested that records having precedential value were more likely to be retained. My own extensive review of the files of several magisterial districts in the Natal Archives suggests that about 5 percent of the original records have been retained. It is impossible to determine what methods may have been used in "scrutinizing" these records. A large proportion of the retained records comprise cases in which a lawyer represented at least one side, but most do not appear to have been appealed. It is quite possible that the records have been retained on a purely random basis according to a quota based on available shelf space. From the point of view of historians seeking to use these records, random decimation is the best decimation, but the unfortunate truth is that we don't know.

What of the lying litigant? People who have sworn to tell the truth often do not do so, despite the threat of legal or spiritual sanctions, but this is a problem only to the extent that one is relying on the record to establish the truth of the matter testified to by that particular litigant. Most of the time, scholars rely on court records to determine what kinds of things people disputed about, in what types of courts, and how they established their claims or defended their innocence; whether any particular litigant is reporting truthfully is usually of considerably less concern to the scholar than it was to the litigants and the judge.[111] In my analysis of NC Court records, for example, it is less important that a particular cow was the subject of a *sisa* (cattle loan) arrangement as opposed to a *lobola* transfer than to see that this matter frequently became a subject of dispute among Natal labor tenants in the 1940s.[112] Furthermore, one of the significant advantages of court records over other types of documents is that by their nature they record multiple points of view. Court records like these show the types of disputes that occur in various communities and how those disputes are conceived and presented to allies, opponents, and judges. Best of all, they record the words of the litigants and their witnesses.

Or do they? The field of African studies has long been obsessed with the search for the African voice. The motivating factor in this search, of course, has been that that voice (or those voices, as we are now inclined to say) has been relatively hard to hear through traditional historical methods. Unfortunately, problems of transcription and translation intervene between us and the words spoken in a 1932 NC courtroom, for instance, by a widow seeking to deny her son's claim to her herd of goats. The handwritten trial records of NC Courts read, at first glance, like verbatim accounts of trials. They are full of the sudden stops and starts, changes of direction and perspective, and surprising conclusions that mark judicial proceedings in the flesh. On closer inspection, however, there are a number of gaps and filters. First, the records are generally in English, although there are occasional phrases or appended documents in *isiZulu*, the Zulu language. Before appearing on paper, then, the words of the litigants passed through two prisms: translation and transcription. It is not clear exactly how this occurred. Testimony must have been given primarily in *isiZulu*, the main language of the litigants and most of the witnesses, although some (especially the men) may also have been familiar with English, Afrikaans, or other languages of South Africa's industrial centers.[113] However, litigants and their witnesses were only part of the dramatis personae in the court. The NC was invariably white, and usually (in Central Natal) Anglophone. Ironically, the professionalization of the NAD from the 1930s may have militated against the linguistic (and cultural) expertise of the commissioners, as officers who had previously been long attached to a particular location were now subjected to a policy of regular transfers.[114] Some of them were probably excellent speakers of *isiZulu*, but this was certainly not uniformly the case.[115] In any event, there were other Anglophones on the stage: the lawyers engaged by a large number of the litigants. Once again, their rural and small-town origins may have given them a linguistic assist, but it is unlikely that most of them were able to communicate exclusively in *isiZulu* with first-language speakers.

The records give only slight indication of the fact of translation. Beyond the inference arising from the fact that most participants were speakers of *isiZulu* and the records are mainly in English, the record sometimes notes the presence, and more rarely the name, of the interpreter.[116] Although there is rarely any indication in the record itself of poor interpretation, it is likely that simultaneous translation from *isiZulu* to English, with the translated words then written down in English, would have resulted in some errors. The difficulty is compounded by the fact that *isiZulu* is a highly allusive language, whereas adversarial questioning in the Western-style courtroom calls for a fairly concrete and narrative structure. Ironically, then, the fact that testimony sometimes makes little sense or seems off the point tends to increase my confidence in the conscientious efforts of the interpreters and transcribers.

Emmanuel Le Roy Ladurie was faced with similar problems of translation in eliciting social history from the Inquisition records in southern France. He described the creation of the record as a three-stage process, with translation occurring as follows:

> The final Latin text of the Fournier Register raises various problems of translation. The accused usually spoke in Occitan. . . . So at some point the scribes translated the words of the accused into Latin. This operation took place either at the first stage, when the first notes were being taken, in a kind of "simultaneous translation," or, at the latest, when the minute was written (the second stage of the process). . . . A spoken translation back into the "vulgar tongue" was made when the accused

had the text of the minutes read out to them so that they could have alterations made in it if they wished.[117]

Ladurie reported this process of multiple stages of transcription and translation, but he makes no further comment on it except, in his conclusion, to call the record "a repressive Latin register that is a monument of Occitan literature."[118] Drawing a complex and intimate portrait of the fourteenth-century European village, he implicitly denied that the record might be distorted in any significant way. He suggested, again implicitly, that it is the fundamental whole rather than particular details that matter. Even more blithely, Steve Stern and William Taylor completely ignored the potential problems of translation in their respective use of court records to write histories of peasants in colonial Mexico.[119]

Beyond translation, a further problem is exclusion. The manner of eliciting evidence in structured, adversarial court proceedings results in a narrow view. Indeed, common law courts see the narrowing of issues as one of their most important functions. Trials and their transcripts exclude information in a variety of ways. First, as Cohen argued, court records provide a sort of tunnel vision of a social conflict because they tend to omit the context and history of the dispute. Second, rules of evidence exclude; that is their purpose. In the Natal NC Courts, however, procedure appears to have been quite relaxed; hearsay testimony is common in the record, as in ordinary conversation. Another category of exclusion, however, is more serious, and it is related to the concern raised by Cohen. Because the colonial state wished to deny the reality of some cognitive categories that were familiar and even essential to those permitted to make use of the customary law courts, testimony dealing with such issues was routinely (though not thoroughly) suppressed. Most pervasively, the courts refused to entertain accusations of witchcraft, except as an indirect or tangential issue.[120] Despite this systematic exclusion, Timothy Lane has produced a fascinating account of "how and why witchcraft accusations continued to manifest themselves as a powerful form of local discourse even in the face of the state's assault on African witchcraft beliefs."[121] In fact, witchcraft was a common subject of witness testimony in the divorce cases I discuss in chapter 5.

Finally, are court records representative? Disputes that end up in court are, of course, exceptional, but these disputes represent the sorts of revealing crises that show the types of strains and alliances that make up the fabric of everyday life. They also reveal the way in which some people used the institutions of the state to pursue personal and group strategies, as well as the way that legal structures—courts and codes—limit or shape remedies and even the way that people conceptualize their conflicts with others. The decimation of South African court records means that it is not generally possible to use the records to draw statistical conclusions, but they remain revealing sources of social tension, with considerable potential to enrich our understanding of how people make their own histories in conditions not of their own choosing.

Court records, like other sorts of historical evidence, are both enlightening and misleading. Court records are potential sources of unequalled power to reveal secret histories of divorce, inheritance, disputes over the ownership of cattle, and the ways in which such disputes intersect with the larger social processes of tenancy, migration, and the enforcement of state policies. They have a great advantage over oral histories in that they record the contemporaneous thoughts and speech of the participants, albeit in a form that contains various degrees of distortion. On their own, however, the records will usually fail to disclose a great many important connections—the history of the dispute and its broader social context as well as larger questions of ethnography and political economy—which are left to the scholar to ferret out by investigation, inference, and intuition. My own method, informed by my training both as a lawyer and as a historian, has involved an extremely close reading of the transcripts, coupled with a deep knowledge of the broader historical and ethnographic contexts in which the disputes took place. I gained a significant part of my understanding of the historical and cultural contexts of the disputes from oral testimony.

The Oral Testimony

A central component of my research was eliciting oral testimony from former labor tenants. I conducted approximately fifty oral interviews with older African men and women; nearly all were labor tenants in Central Natal in the relevant period. Most of the early methodological work on oral evidence concerned the use and interpretation of oral history of events and processes beyond living memory.[122] More recently, social historians and anthropologists concerned with processes within living memory have been concerned with the collection and use of oral testimonies and life histories of participants in those processes.[123] Analysts have noted such problems as the setting and the power relations involved in the interview, as well as the perils of cultural and linguistic translation.[124] Bozzoli, with Mmantho

Nkotsoe, acknowledged these problems in *Women of Phokeng*, but they believed that they had avoided many of them in their work. Nkotsoe, a woman originally from the area (albeit then a young urban academic), had conducted the interviews with elderly African women in rural Phokeng.[125] Van Onselen found it somewhat more difficult to negotiate the parameters of power in his extended series of interviews with Kas Maine, despite their shared gender and seniority; he relied mainly on a team of African student interviewers.[126] Keegan argued that "the difficulties of investigating women's perspectives should not be underestimated" and left that task to others.[127]

As a white, middle-class, foreign male, then in my late thirties, I entered the field with these difficulties in mind but determined to seek the oral perspectives of elderly African women and men who had been involved in labor tenancy. In fact, I faced an even more formidable obstacle: the "low-intensity" civil war then ravaging rural Natal in the dying days of apartheid. This context made the formation of bonds of trust across the above-mentioned differences extremely difficult. I did not throw caution to the wind but concluded, as Van Onselen later said, that "interviewing, like any other instrument at the disposal of the social scientist, has obviously got a distinctive shape and reach but . . . the tool is not, in itself, inherently flawed."[128] I approached the interviews in a manner that I hoped would minimize the inherent difficulties of interviews between a relatively youthful urban Westerner and elderly rural African informants, while accepting that these differences were bound to affect the content of our interactions. Because of widespread political violence, most of which was then occurring in rural areas and towns, I was not able to spend extended time living in the countryside. My wife and I lived in Pietermaritzburg in a former caretaker's cottage we rented on the grounds of a church-related primary school. Our neighbors included working-class former Rhodesians, university undergraduates, and marginally employed Africans escaping the violence of nearby African townships in the Edendale valley. Our little street, ironically one named for Shepstone, was only a couple of hundred meters from the Victorian railway station where Mahatma Gandhi had been thrown from a first-class carriage onto the platform. In another direction, our local supermarket was in the aptly named "Laager Center," not far up the street from the regional headquarters of the South African Defence Forces, itself only a few blocks from the offices of the then-recently unbanned ANC.

These circumstances meant that my interactions with informants, though always cordial, were never intimate. In some cases I was present at the site of the interview for only a few hours; in other cases

I was in the area for several days at a time. Although I tried to be
and to appear sympathetic, I was clearly an outsider. However, I
wanted to ensure that the informants with whom I spoke were as comfortable as possible with the situation and with me. I went to great
lengths to secure introductions to potential informants from people
whom they trusted, and I avoided initiating discussion of contemporary politics or violence. Although I myself was not known to the
men and women I interviewed, in each case the interpreter was someone the interviewee was familiar with, as I describe below. All interviews took place at the homesteads of informants or in nearby public
spaces, at times worked out between them and the interpreter. In some
cases we sat in a group of men or women, but I interviewed one at a
time. More often, those present included only the interviewee, the interpreter, myself, and sometimes one or two family members or friends
of the interviewee. I worked from an outline of questions I wished to
pursue, but I did not stick to a particular order of questions, and I
tried to be open to directions suggested by the informants. In general,
my questions were designed to elicit responses about the informant's
early life history and involvement in labor tenancy. Although I worked
with interpreters, as I became more comfortable in *isiZulu* and with
the social environment, I participated in parts of the *isiZulu* conversation and did not always wait for a translation before responding.

I worked with six different interpreters in various parts of the Midlands and thornveld over a period of several months. At the invitation of
Peter Brown, I conducted interviews at Easingwold, a farm owned by his
son in Lions River district. The elder Brown was a leader of the antiapartheid Liberal Party in the 1950s and later a founder of an NGO that
opposed removals of "black spots" and advocated labor tenant rights, the
Association for Rural Advancement (AFRA).[129] At the farm, I conducted
the interviews with the interpretation assistance of Antony Ntuli, head-
master of the farm school, in his office. Ntuli was a young married man
who had lived on the farm for a few years. He was acquainted with all of
the interviewees, who included both men and women. Sometimes one
other interviewee was present, and on one occasion another teacher was
there.

The one interview with a retired labor tenant at Malanspruit
(Estcourt district) was conducted at the informant's home. Malanspruit
is owned by Graham McIntosh, a former Democratic Party Member of
Parliament, outspoken advocate of unbridled capitalism, and opponent
of labor tenant advocacy groups such as AFRA. Nevertheless, AFRA
suggested that I contact him, and McIntosh invited me to conduct interviews at Malanspruit and on his labor farm, Mkolombe, in Weenen

district. My interpreter was a young farmworker, Nhlanhla Zungu, then studying for matriculation exams. He knew the informant well, and no one else was present during the interview. The interviews at Mkolombe were conducted at the two-room farm school. One of the teachers, a woman named T.J. Zungu (no relation to Nhlanhla), interpreted. The first interview was with two elderly men, including Kotayi Mkhize, the farm *induna* (headman). In a vivid manifestation of the patriarchal relations that are among the subjects of this study, Mkhize insisted on attending my interview with two elderly women of the farm the next day.

The greatest number of interviews was conducted with the assistance of CAPFarm Trust, a rural NGO based on the Msinga border of Weenen district. We interviewed women and men at Waaihoek (a resettlement camp for evicted labor tenants), at Mdukatshani (CAP's farm), in Mpofana, and at Keate's Drift (Msinga). Rauri Alcock, who manages the project, interpreted for most of the interviews; Natty Duma, also a CAP administrator, interpreted for several interviews in Mpofana. Alcock is white and was then in his early twenties. He grew up at Mdukatshani, is fluent in both *isiZulu* and English, and has extensive experience as an interpreter. Duma is an older African woman who is part of CAP's management and often serves as an interpreter. Both knew many of the informants and were known to all of them because of their work.

I conducted one interview in Keate's Drift (Msinga district) at an informant's home. The interpreter was Siyazi Zulu, a performer whose rural home is in Keate's Drift. Zulu's father, a contemporary of the interviewee, was also present.

With the agreement of the informants, I recorded each of the interviews on audiotape. Sifiso Ndlovu, then a master of arts student in history at the University of Natal, translated and transcribed the tapes. I lodged the transcriptions and copies of the tapes at the Killie Campbell Africana Library in Durban; I retain the original tapes. The interviews were of great assistance in getting life histories of labor tenants in terms of conditions of labor and of tenancy, migrancy, marriage, and family size, adding considerably to my understanding of other sources.[130] The knowledge I gained came not only from the interviews themselves but probably more profoundly from being able to spend several days at a time with several informants and interpreters in and around the farmland where they had worked. I was therefore able to absorb a sense of contemporary rural life that is essential in my interpretations and arguments, despite the atmosphere of violence that prevented a deeper rural immersion.

SUMMARY OF THE BOOK

Chapter 2 describes the nineteenth-century development of Natal's six-month system of labor tenancy and goes on to bring into focus its operation in the interwar period. The chapter shows how tensions of gender and generation were exacerbated by the structure of labor tenancy and further fueled by the accelerating pace of farm commercialization and the competing growth of urban labor markets. It draws on evidence collected by the NEC to develop a general picture of the system of labor tenancy and specifically its operation in Natal in the years around 1930. The chapter juxtaposes that official evidence with the context of the memories of former labor tenants who spoke with me in the early 1990s about their experiences of the system in their youth.

Chapter 3 places the six-month system and its familial tensions in the context of Natal's agricultural economy in the 1920s and 1930s. The pressures of agricultural boom in the late 1920s helped to fuel rural radicalism in Central Natal in the late 1920s in the form of the ICU. That movement in turn helped to generate support for tightening controls on rural labor, and the slide into economic depression also encouraged the state to erect a variety of marketing controls. These efforts occurred in the context of a series of ecological disasters in the early 1930s. The damage done to labor tenant security by the weather was exacerbated by diminishing returns for tenants on farms that were expanding commercial production backed by state subsidies. The lack of opportunity for younger members of tenant households increasingly contrasted with the growth of urban economies, while urban environments also offered opportunities to escape familial controls. Here we begin to examine the crisis of control that developed in the 1930s as a public controversy erupted over white farmers' claims of a chronic labor shortage, prompting the government to undertake an extensive inquiry into farm labor. Officials and farmers decried the tendency of labor tenant youth to abandon the farms for the cities, leaving their parents vulnerable to evictions. Large farming interests and modernizing economists took the opportunity to call for an end to the inefficiency of labor tenancy, whereas the state undertook extremely modest efforts toward reform. This detailed look at economic pressures and incentives for Natal's white farmers and their tenants sets the stage for a closer examination of gender and generation conflict in the next two chapters.

In chapters 4 and 5, I use the records of the NC Courts to look more closely at the divisions and alliances of gender and generation arising from this matrix. Chapter 4 further introduces my use of NC Court records and illustrates NAD's adoption of a rigid hierarchical understanding of customary law in the face of unsettling social change in the 1920s and 1930s. It goes on to examine the crisis of control in the context of rural authority and what I call the filial contract. Rural African fathers, along with farmers and the state, expressed increasing unease about the youthful lack of respect and failure to fulfill filial obligations, specifically the obligation to work six months on the farms. This struggle surfaced in the NC Courts in the context of cases between fathers and sons over bridewealth. Fathers refused to provide bridewealth for sons who had not worked on the farm in fulfillment of labor tenancy obligations, because this failure exposed the fathers to risk of eviction. Sons, on the other hand, demanded bridewealth as a quid pro quo from the fathers on whose behalf they had worked. In the background of these disputes, many sons earned their own bridewealth in the cities, whereas farmland was increasingly unavailable to tenants for the accumulation of cattle. Here again, court records demonstrated not a settled version of tradition but one that was shifting and contested in the context of ongoing economic and social change.

Chapter 5 is concerned with gender issues in the NC Courts. I examine a number of cases (mostly among labor tenants) about marriage, divorce, and bridewealth. These cases demonstrate increasing concern on the part of rural African men to exercise control over the movements and sexuality of African women, including daughters, wives, and widows. The NC and appellate courts were usually (but not always) sympathetic to this goal because they saw obedient African women as essential to a stable rural social order. The cases also reiterate the argument made in chapters 2 and 4 that, despite the attempt by the state and African elders to establish a uniform version of custom in the customary law regime, those disadvantaged under the regime constantly contested tradition and custom. Women and juniors contested it both in their actions and, ironically, in the courts designed to ensure the enforcement of the official traditional order.

In chapter 6, I attempt to draw some conclusions and to consider the lessons and legacy of this era for the post-apartheid order in South Africa.

NOTES

1. The setting of this study is the interior of Natal, then a province of the Union of South Africa. Historical changes in jurisdictional boundaries make the

discussion of this area somewhat confusing. Natal was a British colony from 1843 to 1910, and from 1895 it included Zululand. It was a province of South Africa from 1910 to 1994, and in 1994 it entered the "new" South Africa as part of the province of KwaZulu-Natal, which rejoined the province with the Zulu "homeland" that the apartheid state had consolidated from far-flung reserve areas within the provincial boundaries.

2. Colin Bundy, "The Emergence and Decline of a South African Peasantry," *African Affairs*, 71 (1972): 360–88, later expanded into book form as *The Rise and Fall of the South African Peasantry* (London: Heinemann, 1979).

3. Robin Palmer and Neil Parsons, eds., *The Roots of Rural Poverty in Central and Southern Africa* (Berkeley and Los Angeles: University of California Press, 1977).

4. This "cheap labor thesis" was most forcefully stated in H. Wolpe, "Capitalism and Cheap Labour-Power in South Africa: From Segregation to Apartheid," *Economy and Society*, 1, no. 4 (1972): 425–56. For a review of world systems, dependency theory and "articulation of the modes of production," and their influence on African and agrarian studies, see Frederick Cooper et al., *Confronting Historical Paradigms: Peasants, Labor, and the Capitalist World System in Africa and Latin America* (Madison: University of Wisconsin Press, 1993).

5. For the split between social history and structuralism in 1970s and 1980s South African historiography, see Belinda Bozzoli and Peter Delius, "Radical History and South African Society," and Helen Bradford, "Highways, Byways and Culs-de-Sacs: The Transition to Agrarian Capitalism in Revisionist South African History," both in *History from South Africa*, ed. by Belinda Bozzoli and Peter Delius, special issue of *Radical History Review*, 46/7 (Winter 1990), 13–46 and 59–88.

6. William Beinart, *The Political Economy of Pondoland 1860–1930* (Johannesburg: Ravan Press, 1982); Timothy J. Keegan, *Rural Transformations in Industrializing South Africa: The Southern Highveld to 1914* (Johannesburg: Ravan Press, 1986). See also Peter Delius, *The Land Belongs to Us: The Pedi Polity, the Boers and the British in the Nineteenth-Century Transvaal* (Berkeley and Los Angeles: University of California Press, 1984).

7. See William Beinart et al., eds., *Putting a Plough to the Ground: Accumulation and Dispossession in Rural South Africa 1850–1930* (Johannesburg: Ravan Press, 1986). For Natal, see John Lambert, *Betrayed Trust: Africans and the State in Colonial Natal* (Scottsville: University of Natal Press, 1995).

8. Helen Bradford, *A Taste of Freedom: The ICU in Rural South Africa 1924–1930* (New Haven: Yale University Press, 1987); William Beinart and Colin Bundy, *Hidden Struggles in Rural South Africa: Politics and Popular Movements in the Transkei and Eastern Cape 1890–1930* (Johannesburg: Ravan Press, 1987).

9. James Scott pioneered the concept of "everyday resistance" in peasant communities in *Weapons of the Weak: Everyday Forms of Peasant Resistance* (New Haven: Yale University Press, 1985). Gillian Hart criticized Scott's concept of everyday resistance for its failure to consider gender and differential experience within rural households. See Gillian Hart, "Engendering Everyday Resistance: Gender, Patronage and Production Politics in Rural Malaysia," *Journal of Peasant Studies*, 19, no. 1 (1991), 93–121, from which I derive the title of the next subsection.

10. Charles Van Onselen's work is a major exception to this general rule. See Charles Van Onselen, *The Seed Is Mine: The Life of Kas Maine, A South African Sharecropper 1894–1985* (New York: Hill and Wang, 1996). Three other recent exceptions are: Lambert, *Betrayed Trust*; Jeremy Krikler, *Revolution from Above, Rebellion from Below* (Oxford: Clarendon Press, 1993); Colin Murray, *Black Mountain: Land, Class and Power in the Eastern Orange Free State 1880s–1980s* (Johannesburg: Witwatersrand University Press for the International African Institute, 1992).

11. Beinart, for instance, gave considerable attention to contests between seniors and juniors over the accumulation and distribution of bridewealth but did not look directly at gender relations between men and women. *Political Economy of Pondoland.*

12. Belinda Bozzoli, "Marxism, Feminism and Southern African Studies," *Journal of Southern African Studies*, 9, no. 2 (1983): 139–71.

13. Helen Bradford, "Women, Gender and Colonialism: Rethinking the History of the British Cape Colony and Its Frontier Zones, c.1806–70," *Journal of African History*, 37, no. 3 (1997): 351–70.

14. Jeff Guy, "Gender Oppression in Southern Africa's Precapitalist Societies," in *Women and Gender in Southern Africa to 1945*, ed. by Cherryl Walker (Cape Town: David Philip, 1990), 33–47.

15. See Gillian Hart, "Imagined Unities: Constructions of 'The Household' in Economic Theory," in *Understanding Economic Process*, ed. by Sutti Ortiz and Susan Lees (Lanham, MD: University Press of America, 1992), 111–29; Jane Guyer and Pauline Peters, introduction to *Conceptualizing the Household: Issues of Theory and Policy in Africa*, special issue of *Development and Change*, 18 (1987): 197–214.

16. See, e.g., Bozzoli, "Marxism, Feminism." Gendered responses to changing relations of production are also explored in Michael Watts, "Living under Contract: Work, Production Politics, and the Manufacture of Discontent in a Peasant Society," in *Reworking Modernity: Capitalisms and Symbolic Discontent*, ed. by Alan Predd and Michael Watts (New Brunswick, NJ: Rutgers University Press, 1992), 65–105. For the most part, this literature has concentrated on gender divisions within the household, looking at the differential interests, access to resources, and strategies of men and women. I use this concept to look also at generational divisions in the labor tenant household.

17. Cf. Martin Chanock, "A Peculiar Sharpness: An Essay on Property in the History of Customary Law in Colonial Africa," *Journal of African History*, 32, no. 1 (1991): 67. An exception is John Lambert, "The Undermining of the Homestead Economy in Colonial Natal," *South African Historical Journal*, 23 (1990): 54–73. Lambert's work showed that generational tensions have been a hallmark of labor tenancy in Natal from its inception. Benjamin Mazower also viewed the 1940s and 1950s farm labor shortage as a generational crisis. See Benjamin L. Mazower, "Agriculture, Farm Labour and the State in the Natal Midlands, 1940–60," (M.A. thesis, University of Cape Town, 1991), chapter 3. Claude Meillassoux, of course, provided a general structural model of generational tension in African peasant communities but leaves little room for agency or change. See, e.g., Claude Meillassoux, "From Production to Reproduction: A Marxist Approach to Economic Anthropology," *Economy and Society*, 1, no. 1 (1972):

93–105. Sara Berry examined generational dynamics in the context of West African communities in *Fathers Work for Their Sons: Accumulation, Mobility and Class Formation in an Extended Yoruba Community* (Berkeley: University of California Press, 1985). See also Guyer and Peters, "Conceptualizing the Household."

18. Benedict Carton, *"Blood from Your Children": The Colonial Origins of Generational Conflict in South Africa* (Charlottesville: University Press of Virginia, 2000).

19. Beinart, *Political Economy of Pondoland*.

20. Keegan, however, continued to be preoccupied with the question of whether farm workers were proletarians. Keegan, *Rural Transformations*, 121–40.

21. More recently, Patrick Harries did incorporate gender into his analysis of household dynamics among migrant workers from Mozambique, although he gave little space to the views of nonmigrants, including women. Patrick Harries, *Work, Culture, and Identity: Migrant Laborers in Mozambique and South Africa, c.1860–1910* (Portsmouth: Heinemann, 1994).

22. Van Onselen, *The Seed Is Mine*.

23. Meredith McKittrick, *To Dwell Secure: Generation, Christianity, and Colonialism in Ovamboland* (Portsmouth: Heinemann, 2002); Carton, *Blood from your Children*.

24. Bozzoli, "Marxism, Feminism." Bradford, "Women, Gender and Colonialism," similarly argued for the centrality of gender to the colonial history of the Cape.

25. Wolpe, "Capitalism and Cheap Labour."

26. This argument relied on John Wright's research on "Control of Women's Labour in the Zulu Kingdom," in *Before and after Shaka: Papers in Nguni History*, ed. by J.B. Peires (Grahamstown: Institute of Social and Economic Research, 1981), 81–99, discussed below.

27. Cherryl Walker, "Gender and the Development of the Migrant Labour System c.1850–1930," in *Women and Gender in Southern Africa to 1945*, 68–96.

28. See especially, Kristin Mann and Richard Roberts, eds., *Law in Colonial Africa* (Portsmouth: Heinemann, 1991), 3–60; Sally Falk Moore, *Social Facts and Fabrications: "Customary" law on Kilimanjaro, 1880–1980* (Cambridge: Cambridge University Press, 1986); Martin Chanock, *Law, Custom and Social Order: the Colonial Experience in Malawi and Zambia* (Cambridge, UK: Cambridge University Press, 1985); Margaret Jean Hay and Marcia Wright, eds., *African Women and the Law: Historical Perspectives*, vol. 7 of *Boston University Papers on Africa* (Boston: Boston University, 1982).

29. Sara Berry, *No Condition Is Permanent: The Social Dynamics of Agrarian Change in Sub-Saharan Africa* (Madison: University of Wisconsin Press, 1993); Terence Ranger, "The Invention of Tradition Revisited," in *Legitimacy and the State in Africa: Essays in Honour of A.H.M. Kirk-Greene*, ed. by Terence Ranger and Olufemi Vaughan (Houndmills, UK: Macmillan, 1993), 62–111; Sally Engle Merry, "Law and Colonialism," *Law and Society Review*, 25, no. 4 (1991), 889–922; Terence Ranger, "The Invention of Tradition in Colonial Africa," in *The Invention of Tradition*, ed. by Eric Hobsbawm and Terence Ranger (Cambridge, UK: Cambridge University Press, 1983), 211–62.

30. Chanock, *Law, Custom*.

31. Ibid.; Martin Chanock, "Making Customary Law: Men, Women and Courts in Colonial Northern Rhodesia"; and Marcia Wright, "Justice Women and the Social

Order in Abercorn, Northeastern Rhodesia, 1897–1903," both in *African Women*, ed. by Hay and Wright, 53–67 and 33–50.

32. Chanock, *Law, Custom*; see also Elizabeth Schmidt, "Negotiated Spaces and Contested Terrain: Men, Women and the Law in Colonial Zimbabwe, 1890–1939," *Journal of Southern African Studies*, 16, no. 4 (Dec. 1990): 622–48.

33. Moore, *Social Facts*.

34. Ibid.

35. This point has been made by Iris Berger, "'Beasts of Burden' Revisited: Interpretations of Women and Gender in Southern African Societies," in *Paths toward the Past: African Historical Essays in Honor of Jan Vansina*, ed. by Robert Harms et al. (Atlanta: African Studies Association Press, 1994).

36. William H. Worger, *South Africa's City of Diamonds: Mine Workers and Monopoly Capitalism in Kimberley, 1867–1895* (New Haven: Yale University Press, 1987). Bradford, *Taste of Freedom*; Beinart and Bundy, *Hidden Struggles*.

37. See e.g. Diana Jeater, *Marriage, Perversion and Power: The Construction of Moral Discourse in Southern Rhodesia 1894–1930* (Oxford: Clarendon Press, 1993); Elizabeth Schmidt, *Peasants, Traders and Wives: Shona Women in the History of Zimbabwe, 1870–1939* (Portsmouth, NH, 1992); Sean Redding, "The Making of a South African Town: Social and Economic Change in Umtata, 1870–1950" (Ph.D. dissertation, Yale University, 1987).

38. Martin Chanock, "Writing South African Legal History: A Prospectus," *Journal of African History*, 30, no. 2 (1989): 265–88; see also Chanock, "A Peculiar Sharpness." The project has now appeared as *The Making of South African Legal Culture 1902–1936: Fear, Favour, and Prejudice* (Cambridge: Cambridge University Press, 2001).

39. Mahmood Mamdani, *Citizen and Subject: Contemporary Africa and the Legacy of Late Colonialism* (Princeton: Princeton University Press, 1996).

40. Sandra Burman, "Fighting a Two-Pronged Attack: The Changing Legal Status of Women in Cape-Ruled Basutoland, 1872–1884," in *Women and Gender*, ed. by Walker, 48–75; John Mason, "Hendrik Albertus and His Ex-Slave Mey: A Drama in Three Acts," *Journal of African History*, 31, no. 3 (1990), 423–46; Pamela Scully, "Rape, Race and Colonial Culture: The Sexual Politics of Identity in the Nineteenth Century Cape Colony, South Africa," *American Historical Review*, 100, no. 2 (Apr. 1995): 335–59; Pamela Scully, *Liberating the Family? Gender and British Slave Emancipation in the Rural Western Cape, South Africa, 1823–1853* (Portsmouth, NH: Heinemann, 1997).

41. This is also, of course, an issue of gender, bound up with constructions of masculinity.

42. Jeater, *Marriage, Perversion and Power*; Schmidt, *Peasants, Traders and Wives*.

43. Schmidt, *Peasants, Traders and Wives*, esp. 98–121.

44. Cf. Berry, *No Condition Is Permanent*, 40.

45. Cf. Harries, *Work, Culture and Identity*, xv–xix.

46. This section relies on the work of several scholars of nineteenth-century Natal: Lambert, *Betrayed Trust*; John Wright and Carolyn Hamilton, "Traditions and Transformations: The Phongolo-Mzimkhulu Region in the Late Eighteenth and Early Nineteenth Centuries," in *Natal and Zululand from Earliest Times to 1910: A New History*, ed. by Andrew Duminy and Bill Guest (Pietermaritzburg:

University of Natal Press, 1989), 49–82; David Welsh, *The Roots of Segregation: Native Policy in Colonial Natal, 1845–1910* (Cape Town: Oxford University Press, 1971). Their views are confirmed by my own examination of the relevant legislation of Natal Colony; commissions of enquiry into Natal's nineteenth century "native affairs"; and files of the colony's Secretary for Native Affairs (SNA) pertaining to customary law.

47. Cf. Berry, *No Condition Is Permanent,* 22–42.

48. Berry, *No Condition Is Permanent,* 22–42.

49. Mamdani, *Citizen and Subject*; Chanock, *Law, Custom, and Social Order.*

50. Jeff Guy, "An Accommodation of Patriarchs: Theophilus Shepstone and the Foundations of the System of Native Administration in Natal," paper presented at Conference on Masculinities in Southern Africa, University of Natal, Durban, July, 1997. See also Carton, *"Blood from your Children."*

51. Guy, "Gender Oppression;" Wright, "Control of Women."

52. Schmidt, *Peasants, Traders, and Wives*; Berger, "'Beasts of Burden' Revisited."

53. John Wright, "Control of Women's Labour;" Eileen J. Krige, *The Social System of the Zulus* (Pietermaritzburg: Shuter & Shooter, 1950); A.T. Bryant, *The Zulu People As They Were before the White Man Came* (Pietermaritzburg: Shuter and Shooter, 1949).

54. Bryant, *The Zulu People,* vii.

55. See Lambert, "Africans in Natal"; Jeff Guy, "The Destruction and Reconstruction of Zulu society," in *Industrialisation and Social Change in South Africa: African class formation, culture and consciousness 1870–1930,* ed. by Shula Marks and Richard Rathbone, 167–94 (London: Longman, 1979).

56. Guy, "Gender Oppression."

57. Ibid., 33.

58. Ibid., 39.

59. *Ordinances and Laws of Natal,* 2, 1870–1878, Code of Native Law as at present (1876–1878) administered, preface.

60. For instance, among Zulu speakers (in contrast to Tswana speakers) it is a young woman who "chooses" and "marries," in contrast to the young man, whose role (as suggested by language) is less direct. Adam Kuper, *Wives for Cattle: Bridewealth and Marriage in Southern Africa* (London: Routledge & Kegan Paul, 1982), 128–29. Cf. Jean Comaroff and John Comaroff, *Ethnography and the Historical Imagination* (Boulder: Westview Press, 1992), 127–54 (concerning Tshidi culture); Regina Smith Oboler, *Women, Power, and Economic Change: The Nandi of Kenya* (Stanford: Stanford University Press, 1985).

61. See Guy, "Gender Oppression," 45–47; Wright, "Control of Women's Labour," 93–95.

62. Guy, "Gender Oppression," 45.

63. Ibid., 46.

64. See Wright, "Control of Women's Labour," 85.

65. Krige, *Social System of the Zulus,* 30.

66. Guy, "Gender Oppression," 34–35.

67. This section relies on Wright and Hamilton, "Traditions and Transformations," and Guy, "Gender Oppression." It is not clear to what extent these changes affected areas like Natal, which was outside the Zulu heartland but subject in varying de-

grees to its dominance and also to the dominance of chiefdoms that had relocated from the Zulu heartland, such as the Qwabe and the Chunu. For an analysis of the variable extent of Zulu power in the region, see John Wright, "The Dynamics of Power and Conflict in the Thukela-Mzimkhulu Region in the Late 18th and Early 19th Centuries: A Critical Reconstruction," Ph.D. dissertation, University of the Witwatersrand, 1989.

68. *Inkosi*, an *isiZulu* word usually translated as "chief," may also be translated as "king" or "lord." The nineteenth-century Zulu kings were overlords of chiefdoms that had been amalgamated under Zulu authority.

69. Lambert, *Betrayed Trust.*

70. Cf. Schmidt, *Peasants, Traders and Wives*; Carton, *"Blood from Your Children."*

71. Beinart, *Political Economy of Pondoland.*

72. See Harries, *Work, Culture and Identity.*

73. Lambert, *Betrayed Trust.*

74. Berry, *No Condition Is Permanent*, 29.

75. Pietermaritzburg Archives Repository (PAR), SNA, Instructions Issued to Administrators of Native Law, "Regulations Issued Under Law No. 1, 1869, for the Registration of Native Marriages, Divorce, and Translation, in the Colony of Natal"; PMB, SNA 1/7/8; Lambert, *Betrayed Trust*; Welsh, *Roots of Segregation*, 103–5. The colonial state in Rhodesia made similar forays into regulating marriage and adultery. See Jeater, *Marriage, Perversion and Power*; Schmidt, *Peasants, Traders and Wives.*

76. Cf. Chanock, *Law, Custom, and Social Order.*

77. *Ordinances and Laws of Natal*, 2, Code of Native Law as at present (1876–1878) administered; *Ordinances and Laws of Natal*, 5, Code of Natal Native Law, No. 19, 1891. See Welsh, *Roots of Segregation*, 1971. Mamdani, *Citizen and Subject*, mistakenly characterizes the 1878 codification as the issuance of mere guidelines.

78. Natal Code, 1878, preamble.

79. Carolyn Hamilton, *Terrific Majesty:* The Powers of Shaka Zulu and the Limits of Historical Invention (Cambridge, MA: Harvard University Press, 1998); Worger, "Law at the Margins of Empire," paper presented at African Studies Association Annual Meeting, San Francisco, November, 1996.

80. Carton, *"Blood from Your Children"*; Shula Marks, *Reluctant Rebellion: The 1906–08 Disturbances in Natal* (Oxford: Clarendon Press, 1970).

81. Welsh, *Roots of Segregation.* Dubow tends to dismiss the Shepstonian heritage of segregation, emphasizing instead the Cape bureaucratic tradition. Saul Dubow, *Racial Segregation and the Origins of Apartheid in South Africa, 1919–36* (Houndmills, UK: Macmillan, 1989).

82. Shula Marks, *The Ambiguities of Dependence in South Africa: Class, Nationalism, and the State in Twentieth Century Natal* (Baltimore: Johns Hopkins University Press, 1986); Saul Dubow, *Scientific Racism in Modern South Africa* (Cambridge: Cambridge University Press, 1995).

83. The Union of South Africa united the two former British colonies, the Cape and Natal, with the two former Boer republics, the Transvaal and the Orange Free State. The reserve-based policies of the former British colonies were the most influential in the post-Union period.

84. Dubow, *Racial Segregation*, 21–50.

85. Ibid.; Beinart and Bundy, *Hidden Struggles*.

86. The Natives Land and Trust Act of 1936 is discussed in chapter 3.

87. *Report of the Department of Native Affairs for the Years 1935–36*, U.G. 41-1937, 12.

88. In this period the government also enacted a uniform system of native taxation under the rubric of the Natives Taxation and Development Act of 1925. The act provided for a one-pound poll tax payable by every African male over eighteen years of age, plus an additional ten shillings for reserve dwellers. The poll tax was designed to finance the costs of native administration. Ibid., 13.

89. Labor tenancy, in the form discussed here, was officially abolished between 1964 and 1980. Gavin Williams, "Transforming Labour Tenants," in *Land, Labour and Livelihoods in Rural South Africa: Vol. 2, Kwazulu/Natal and Northern Province*, ed. by M. Lipton and F. Ellis (Durban: Indicator Press, 1996), 215–38. Present-day labor tenants are usually full-time workers who reside on the farms where they work, but the "six-month system," as discussed in this study, persists in isolated pockets. Laurine Platzky and Cherryl Walker, *The Surplus People: Forced Removals in South Africa* (Johannesburg: Ravan Press, 1985), 30–31. The post-apartheid government has passed legislation to secure the rights of labor tenants and to distribute land to some of them. See The Land Reform (Labour Tenants) Act, No. 3 of 1996. Williams has identified serious conceptual and practical difficulties with this legislation.

90. Cf. James C. Scott, *Domination and the Arts of Resistance: Hidden Transcripts* (New Haven: Yale University Press, 1992).

91. In order to reduce bulk, the Archives Service "scrutinised" the court records and discarded most of them, leaving only a few cases per year per district. I take up this issue in more detail below.

92. Reserves were then part of the KwaZulu homeland ("Bantustan") and are now included within lands administered by the Ngonyama Trust. In apartheid theory, these lands were not part of "white" South Africa.

93. The area is in the southwestern portion of the present province of KwaZulu-Natal, but it is central with reference to the former Natal Colony—that is, the portion of the province southwest of the Thukela River. Apart from the sugar-growing coast, Natal was dominated more by white farming and less by reserve land than was Zululand (the portion of the province northeast of the Thukela).

94. The possibilities for agriculture in Natal are largely determined by rainfall patterns and topography. The best agricultural land lies in the rolling coastal and Midlands regions below 3,000 feet. This belt has good soils and warm to hot summer growing seasons with reliable summer rains and some winter rainfall, although hilly topography limits cultivation in some parts of the region. Much of the northern interior is dominated by medium-quality land, a "gently undulating grassland" between 3,000 and 4,000 feet, where limits are set by hot summers and the lack of winter rainfall. This area is mainly used for cattle grazing. The transverse river valleys—for example, the Thukela River in the interior districts of Weenen and Msinga—feature generally poor land. Summers are very hot, rainfall is both low and unreliable, and the land is rugged and mountainous. The Drakensberg range is also too rugged for agriculture, but there is summer grazing and forestry in some areas of the mountains. T. J. D. Fair, *The Distribution*

of Population in Natal, vol. 3 of *Natal Regional Survey* (Cape Town: Oxford University Press, 1955), 30–32.

95. More recently, agricultural enterprises have used Midlands areas for intensive chicken farming, more forestry (including gums and pines), and sugarcane. In the wake of apartheid, the area has emerged strongly as a region for tourism, offering crafts and bed-and-breakfast accommodation, and serving as a gateway to the Drakensberg.

96. Unless stated otherwise, I am referring to the magisterial districts, not the towns of the same names. Mooi River district was a part of Estcourt district in the time period of my study. The boundaries of other districts have also shifted several times.

97. Lambert, *Betrayed Trust.*

98. N. Hurvitz, *Agriculture in Natal 1860–1950*, vol. 12 of *Natal Regional Survey* (Cape Town: Oxford University Press, 1957), 12.

99. Interview with Don Hall, Willow Grange, 18 Feb. 1992.

100. To *khonza* is to offer allegiance to and seek the protection of: "pay respect to; . . . be a tenant." G.R. Dent and C.L.S. Nyembezi, *Scholar's Zulu Dictionary* (Pietermaritzburg: Shuter and Shooter, 1969), 392. Some industrial concerns and sugar farmers also owned labor farms in the thornveld, as did some farmers from the Orange Free State. See the discussion of labor farms in Bradford, *Taste of Freedom,* 55–56 and 189–90.

101. Cf. Schmidt, *Peasants,* 2.

102. Mann and Roberts, *Law in Colonial Africa.*

103. David William Cohen, "A Case for the Basoga: Lloyd Fallers and the Construction of an African Legal System," in *Law in Colonial Africa*, ed. by Mann and Roberts, 239–54.

104. James Clifford, *The Predicament of Culture: Twentieth-Century Ethnography, Literature, and Art* (Cambridge, MA: Harvard University Press, 1988).

105. Richard Roberts, "Text and Testimony in the *Tribunal de Premiere Instance*, Dakar, during the Early Twentieth Century." *Journal of African History* 31, no. 3 (1990): 447–63. The article preceded the publication of *Law in Colonial Africa*, so it is therefore not a revision, but it takes a more focused look at the problems of interpreting court records.

106. Ibid., 462.

107. Stephan Miescher, "Gender, Personhood, and Legal Consciousness in Colonial Ghana," paper presented at Symposium on Law, Colonialism, and Human Rights in Africa, Stanford University, 8 May 1999.

108. Roberts, "Text and Testimony."

109. Cohen, "A Case for the Basoga," 254.

110. Act 43 of 1996, the National Archives of South Africa Act, now prohibits destruction of public records "without the written authorisation of the National Archivist." The Archivist appears, therefore, to have discretion to destroy some public records. I do not know whether the National Archives has continued to throw out court records in the post-apartheid era.

111. One of the major exceptions to the exclusion of hearsay evidence at common law takes a similar approach; hearsay evidence may be admitted when it is used, for example, to establish the state of mind of the speaker rather than the truthfulness of the statement.

112. Thomas McClendon, "'Hiding Cattle on the White Man's Farm': Cattle Loans and Commercial Farms in Natal, 1930–1950," *African Economic History*, 25 (1997): 43–58.

113. In McClendon, "'Hiding Cattle,'" the witness who gave the unusual definition of *ukusisa* reflected in the title blamed his statement on poor translation (and the absence of his lawyer). In another case, a witness caught in a contradiction protested that "I understand the interpreter and all that he says," PAR, 1 EST 2/1/2/1, *Nene v. Ndhlovu*, case 31/1942.

114. Dubow, *Racial Segregation*.

115. A 1946 court record notes the absence of a Zulu interpreter as a reason to delay resumption of the case, PAR, 1 EST 2/1/2/1, *Koza v. Mapumulo*, case 106/1943.

116. PAR, 1 WEN 2/1/2/1, *Nene v. Ngqulungu*, case 18/1936, reports the reasons for judgment by the chief's deputy Mbuzi Mzolo, "interpreted by F.W. Birkenstock." The "acting clerk and Zulu interpreter" of the Lions River NC Court in 1920 was Algernon Roach, 1 HWK 2/1/2/1, *Luvuno v. Luvuno*, case 8/1920. Joseph George Pullen held that position in 1930, *Nsutsha v. Sokela*, case 22/1930. By 1933, it was J.H. Schafer, *Madhlala v. Tshangase*, unnumbered 1932 case. By the 1940s, more Zulu-surnamed men begin to appear as interpreters, such as Edgar Sydney Kunene in *Zuma v. Ndhlovu*, case 5/1939 (the notation appearing in a 1946 revival of the case). Someone named Williams interpreted in Weenen in 1942, *Mkize v. Mkize*, 1 WEN 2/1/2/1, case 20/1942, while in the same year Herbert Masuka appears as interpreter in a criminal case appended to *Mkize v. Mcunu*, case 23/1942, and "native clerk" Ongubane [sic] in *Majola v. Mcunu*, case 60/1943.

117. Emmanuel Le Roy Ladurie, *Montaillou: The Promised Land of Error* (New York: Vintage Books, 1979), xvii, n. 2.

118. Ibid., 356.

119. Steve J. Stern, *The Secret History of Gender: Women, Men and Power in Late Colonial Mexico* (Chapel Hill: University of North Carolina Press, 1995); William Taylor, *Drinking, Homicide and Rebellion in Colonial Mexican Villages* (Stanford: Stanford University Press, 1979).

120. For colonial legal attitudes to witchcraft and the perverse effects of the non-recognition of witchcraft in colonial legal systems in Africa, see Chanock, *Law, Custom and Social Order*, 85–102. The Royal Instructions pertaining to Natal in 1848 referred, characteristically, to "pretended witchcraft." Taylor came up against the same problem working with criminal records from colonial Mexico, but he did not pursue the issue. Taylor, *Drinking, Homicide*, 73.

121. Timothy Lane, "'A Reasonable Amount of Harmony': Conflict, Witchcraft Accusation, and Violence in Rural Households, 1910–1920," paper presented at Symposium on Law, Colonialism and Human Rights in Africa, 8 May 1999.

122. See, e.g., Jan Vansina, *Oral Tradition As History* (Madison: Wisconsin, 1985); Jan Vansina, *Oral Tradition: A Study in Historical Methodology*, trans. by H.M. Wright (London: Routledge and Kegan Paul, 1965); Joseph Miller, ed., *The African Past Speaks: Essays on Oral Tradition and History* (Folkstone, UK: 1980); David Henige, *The Chronology of Oral Tradition: Quest for a Chimera* (Oxford: Clarendon Press, 1974).

123. See, e.g. Susan Geiger, *TANU Women: Gender and Culture in the Making of Tanganyikan Nationalism, 1955–65* (Portsmouth: Heinemann, 1997); Harries, *Work, Culture and Identity*; Belinda Bozzoli with the assistance of Mmantho Nkotsoe, *Women of Phokeng: Consciousness, Life Strategy and Migrancy in South Africa, 1900–1983* (Johannesburg: Ravan Press, 1991); Luise White, *The Comforts of Home: Prostitution in Colonial Nairobi* (Chicago: University of Chicago Press, 1990); Sarah Mirza and Margaret Strobel, eds., *Three Swahili Women: Life Histories from Mombassa, Kenya* (Bloomington: Indiana University Press, 1989); Timothy J. Keegan, *Facing the Storm: Portraits of Black Lives in Rural South Africa* (Cape Town: David Philip, 1988). For a brief overview of the use of oral history in South Africa up to the late 1980s, see Paul La Hausse, "Oral History and South African Historians," in *History from South Africa*, ed. by Bozzoli and Delius, 346–57.

124. See, e.g., Bozzoli, *Women of Phokeng*, 1–15.

125. Ibid., 4–10.

126. Charles Van Onselen, "The Reconstruction of a Rural Life from Oral Testimony: Critical Notes on the Methodology Employed in the Study of a Black South African Sharecropper," *Journal of Peasant Studies*, 20, no. 3 (Apr. 1993): 494–514. See also Miranda Miles and Jonathan Crush, "Personal Narratives As Interactive Texts: Collecting and Interpreting Migrant Life-Histories," *The Professional Geographer*, 45 (Feb. 1993), 84–94.

127. Keegan, *Facing the Storm*, 160.

128. Van Onselen, "Reconstruction," 513.

129. AFRA had its origins in the Surplus People's Project and now works for restoration of land to dispossessed titleholders and labor tenants.

130. I also conducted interviews with three white farmers in Willow Grange (Estcourt district). In addition, I interviewed a retired white magistrate in Eshowe. Finally, I have closely reviewed the transcripts of interviews conducted with Natal labor tenants by Helen Bradford in 1980 and by the University of Natal Oral History Project in the 1979–1981 period.

2

GENDER AND GENERATION IN THE SIX-MONTH SYSTEM THROUGH THE 1930s

> Well the six-month system was good as far as the fact that you were working for your father, helping him secure a place to stay with the family as tenants in a farm. Also the father could pay *lobola* for you. . . . The bad part of it was that you became a laughing stock to your peers because of the low wages you were receiving after the six-month period.[1]

By the early decades of the twentieth century, labor tenancy was the dominant system through which Africans gained access to nonreserve land and white farmers gained access to labor. The system emerged in the nineteenth century as a means for African peasants to retain their place on white-owned farmland by paying rent in the form of labor, enabling white farmers to have access to a workforce at minimal cost, measured mostly in land dedicated to tenants' homesteads and grazing. The resulting compromise was a system in which an African homestead provided some of its members—especially the young men—as labor for the white farmer for six months of the year. Tenant workers were paid nominal wages, if any, and often went into debt to landlords who provided advances in cash or in kind. During the six months "off," the men either "rested"—that is, worked on their own homesteads on the farm—or migrated to the cities, especially Johannesburg and Durban, for work at considerably higher wages. This arrangement came to be known as the "six-month system," or

ukusebenza isithupa (working six months). As the implementation of
the 1913 Natives Land Act gradually eliminated the greater independence available under rent tenancy, most rural Africans outside the
reserves became labor tenants. The combination of industrial expansion in the cities with more commercial use of farmland, leaving less
land available for the use of tenants, led increasing numbers of young
men and women to leave the farms as migrant workers or permanent
emigrants. After the commodities boom of the late 1920s, followed
immediately by the Great Depression and then by an industrial upsurge from the mid-1930s, this farm labor system entered a prolonged
period of crisis, fueling cries for its abolition in the 1940s and 1950s.
Because of distinct advantages to both white farmers and black labor
tenants, however, labor tenancy survived until its forced demise in the
1960s, and traces of it linger in the thornveld and in northern Natal.[2]

The labor tenant system depended on the ability of *abanumzane* to
commit the labor of their juniors—sons, daughters, and wives—to
work in response to the demands of white landowners. In return for
promising family labor, *abanumzane* gained access to land for growing subsistence food crops and grazing stock, tasks which were also
performed primarily by wives and children. Most *isithupa* labor was
performed by sons, from adolescence until they married and moved
away to establish their own homesteads. These same young men usually spent the months in which they were free of *isithupa* obligations
engaged in migrant labor in urban areas, in order to earn cash for tax
payments, clothing, luxuries, and marriage payments. Diminishing
opportunities for peasant production and accumulation on white-owned
farms made urban labor both more necessary and more attractive. As
a result, farmer-landlords and *abanumzane* often found it difficult to
get labor tenant sons to return from urban sojourns for the performance of *isithupa*. If sons failed to return, fathers and their other dependents were likely to suffer the consequences in the form of
eviction, reducing them to wandering in search of a new labor tenant
agreement or seeking entry into overcrowded reserve areas. Wives and
daughters also carried a heavy burden under labor tenancy and exercised choices that frustrated patriarchal arrangements. Labor tenant
wives did not engage in *isithupa* labor, since they were responsible
for crop production and domestic reproduction in labor tenant homesteads, with daughters by their sides. Daughters, however, often did
perform *isithupa* as household servants, whereas wives were called on
to perform *togt* (casual labor), especially in the farmer-landlord's
house and garden and at harvest time. Women did not migrate to urban areas to work because there was little formal urban work avail-

able for them and urban journeys by single women were seen as corrupting, which often resulted in loss of familial ties. *Abanumzane* and
younger married men nevertheless worried about the potential waywardness of wives and daughters because their security rested on the
stability of female production and reproduction. Control of the movements and sexuality of wives and daughters was as crucial to labor
tenant patriarchs as was control of the labor of younger men.

This chapter will describe the system of labor tenancy and outline
its historical development in Natal. It will examine the way the system worked in the 1920s and 1930s through the remembrances of labor tenants and contemporary witnesses to government commissions,
demonstrating the nature of the labor tenant household and its lines of
tension. Chapter 3 will explore the way in which these tensions were
exacerbated by economic developments in the 1920s and 1930s, leading to a crisis of control that is explored both in that chapter and
through more detailed examination of NC Court litigation in chapters
4 and 5.

THE ORIGINS OF LABOR TENANCY IN NATAL

The system of labor tenancy developed in nineteenth-century Natal
from the need of rural Africans for land and the need of white farmers for flexible labor. Like sharecropping in the southern United States,
labor tenancy represented a compromise between white landowners and
the resident black labor force.[3] Rural African homesteads were unable
to retain complete independence and self-sufficiency, whereas white
farmers were unable to achieve the total dominance that would have
enabled them to require full-time labor while continuing to pay extremely low wages. The six-month system represented a balance of
power between workers, who saw themselves as independent, and
landowners, who saw themselves as commercial farmers commanding
a labor force, not as "*kaffir* ["African," derogatory] farmers" dependent on rent from African homesteads.[4]

Before white commercial agriculture became viable in the 1880s, however, the colonial state, white settlers, and speculating landowners all
depended heavily on the rise and continued success of an African peasant
class in Natal.[5] In the first part of the colonial period in Natal (1843–
1880), the settler population ate, the state filled its coffers, and land
speculators reaped revenues through the efforts of this Natal peasantry.[6]
The failure of mid nineteenth century immigration schemes to stimulate
white farming resulted in large tracts of land in Natal falling into the
hands of absentee land speculators, especially large investors such as the

Natal Land and Colonisation Company.[7] Even on those lands actually occupied by their white owners, there was little white investment in agriculture before the 1880s. Transportation of goods to market was difficult until the completion of the railway line from Durban to the Transvaal gold fields in the 1880s. In addition, the settlers until then failed to develop any successful export crops, and land speculation remained a profitable "use" of the land.[8]

Although white settlers were not producing much food for their colony, they did constitute a market for agricultural products. Africans living near areas of white settlement filled the market vacuum created by the failure of whites to engage in productive farming in the early colonial period, and African homesteads remained in possession of most white-owned and Crown land. Lambert describes "a remarkable flowering of the African homestead economy" from the 1850s to the 1870s, especially in the Midlands area of Natal with convenient access to Pietermaritzburg, the capital and principal town of the interior. In more outlying areas of the Midlands, African producers sold grain to white farmers.[9] African prosperity in this period was built on surplus production of the homestead staple, maize. *Abanumzane* used their profits to build up cattle herds, the traditional form and expression of wealth.[10] Successful *abanumzane* were therefore able to increase the size of their homesteads by marrying additional women and transfering bridewealth cattle to new in-laws. At the same time, the presence of white farms seeking African tenants to pay rent, provide labor, or both offered an opportunity to young men seeking to establish new homesteads.

The infertility and small size of the reserves relative to the population meant that from an early date a large proportion of African homesteads were located on Crown land or white-owned farms.[11] As white farming developed, much of the Crown land occupied by Africans was sold to white farmers, who then attempted to collect rent or labor services. African homesteads on white-owned lands in the late nineteenth century fell into two categories: squatters and labor tenants. The two categories were sometimes conflated in the contemporary literature, but in precise usage *squatters* referred to rent-paying tenants, whereas *labor tenants* gained access to arable and grazing land by supplying labor to the farm owner for an agreed number of person-days per year.[12] Both forms of tenure on white farms conferred some advantages on African homesteads, but tenant families preferred squatting, as it provided the greatest degree of autonomy for homestead activities and production. Squatters were subject to the threat of eviction, but otherwise they suffered little interference with their agricultural or pastoral practices as long as they paid the required rent. Of course, the best land, especially land close to urban markets, carried a premium.[13] As white agriculture developed from the 1880s, many squatters were evicted or were forced to enter into labor tenancy agreements. This trend accelerated after the 1913 Land Act outlawed new rent tenancies.

Although most Africans viewed labor tenancy as less desirable, it was nevertheless mutually advantageous to white farmers and African tenants, which helps to explain its survival into the late twentieth century. In the nineteenth century, its most obvious advantage for labor tenants was that they were exempt from being called out by their chiefs for *isibalo* on the colonial state's public works, mainly roads.[14] In this respect, labor tenancy restored the homestead as the fundamental political unit, supplanting the power of chiefs. To some degree, however, the authority of the chief was replaced by the authority of the farmer as the person who could distribute or withhold land and who was the ultimate arbiter of justice in his realm.[15] Initially, as suggested above, labor tenancy (like squatting) offered an advantage to young men seeking to escape the authority of their fathers and chiefs and trying to find suitable land on which to establish a new homestead. As the system developed, however, it was fraught with generational tensions that weakened the homestead as a unit. Although moving to another farm remained an option for those seeking to establish a new homestead, analogous to the practice of relocating and offering to *khonza* a new chief, the labor tenancy system was built on an alliance between white farmers and African homestead heads seeking to command the labor and deference of young men.

This tension between fathers and sons over labor and the disposition of earnings, present at the outset, was to grow into a full-blown crisis by the 1930s. Although it contained this seed of conflict, the labor tenancy system flourished because it offered Africans access to land and grazing outside the overcrowded and increasingly impoverished reserves, and it gave white farmers access to a cheap dependent labor supply. The system reached its peak in the 1920s and 1930s, bringing its contradictions to the fore.

LABOR TENANCY IN THE 1920s TO EARLY 1930s

By the time of the 1930–1932 NEC, labor tenancy was the dominant system of African land tenure and of agricultural labor outside the reserves. This remained true in the late 1950s, when the University of Natal conducted its regional survey.[16] The decisive event intervening between the first growth spurt of commercial farming in the late nineteenth century and the boom of the late 1920s was the passage of the 1913 Natives Land Act.[17] Debates over the effect of the act have shown that it did not undo the independence of South Africa's peasantry by fiat, or overnight.[18] Although the act gave increased leverage to white farmers, "it did not immediately transform the countryside."[19] Over time, however, in combination with economic forces that increased the amount of land put into production while drawing labor to the cities, the Land Act decisively changed the balance of power in favor of white farmers and against African tenants. The law prohibited "squatting," or rent tenancy, by requiring that African residents on white-owned land render "service" to the owner for at least ninety days each year.[20] Henceforth, a legal tenancy was one that required labor service from the tenant. Although this requirement continued to be evaded, and although existing rent tenancies were exempted, the legislation tilted the scales in favor of labor-seeking farmers.[21] The Land Act prohibited new rent tenancies, but it did not proscribe existing tenancies, so many rental arrangements continued as before. As white farmers brought more land into production in the 1920s, however, they terminated rent tenancies and required their tenants to enter relations of labor tenancy; as a result of the act, tenants were left with fewer options to resist these changes.[22]

The NEC Report, published in 1932, discussed labor tenancy at length. In an unintentionally ironic aside on the way that race and class shaped the hearing of testimony, it commented that although witnesses had complained about the conditions and pay of labor tenants, "very few of these witnesses were themselves labour tenants."[23] The report noted that the "head of [the labor tenant] family" generally did not work if he had adult children. His wives and daughters were often called on to "do the house work and the washing" at the home of the white farmer, in addition to the domestic labor they performed at their own homesteads (which the report left unmentioned). In the main, however, the labor supplied by the *kraal* head was that of his sons:

> The principal source of labour for the farmer is the sons of the kraal head, who can be usefully employed at a fairly early age. The flight of many young Natives from the farms to the towns is referred to elsewhere. This gives rise to considerable difficulties and friction between employer and tenant.[24]

In addition to the payment of wages, if any, the NEC reported that labor tenants were given food while at work, and they were allowed to eat stock that died on the farm. They also got variable amounts of land for plowing and grazing, sites on which to erect dwellings, and the use of building materials, fuel, and water found on the farm.[25] These details purported to show that the minimal wages received by tenants did not fully measure their compensation.

Commissioner F.A.W. Lucas's addendum took a more realistic view of the economic predicament of labor tenants. To counterbalance the commission's emphasis on the disadvantages for the farm owner, Lucas provided a useful summary of the disadvantages of the system for the tenant:

> [I]n many areas he has to work for the owner of the land at the time when he should be attending to his own agricultural needs and his crop is often neglected. In any event he often does not get enough land to provide for the food requirements of himself and his family, certainly seldom enough to enable him to produce a surplus to sell. . . . A good season may give him enough food, a bad season will not, and he has then to depend on the goodwill of his employer to feed him and his family. The labour tenant has no security of tenure and no chance to carry over anything to the next year. To a farmer who has more land than he can work the cost of a labour tenant is little or nothing. . . . The labour tenant must give services which on a three monthly basis in the Transvaal and a six monthly in Natal often constitute a very high rent.[26]

Many African witnesses complained of the low pay, inadequate lands and grazing, and poor conditions for labor tenants, but the NEC Report nevertheless asserted that "[t]he bulk of farm Natives are not dissatisfied with their conditions."[27] The most important benefit to tenants was the right to graze their stock, so for farm owners this was "an important consideration from the point of view of obtaining a labor supply for the farm." These rights were nevertheless undervalued by tenants, according to the NEC, because "the Native does not in the first instance regard his stock from an economic angle and he therefore does not get the income from them which he should."[28] Nevertheless, the commission realized that the "desire to stay where he can get grazing" led "the Native" to put up with considerable economic hardship. The NEC evidently failed to understand the basis of this "love of the Native for his cattle," seeing it as inherently irrational rather than as integral to social prestige and interconnections.[29]

Farmers and farmers' associations testifying to the commission characterized labor tenancy as a "necessary evil," which they uniformly condemned as uneconomical, while they continued to employ labor tenants. "It involves waste, inasmuch as it is generally necessary to keep more labour on the farm than the work warrants." According to the report, the rise of intensive cultivation and consequent decrease in grazing land meant that the system was economically doomed. White farmers, bringing more land under cultivation, would increasingly restrict grazing and plowing for tenants, "and the basis of the Native labour tenant system will disappear."

> Where land values have risen and intensive cultivation is coming in, it is no longer economically possible for the farmer either to give the grazing which the Native wants or to allow him to work any portion of the land according to his own primitive methods. In such areas therefore labour shortage is beginning to be felt owing largely to the farmers' inability to remunerate in the manner which Natives prefer. In other areas the number of cattle, which the Native is allowed to graze, is being severely limited. This again brings conflict between farmer and labour tenant. The farmer looks at the question from the point of view of the *value* of the land; the Native of the *number* of his cattle.[30]

The NEC's prediction of demise was not wrong, but as we shall see, it was premature. For the next four decades and more, labor tenancy would sputter along, despite these conflicts, contradictions, and complaints.

Concerning another major trend that augured the demise of labor tenancy, the report contained a section entitled "The Drift of Young Natives to Towns." Here, for the first time in its analysis, the NEC called attention to the fact that payments in kind, on which it had placed so much emphasis to show that compensation for labor tenants was both adequate and fair, were in fact payments to the *umnumzane* (referred to in the report as "*kraal* head"). The NEC noted that "family unity," which ensured that all would benefit from such a system, had broken down under white influence (although it failed to discuss how that influence operated), and reported that "the young men, and even the young women, are frequently dissatisfied with their position in the family." As a result the movement of young men and women from farm tenancies to towns was one of the "outstanding migrational movements" of the time. "They frequently abscond from their homes leaving their work unfinished, leaving the cattle untended, and giving no notice to their parents of their intention." Whereas farmers and labor tenants were in conflict over cultivation, grazing and (to a lesser extent) wages, *abanumzane* were in conflict with youth over labor, *lobola*, and remittances.

> Parents complain that they have frequently to find *lobolo*-cattle and even money for taxes for their prodigal sons. The older Natives complain bitterly throughout the country that their children are not sending back money [from urban labor centers] as they used to do.[31]

This generational tension introduced another conflict, "between farmer and labour tenant," since the *umnumzane* obtained his place on the farm by promising the labor of his children:

> The farmer takes on a labour tenant in order to obtain the labour of his children; the children abscond or do not come back when it is their turn to put in their period of labour; the farmer, finding that he does not get the labour which he requires, ejects the head of the family and *this causes ill feeling*.[32]

The NEC also recognized, somewhat grudgingly, that the small or nonexistent cash wage had a detrimental effect on the supply of farm labor.[33] The smallness of the wage made migrancy a necessity, not a mere whim of youth seeking the proverbial bright lights. "Generally the amount is not enough for the cash requirements of the labour tenant, and he must necessarily increase it by going to work elsewhere." The NEC believed that "natives" were overly concerned with this factor, however, as they tended to undervalue in-kind benefits, such as the use of land, which was "free" in what it called the "tribal state." The commission understood, however, that payment in kind could be detrimental because it hinged on the country's very fickle climate: "When there is a crop failure the Native is left very badly off." In drought the farmer would often lend grain to his tenants, creating a debt to be worked off, sometimes with "usurious rate[s] of interest."[34]

The NEC also cited its stereotypical understanding of African gender roles as an underlying reason for "drift." The commission believed that "native" men were drawn away from farms by their "gregarious instincts" and because "in the tribal state" most of the work was done by women, so men were unused to hard physical labor.

> The Native male is no more fond of hard physical exertion than most Europeans, and prefers the less strenuous nature of many town jobs, like house work [then predominantly done by male domestic servants], newspaper selling, delivery work, to the relatively harder farm work.[35]

Because of this preference, according to colonial reasoning, there tended to be a labor shortage in "strenuous" occupations such as farming and mining.[36] The first paid miserably and the second was quite dangerous while paying no better than domestic service, but apparently that did not strike the commissioners as important.

LABOR TENANCY IN NATAL

Labor tenancy was especially prevalent in the dry interior of Natal, including the thornveld that lay to the northeast of the Midlands. White farmers and businesses needing a reserve supply of labor held thornveld farms, in the districts of Weenen and parts of Estcourt and Umvoti, as labor farms.[37] Labor tenants on the thornveld farms were required to supply labor to the working farms owned by their landlords in the neighboring districts of the Midlands or sometimes in the Orange Free State.[38] The young men, and sometimes the young women, would migrate from their thornveld homesteads to these commercial farms for *isithupa* stints for which they would receive little or no compensation. In return, the *abanumzane* had access on the thornveld farm to land and grazing, limited only by overcrowding and by the persistent drought conditions of the region. Thornveld homesteads were subject to little supervision, but there was usually a farm *induna*, a foreman who assigned plots and called out labor for the farmer much as a chief's *induna*, a deputy, would do for the chief.

In 1926 the Weenen Magistrate described the operation of labor farms in his district as follows:

> So far as I am aware there are no rentpaying natives on farms in this district. Nearly all . . . may be described as labour tenants. They are as a general rule permitted to reside on a farm with their families, to graze their stock and to cultivate lands . . . on the understanding that all ablebodied inmates of the kraals render service to the farm owners for about six months during each year for a small wage. During the winter months the farmers run their stock on these farms but otherwise they are not made use of by the owners.[39]

A few years later, Weenen's Magistrate, now also serving as NC, again described the system in his report to the NEC.[40] He reported that the "majority of farms in this district are owned by absentee landlords and are used solely as labour farms." The "custom" was "for native tenants to work six months each year," although on some they performed labor service less often, every year and a half or two years.

He reported that the normal wage for adult males was ten shillings per month, although some paid only five shillings. Adolescents were paid about half of the adult rate. Even the NC was appalled at these wage rates:

> The farmer's view is that natives leave kin on the farm, can plough as much land as he likes, and graze as many cattle as he likes. It is true that when a tenant has large flocks the farmer comes out on the wrong side but where a tenant has no stock the wages paid are too low. It is impossible for a native to support a wife and children on 10/ per month especially in this district where failure of crops is practically a yearly occurrence.[41]

The only exception to these wage rates was on the three irrigated citrus farms in the district, which paid one pound (twenty shillings) per month.[42]

The most telling part of the report for understanding the system of labor tenancy was the magistrate's statement about who performed the labor obligation. Although "labor tenant" was often equated in the words of officials and farmers with the *kraal* head (*umnumzane*), it was not normally he who labored for the farmer:

> *The kraal head is usually exempted if there are other inmates who render service.* As soon as the boys are old enough to work they are also called upon to work. . . . Some farmers contract with the tenants for their wives to render service once a week cleaning up in his household or laundry work (emphasis added).[43]

The *umnumzane*, then, while known in official discourse as "the" labor tenant, was usually the person who commanded the labor of others in order to secure his place, including rights to fields and grazing, on a farm. The adult sons and younger brothers of *abanumzane* were the main workers. Young married men, who lacked children old enough to work but who had established their own homesteads, rendered service themselves if they could get a place on a farm. Children of both sexes worked on the farm, although boys did so with more regularity than girls. Wives were called upon for *togt* in the gardens and as domestics and were also expected to work at planting and harvest times.

This system, whereby the *abanumzane* gained and retained their place on the farm through the labor of members of the homestead, exacerbated existing lines of tension within African tenant households.

This was especially so with regard to generational tensions. The labor of sons ensured the security of fathers on the farm yet did little (due to the low wages) to enable the sons to accumulate *lobola* to establish homesteads of their own. For this purpose, as well as to earn funds for taxes and other necessities as well as consumer luxuries, such as bicycles and concertinas, sons migrated to the cities in the six months off. Fathers and sons, as well as older and younger brothers, continually struggled over remittances and over the timing of the sons' and younger brothers' return from the city. Fathers and older brothers ensured compliance by threatening to withhold "customary" *lobola* support, by disinheriting recalcitrant juniors, and by seeking the state's coercive police powers for the return of young men "overstaying" in the city.[44]

Under this system, wages were so small that it was clear that labor tenants were working for access to land, not for money. That is, labor was itself a form of rent. On one farm in the district, the owners told the NC that when they offered their tenants a choice between six months work at ten shillings per month or three months with no wages, the tenants chose the latter.[45] An Estcourt farmer told me in 1992 that before World War II labor tenants earned no wages on his farm, as they were able to produce what they needed on the labor farm, where they kept cattle without restriction. Workers on six-month stints were "fed and housed," and mealie meal was taken to them. They obtained milk and could eat stock that died.[46] A neighboring farmer, of a somewhat more progressive cast, said that labor tenants during *isithupa* were paid one pound per month, although girls, who worked as domestics, earned ten shillings per month.[47] Another local farmer reported that few continued to work on the farm during the "free" six months, although many worked at the nearby food processing plants (Nestles and a bacon factory) in the town of Estcourt.[48]

Tenants valued the land for the independence it offered to raise subsistence crops and for grazing. Although some tenants were able to accumulate large enough herds to sell some of the cattle from time to time, labor tenants on dry, rocky, and hilly Weenen farms were not able to raise surplus crops.[49] Don Hall's tenants, at his commercial farm in Estcourt, had land to plow (three acres per working "boy" and the loan of a plow; they used their own oxen) and were allowed five head per *kraal*. They would sometimes keep a few extra head when marriage arrangements were being made. (Sometimes he provided cattle for *lobola* on partial credit.)[50] Godfrey Symons recalled that tenants on his three labor farms had ten acres for growing "mealies and kaffir corn" and up to fifteen head per kraal. He claimed that labor tenants were "self-sufficient," in mealies, although he admitted that they also bought mealies from him.[51]

Because wages were so low during the six months of service, labor tenants were compelled to work elsewhere during the six months "off." One solution was to continue working on the farm, usually at double the wage offered during the required period of service. However, Africans could get really good wages only in the cities, so the young men migrated for at least a few seasons to work in Johannesburg, Durban, or another town. The Weenen NC reported on this aspect of labor tenancy in his 1932 annual report: "A large number of natives leave the district each year to work for their landlords. Others go to Durban, Johannesburg and Kimberley."[52] Former tenants with whom I spoke confirmed this life of oscillation, as well as tensions of gender and generation that resulted from the tenant condition.

ORAL ACCOUNTS OF LABOR TENANCY

Interviews with former labor tenants from central Natal, some of whom continue to live on "white" farms but now work full-time, and many of whom were evicted from thornveld farms during the forced removals era in the 1970s and 1980s, confirm these general outlines of the conditions of labor tenancy, while they add the variation of their lives and the richness of individual perspectives.

John Dladla

John Dladla was born on a stock farm belonging to a white man named J. Vermaak in Middelrus, between Mooi River and Weenen, in 1922.[53] His father had four wives but had become Christian by the time the fourth wife gave birth to John. John recalls that there were more than ten homesteads on the farm. "There were many *imizi*, besides us the Dladlas there were the Magubanes, the Zithas, the Nshangases, the Nenes, the Nzimandes, the Mongadis, the Shangases, the Phungulas, the Sitholes." His father's polygyny was the norm. "No, most people, nearly everyone had more than one wife, as polygamy was practised in former times." These *imizi* had sufficient arable fields—one per wife—and were allowed to raise stock without any arbitrary limit.

> Each wife was given a plot of her own—if they got along well they used to join hands and end up with bigger plots. Stock ownership was not restricted to a certain number; they kept as many as they liked.[54]

John remembered his own father as having more than one hundred head of cattle, as well as sheep and goats, and said that this amount was not unusual. The fields enabled them to produce "enough crops to feed ourselves," but no surplus for sale. For two years (probably 1932–1934), though, famine resulting from floods and locusts forced them to buy food from white farmers and Indian traders.

As a child, John attended the farm school for one year. This was the sum of his formal education. At age six or seven, he began working for the farmer's family, first as a child minder, looking after their young daughter. Later, he herded the farmer's sheep and also herded cattle for his father. At age twelve, he began to do *togt* during his six months "off," probably in nearby towns or on other farms. He remembers his wage on the farm during the *isithupa* period as five shillings a month, or one pound ten shillings after six months. Working during the "free" period on the orange farms at Muden, he earned between a pound and a pound and a half per month. As he and his siblings grew up, John's father discontinued his own work on the farm. John's sisters as well as his brothers worked *isithupa*, exchanging with one another on a rotating basis. The sisters worked as domestic servants.

When he was about twenty years old, John went to Natalspruit, on the East Rand, for one year. There he worked as a domestic servant and gardener for a white family "in order to raise enough money to pay *lobola* for my wife—MaNene."[55] While he was gone, he got his brother to substitute for him on the farm for his *isithupa* service and compensated him with a cow. Meanwhile, he earned three pounds per month for his work in Johannesburg, using about eight pounds of this to buy gifts for his in-laws. Other funds went toward the eleven cattle he *lobola*'d with and for clothes for himself when he got married, around the end of World War II. His father supplied some of the *lobola* for his first marriage, because he had worked *isithupa* on his father's behalf and had sent wages home from other jobs. When he later married a second wife, he supplied his own *lobola*.

After he got married, John went to live on the Browns' farm in Mooi River (then in Estcourt district), where he still lived in 1992.[56] Moving to the Browns' meant the imposition of stock restrictions—they were allowed three head, and smaller fields, "I guess because the farm was small."[57] Mrs. Brown, a widow, was raising both beef and dairy cattle on her mist-belt farm, as well as horses. John was induced to come to the Browns' farm by his nephew and brother-in-law, who already worked there. They advised him of the Browns' fairness and of "opportunities to travel around the country to places like Cape

Town, etc., whilst attending the horses." Despite the restrictions, this more productive farm paid better wages and eventually supplied tenants with rations.

He recalled that when he was young (before his marriage and move to the Browns'), a great many young men left the farms due to low wages and the six-month system, leaving fathers who "suffered and faced the consequences," often meaning eviction:

> Many people were evicted during my stay on the farm. The farmer either evicted the family or beat up the young men who did not want to work on their farm and chased them away. You could return back to the farm and the farm owner would ask you to pay a fine of one cow.[58]

People who were "chased away" went to other farms or to the cities. Unlike many other witnesses, John remembered that "Women also left the farms, and went back home to other farms and cities. Married couples also left in droves." Still, compared to the present, John offered the perennial complaint of elders that his youth was "better because of the respect which existed between children and parents. . . . Nowadays we are sorrowful because our children do not want to give us money." By the 1990s, however, this sort of complaint had taken on the added twist of growing class differences between older rural Africans and younger urban professionals. "They do not care about us, even though you sent them to school and now they are professionals, teachers, etc., they do not want to give us money."[59] On the other hand, John clearly preferred working *draai* (full-time)[60] to *isithupa*, due to the better wages and the more stable home life fostered by full-time work:

> I do not have to vacate the place and look for work elsewhere for six months. It is better now that we are working full time, the whole year, as compared to the time when we were working for six months. I prefer this present-day system. You are always with your wife, the money is also better. Before you used to work harder, and [were] paid less money.[61]

Bettina MaNene Dladla

Bettina MaNene Dladla, John's spouse, had a slightly different perspective on this history and the issues raised by it.[62] She was born in 1925 on the same farm, Rietvlei, near Greytown (Mbulane), where her grandparents and parents were born. Her parents had been married at the time of the epidemic of 1918, the Great Flu, "which killed brides." Bettina's mother was the senior of her father's two wives, who together were the mothers of twelve children. Nevertheless, her parents were *kholwa*, belonging to an independent African church under a minister named Meshack Ndlovu.[63] Her father worked *isithupa* for the white farmer, Mr. Roy. He was in charge of domestic chores until the farm was sold. During the six months "off," Bettina's father worked in Pietermaritzburg. There were perhaps fifteen *imizi* on the farm, with fields and considerable amounts of stock. The fields were "too big to be tilled by boys and girls," and so the labor tenant families worked out a communal arrangement to help each other with cultivation. She recalls her father plowing the fields with oxen. As a girl, Bettina did *togt* while she attended a mission school on a neighboring farm. She attended for three years, up to Standard 1 (equivalent to third grade in the American system), which she believed "was the last standard for Africans then." Her brothers began to work at about age twelve. As a *togt* worker, she received five pence a day in wages for tasks such as weeding, which she turned over to her mother. This money was used in part for trousseau items, such as the mats (*amacansi*) a bride was supposed to bring to the marriage.

Bettina married in 1943 at age eighteen. When she married, her father received twenty goats, eight head of cattle, and a horse, making the equivalent of the standard eleven head of cattle ("ten goats equals one cow and one horse equals one cow"). Her father also paid *lobola* for her brothers, "according to custom," as they had given their wages to him. She then moved with her new husband to his *umuzi* on the farm where he had been born. Initially, they had about ten head of cattle, and fields. She did *togt* in the farmer's garden during planting and harvest seasons and was paid not in cash but with salt. Her husband, working *isithupa*, got some wages, but he earned more while working away in Durban for the six months "off." Two years into her marriage, her husband took a second wife, MaKhanya. Bettina recalls getting along with her co-wife well enough, saying, "We used to stay together and cook together." However, many years later, after Bettina's son had married, MaKhanya separated from their husband and went to live in Pietermaritzburg.

She recalls evictions as a result of "the usual laborer-farmer misunderstandings," but she does not recall large-scale evictions or people leaving the farms without permission or without securing a substitute to work for them while they were away. Moving from Middelrus to work for the Browns in Mooi River and then at Easingwold meant a transition to full-time labor, which was better because of the money. It also meant a change to the Presbyterian Church, as "there was no African [independent] church around . . . and we couldn't stay without going to church."

Domby MaButhelezi Phungula

Domby MaButhelezi Phungula, who also lived on Easingwold farm in 1992, was born on a Weenen (Nobamba) farm.[64] Her father had just one wife, but her parents were not *kholwa*. They had abundant cattle, as there were no limits. Her four brothers worked *isithupa*, having taken over work from their father. Working for the white farmer, they cultivated bananas, cabbages, potatoes, and the like (indicating that the commercial farm was in the irrigated "town lands" near the town of Weenen). Domby and her three sisters worked first looking after fowl, later graduating to the kitchen, enduring the *baas*'s (boss) epithet for them, "Pikini." She at first earned ten shillings in three months, while her older sisters and brothers got that amount each month.[65] Meanwhile, her father went away to work in the wattle plantations near Greytown, but he died by the time she reached maturity. Her brothers used to go to Durban to work at Huletts (sugar processors), and on their return they would give their wages to the father. None of her siblings went to school, for although there were schools, only religious people attended them. She doesn't recall evictions, divorce, or the flight of young men to the cities, all of which she says began quite recently.

She recalls the time of her marriage as falling between two "wars" among local chiefdoms, Ngongolo (1944) and Isimambe (date unknown). They celebrated the marriage with a traditional dance and went to the courts at *Nobamba* (Weenen) to register the marriage. Her husband was a Christian, and as a result Domby converted when her mother-in-law was seriously ill, joining the Nazarene church. Despite the husband's affirmation of Christianity, he took three wives, the second after Domby's first child and the third when her children were already grown. Questioned on her feeling about her husband's polygyny, Domby, speaking in the presence of two men (myself and our interpreter, Antony Ntuli) gave a response that was typical of the women I spoke to on this issue: "I was fine, and was still loyal, as my father had told me."[66] After the wedding, Domby and her husband moved to an orange farm near Muden, and her husband began to work *draai*. They had cattle, but fewer than her father had owned, because her husband was paying *lobola* for Domby's co-wives.

On the whole, she assessed life in 1992 as better than it was back then, because there was now more food and money. However, she was nostalgic about the more traditional life of her youth, which she recalled as more carefree and perhaps more colorful: "We used to go to a feast and dance, wearing our *izidwaba* (pleated black hide skirts) and traditional hats. . . . I'd take off my [modern] clothes right now, and go back there."[67]

Ntshaba

Mr. Ntshaba was born on a farm in the Weenen area during the First World War, before the Great Flu, "when Chiefs died, and I nearly also died, but I survived it."[68] His father worked *isithupa* for the white farm owner, known to them as Semane, at his cattle and sheep farm in Mooi River. He earned six pounds for six months. During his free six months, Ntshaba's father worked in the diamond mines in Kimberley. His father had two wives, and Ntshaba was the eldest son of the senior wife, and therefore the general heir. His family was not *kholwa*. "No, we wore *amabheshu* (goat skins). . . . Christianity only came now (recently)." Elaborating, he explained that men wore *amabheshu* and *izinene* (front covering of fur strips hanging from waist) whereas women wore *izidwaba* and *amabhayi* (cloth capes) like that worn by the woman in Photo 2.1.[69] Houses were also different when he was young. Huts were made of grass in the traditional Zulu beehive style, as shown in Photo 2.2. Later, people started building round houses with wood and mud. Ntshaba placed this change at the time their huts were burned and they were evicted from the farms, around 1980. Other informants suggested that this change came in the 1940s, as a result of the difficulty of getting the grass necessary to build in the old style due to overgrazing and erosion. One woman laid the blame on "white ants." One can easily imagine symbolic overtones of this image, relating to the color, habits of industry, and destructive qualities of white people.[70]

When he was old enough to herd cattle, Ntshaba's family had been evicted from the farm he grew up on due to his father's membership in the ICU, but he was too young to remember what the ICU was, other than its token: a red membership card.[71] After being evicted, the family moved on to a labor farm whose owner required *isithupa* on his wattle farm in New Hanover. They stripped bark, cut wood, "plowed the fields, plant[ed] yams, removed weeds, [and] planted sweet potatoes." At home, however, they were allowed to have as much stock as they wanted. Soon after they moved to the new farm, Ntshaba's father was arrested and

Photo 2.1 Married woman, wearing *ibhayi*, weaving *icansi*, seated in front of traditional-style grass hut. (Photograph by L. Acutt. Supplied and reproduced by kind permission of the Campbell Collections of the University of Natal [D10.067].)

imprisoned for six months for illegally possessing a gun, found among his belongings while he was working *isithupa*. He had acquired the gun in Kimberley in accordance with an established tradition among workers who migrated to the mines there.[72] After he replaced his father in performing *isithupa*, Ntshaba went away to work in a bakery in Johannesburg and secured a replacement worker on the farm for the price of a cow. Ntshaba eventually married two wives. His father paid *lobola* for the first wife, but for the second, "I paid *lobola* myself with the cattle I bought [from wages earned] *eGoli*."[73] In the meantime, his father had died as a

Photo 2.2 Women posed in *umuzi*, near traditional beehive-style grass hut. A modern rectangular building is in background. The women's clothing also reflects a mix of Western and indigenous influences. The beer strainer held by the woman seated at left, the bowl of mealie cobs, and the beer pot resting on the head of the woman standing at center all reflect women's domestic responsibilities. (Courtesy of the Pietermaritzburg Archives Repository [C757].)

result of being shot during the Ngongolo war in 1944, where Ntshaba also fought.

Nokwabiwa Dlada

Some older female informants from the Mpofana-Weenen area provided further perspective on labor tenancy in the thornveld in this period.

One such woman, Nokwabiwa Dlada, said she was born at the time of the Mists (the locusts) before the Bambatha rebellion.[74] This may refer to the locust outbreak following Rinderpest in 1897. Nokwabiwa was born in the location, in Gujini *isigodi* (district), Mpofana, and moved onto a nearby farm, Ncunjana, when she married. She characterizes her father as "lazy" because he did not go away to work in the cities even though his neighbors did. It was not necessary, however, as her grandfather had plenty of stock. Her father had two wives, who gave birth to a total of fourteen children. When she got married, she moved to her father-in-law's *umuzi* on the farm, and she recalls that he was an ICU member. Her husband, the eldest son, was working *isithupa*. They were not *kholwa*, but her husband did not take another wife. Like her father, her husband did not go away to work in the cities, although she wanted him to do so to get money.

After her first child, Nokwabiwa was in training to become a *sangoma* (diviner), from which she later earned money, "and I fed him [her husband]." When two of her children, a girl and a boy, died in the Great Flu,[75] she gained power from them to become an *umthandazi*, a prophetess. Her husband committed suicide, apparently as the result of witchcraft accusations by young men of the area (perhaps connected to her magical work as a *sangoma-umthandazi*). The surviving children worked on the farm until the apartheid-era evictions "in the time of GG."[76] When they were still labor tenants, her children also went to work in the cities, exchanging with siblings who were working on the farm. Nokwabiwa remembered that some people were evicted when their children failed to return from working in the cities to work *isithupa*. In fact, one of her own children failed to return, creating problems with the farmer, and "was brought back immediately." Sometimes husbands failed to return to their wives, who then had to work on their own at their (fathers') homes.

Nocokololo Masoga

Another woman, Nocokololo Masoga, who was a small child at the time of the Great Flu (1918), was born on the farm the previous informant later moved to, Ncunjana, in Weenen.[77] Her father, who had three wives, worked *isithupa* and was the farm *induna*, appointed by the farmer. He stayed at home after *isithupa* to look after his stock rather than going to work in the cities. Nocokololo worked in the farmhouse as a domestic, receiving three pounds for six months labor (ten shillings per month). She exchanged with her sister, doing *isithupa* five times. Her brothers, also working *isithupa*, worked *eGoli* in the free months and brought home a small amount of money. She married about age twenty, as there was "a custom that we weren't supposed to marry while still young." When she married, her husband had to pay sixteen head of cattle for *lobola* because her father was a farm *induna*. Her husband worked *eGoli*, paying someone a cow to replace him for *isithupa*. Eventually he married a second wife, an event she speaks of with resignation. "I couldn't do anything because he loved her." Her husband was not a *kholwa*, but she had become one by that time. Nevertheless, she said she got along very well with the other wife. At one time, they had plenty of cattle, as there was no limit, but the cattle eventually died. While the children were young, her husband died suddenly from stepping on some *umuthi* (medicine) as the result of witchcraft. By that stage, he had left with the other wife to live in the reserve, and Nocokololo was left on the farm with her daughter working for her. She was forced to leave the farm when her daughter got married and moved away.

CONCLUSION

The memories of the men and women I spoke with in 1992 provide us with a textured portrait of labor tenancy in Central Natal during the second quarter of the twentieth century. It is striking that many of them remember labor tenancy fondly, especially in the time of their youth, recalling it as a system that enabled their families to accumulate stock and grow abundant crops through cooperative labor. The nostalgia of these remembrances is by no means surprising in view of the hardships that came later in life. Recall that I was interviewing these elderly men and women at a time of political uncertainty and pervasive but seemingly random violence. It was also a year of extreme drought, said to be the worst in a century. The previous decades had seen a steady loss of land, privileges, and "free" time for labor tenants, as farmers evicted "surplus" tenants and converted the remainder to full-time work. Nevertheless, the pain and the conflicts associated with the *isithupa* system did surface regularly in the recollections of these informants. These memories establish the substance of the NEC Report's discussion of the movement of "young natives" to urban areas, "in droves" according to John Dladla. These witnesses help us to understand how young Africans on the white-owned farms were caught between the expectations of their elders, the violence of their landlords, and the financial incentives of urban work. They also prepare us to understand the generational acrimony and gendered violence that surface in the NC Court cases discussed in later chapters.

Before delving into those cases, however, we will examine the economic and social pressures on labor tenancy in the 1920s and 1930s. As we have seen, pressures from the expansion of white commercial farming, combined with the loss of access to land signaled by the 1913 Land Act, brought most rural Africans outside the reserves into relations of labor tenancy in the 1920s. Although this process was well established by the end of the First World War, we learn in chapter 3 that the wattle and sheep boom of the late 1920s led to wide-scale evictions and conversion of rent tenancies to labor tenancies. The late 1920s brought considerable alarm to white authorities and farmers as rural Africans swelled the ranks of the ICU with its combination of labor militancy and millennial rhetoric. As Natal entered the Great Depression, African tenants found that they had less grazing land available even though they continued to earn minimal wages for *isithupa* work. The loss of tenant privileges combined with the increasing opportunities in industrializing urban areas led to the exacerbation of the tensions within tenant households that we have discussed in this chapter. White farmers became increasingly concerned over the "drift of natives" to urban areas and sought increasingly harsh measures to control farm labor. At the same time, African patriarchs worried about their own loss of control over wives and juniors in the turbulence created by the social and economic pressures of the late 1920s and 1930s. The fears of the state concerning African radicalism, and of African elders over respect and obedience, were to lead to enhanced efforts designed to reinforce "traditional" hierarchies, as we shall see in chapters 4 and 5. The efforts of the NAD and rural patriarchs to use tradition as a counterweight to social change were partially successful but were constantly challenged by litigants whose understandings of tradition and experiences of the world did not conform to the template of the Natal Code. Before delving into the NC court litigation in chapters 4 and 5, we will see in the next chapter that state sponsorship of rural traditionalism blended with other strategies—equally under challenge—to discipline and retain labor on the farms as young Africans increasingly departed for urban opportunities in the 1930s. The lines of tension in the labor tenant household therefore became the object of state policy even as those lines became more visible in the 1930s, a decade of considerable change and stress. It is to these economic processes and social conflicts that we now turn our attention.

NOTES

1. Interview with John Dladla, Nottingham Road, 27 Feb. 1992.

2. In contemporary South Africa, the term *labor tenancy* is used to refer to all working tenants on commercial farms, whether or not the tenants work full time. In this book, however, I use the term to refer to the six-month system, unless otherwise indicated.

3. Cf. Eric Foner, *Nothing but Freedom: Emancipation and Its Legacy* (Baton Rouge: Louisiana State University Press, 1984); Van Onselen, *The Seed Is Mine.*

4. "*Kaffir* farming" referred to the practice of whites renting rural land to African tenants instead of farming it directly. It was increasingly a term of abuse directed by "progressive" white farmers against, first, absentee speculators, and later poorer farmers who lacked the resources to capitalize their farms.

5. The importance of African peasants in the nineteenth-century Natal economy was first suggested by the 1970s work of Henry Slater, Norman Etherington, and Colin Bundy. See Henry Slater, "Land, Labour and Capitalism: The Natal Land and Colonisation Company, 1860–1948," *Journal of African History*, 16, no. 2 (1975): 257–83; Norman Etherington, *Preachers, Peasants and Politics in Southeast Africa: African Christian Communities in Natal, Pondoland and Zululand* (London: Royal Historical Society, 1978); Bundy, *Rise and Fall.* More recently, this thesis has been refined by the work of John Lambert on the African homestead economy in late nineteenth-century Natal. Lambert, *Betrayed Trust*; Lambert, "Undermining of the Homestead Economy."

6. Lambert, *Betrayed Trust*, 10–20; Norman Etherington, "The 'Shepstone System' in the Colony of Natal and beyond the Borders," in *Natal and Zululand*, ed. by Duminy and Guest, 174–76.

7. Slater, "Land, Labour;" Hurvitz, *Agriculture*, 5, 20.

8. Lambert, *Betrayed Trust*, 7–9. On the Natal Coast, by contrast, sugar plantations achieved success in the 1860s but depended heavily on migrant labor from Mozambique and indentured labor from India. See Bill Freund, *Insiders and Outsiders: The Indian Working Class of Durban, 1910–1990* (Portsmouth: Heinemann Press, 1995).

9. John Lambert, "Africans on White-Owned Farms in the Mist Belt of Natal, c.1850–1906," paper No. 4 presented at Workshop on Regionalism and Restructuring in Natal, University of Natal Durban, 28–31 January, 1988, 3–4; Lambert, *Betrayed Trust*, 43–45.

10. Cf. Comaroff and Comaroff, *Ethnography*, 127–154; Thomas McClendon, "'Hiding Cattle on the White Man's Farm': Cattle Loans and Commercial Farms in Natal, 1930–1950," *African Economic History*, 25 (1997): 43–58.

11. According to Lambert, from the outset the two million acres set aside as reserves was adequate for only half of the African population of the colony at best. *Betrayed Trust*, 11. Norman Etherington has recently developed a new interpretation of the areas that became the "homelands" under apartheid. He suggests that determined resistance enabled African chiefdoms to retain some good land, in areas of relatively good rainfall and fertility, in the face of conquest. Norman Etherington, "South Africa's Bantustans: A Legacy of African Resistance to Colonial Rule," paper presented at the African Studies Association annual meeting, Chicago, 1998.

12. Cf. Tabitha Kanogo, *Squatters and the Roots of Mau Mau* (London: James Currey, 1987), where "squatters" refers to independent African producers on white-owned farms who were squeezed into relations of labor tenancy.

13. Lambert, *Betrayed Trust*, 15–16; 72.

14. Lambert, *Betrayed Trust*, 30. For a discussion of *isibalo*, see Marks, *Reluctant Rebellion*. *Isibalo* is a cognate of *chibaro*, the Shona word for forced labor. See Charles van Onselen, *Chibaro: African Mine Labour in Southern Rhodesia 1900–1933* (London: Pluto Press, 1976), 99. Donald S. Moore discussed the genealogy of the word in "Contesting Terrain in Zimbabwe's Eastern Highlands: The Cultural Politics of Place, Identity, and Resource Struggles," Ph.D. dissertation, Stanford University, 1995, 320–22. The Swahili language of slavery included a term that appears to be another cognate associated with low-status labor. See Jonathon Glassman, *Feasts and Riot: Revelry, Rebellion, and Popular Consciousness on the Swahili Coast, 1856–1888* (Portsmouth: Heinemann, 1995), 85–96.

15. Cf. Lambert, *Betrayed Trust*, 13–14, 97.

16. Mazower, "Agriculture, Farm Labour and the State"; Hurwitz, *Agriculture*, 28.

17. Act 27 of 1913. In addition to the squatting restrictions discussed below, the 1913 Natives Land Act most notoriously restricted African rights in land to the existing native reserves, then about 7 percent of the total area of the Union of South Africa. Leonard Thompson, *A History of South Africa*, 2nd ed. (New Haven: Yale University Press, 1995), 163.

18. Van Onselen, "Reconstruction of a Rural Life"; Keegan, *Rural Transformations*, 182–95, 204.

19. William Beinart and Peter Delius, "Introduction," in *Putting a Plough to the Ground*, ed. by William Beinart et al. (Johannesburg: Ravan Press, 1986), 38.

20. Bundy, *Rise and Fall*, 230–32.

21. PAR, 1 WEN 3/3/1/2; 2/7/6, Weenen Magistrate (Mag.), 11 Mar. 1935. Commissioner F.A.W. Lucas's addendum to the Native Economic Commission (NEC) report noted that illegal rent tenancies persisted in various parts of the country, but that it was impossible to quantify the extent of evasion. *Report of the Native Economic Commission 1930–32 (NEC Report)*, U.G. 22-1932, 185.

22. The act also prevented Africans from buying land except in areas designated as "released areas" pursuant to the recommendations of the Beaumont Commission in 1916 and its provincial committees in 1918. The released areas were generally adjacent to "scheduled" reserves, and were being considered for inclusion in a future expansion of the reserves envisioned by the framers of the 1913 Act. In the event, the expansion was not authorized until passage of the Natives Trust and Land Act in 1936. For further discussion of the latter act, see chapter 3.

23. *NEC Report*, 51.

24. Ibid., 52.

25. Ibid.

26. Ibid., 186. Lucas noted, "One effect of the Land Act has been to substitute this six months' service for a rent of £2 or £3 a year." Ibid., 203.

27. Ibid., 53.

28. Ibid., 54.

29. Ibid., 55. Cf. Comaroff and Comaroff, *Ethnography*, 127–54; McClendon, "'Hiding Cattle.'"

30. *NEC Report*, 55. (emphasis in original).

31. Ibid., 56.

32. Ibid. (emphasis added).

33. Whereas grazing opportunities attracted Africans to labor tenancy, white farmers were compelled to the system by the low or nonexistent cash wage, since cash was "generally somewhat scarce on the farms." Ibid., 55.

34. Ibid., 56–57. Debt bondage was apparently quite common even without drought conditions. One magistrate reported that "[a] custom has arisen here whereby a Native invariably wants an advance of money before starting work and in order to obtain his services the master is almost bound to make the advance. Most of his labour tenants are indebted to masters in amounts beyond their means," and while in debt earn significantly lower wages. *NEC Report*, 194. Private farmers' papers confirm that loans to tenants were common. See, e.g., 1930s diaries of Underberg farmer Henry Callaway Gold, Killie Campbell African Library; 1933 diaries of Howick farmer A.H. Parkinson, PAR, Accession A874, vol. 67; and 1921–33 diaries of Richmond farmer J. Scofield, PAR, Accession 203, vol. 101–111.

35. *NEC Report*, 57.

36. Ibid.

37. PAR, 1 WEN 3/3/1/10, 17/2/3, Weenen Mag., 11 Feb. 1926.

38. PAR, 1 WEN 3/3/1/3; 2/15/2 Weenen Mag., 20 Jan. 1930.

39. PAR, 1 WEN 3/3/1/1; 2/3/23, Weenen NC to Secretary for Native Affairs (SNA), 30 Sept. 1926.

40. PAR, 1 WEN 3/3/1/1; 2/3/18, Weenen NC to NEC, 1931.

41. Ibid.

42. Ibid.

43. Ibid.

44. Chapter 4 elaborates on this theme.

45. PAR, 1 WEN 3/3/1/1; 2/3/10A, Weenen NC to Chief Native Commissioner (CNC), 13 Jun. 1933.

46. Interview with John Haw, Willow Grange, 18 Feb. 1992.

47. Interview with Don Hall, Willow Grange, 18 Feb. 1992.

48. Interview with Godfrey Symons, Willow Grange, 18 Feb. 1992.

49. PAR, 1 WEN 3/3/1/1; 2/3/18, Weenen NC, 1931.

50. Interview with Don Hall.

51. Interview with Godfrey Symons.

52. PAR, 1 WEN 3/3/1/3; 2/3/3, Weenen NC annual report, 26 Jan. 1932.

53. Interview with John Dladla.

54. Ibid.

55. Ibid. Zulu speakers refer to married women by the woman's father's *isibongo* (praise name, surname), prefixed by "Ma." MaNene, therefore, is the married daughter of Mr. Nene. Some Christian women, however, have adopted the Western practice of taking the husband's surname, and some use both names.

56. When he arrived, the farm was owned by the mother of Peter Brown, a founder of the Liberal Party in the 1950s and still a prominent political figure and farmer in Kwazulu-Natal.

57. Ibid. Indeed Midland farms, being more intensively farmed and on more expensive land, tend to be smaller than those in the thornveld.

58. Ibid.

59. Ibid.

60. *Draai* is Afrikaans for "turn" and is used to refer to full-time farmwork. In Zulu the term is rendered as *idilayi*, as L usually substitutes for R in translating into Zulu. Rauri Makhonya Alcock, personal communication.

61. Interview with John Dladla.

62. Interview with Bettina MaNene Dladla, Nottingham Road, 1 Mar. 1992.

63. *Kholwa* were still a small minority at this time in the thornveld. One index of mission Christianity, though not necessarily of other forms, was the literacy rate, as missionary work included Western-style education. In 1921, 6.1 percent of Natal's African population was reported as literate (compared to 9.7 percent in the Union as a whole). *Third Census of the Population of the Union of South Africa* (*1921 Census*), U.G. 15-1923, 105. The census showed 77 percent of Natal's Africans as "heathen." The largest numbers of Christians, according to the census, were Methodists (knows to my informants as *amaWesli* (the Wesleyans), followed by Anglicans. *1921 Census*, U.G. 15-1923: 137. By 1951 those reported with "no religion" (meaning traditionalists) were less than half the total; by far the greatest increase occurred among "Bantu Separatist Churches," which by then had more than 390,000 adherents. *Union Statistics for Fifty Years 1910–1960* (Pretoria: Union of South Africa, 1960), A-29.

64. Interview with Domby MaButhelezi Phungula, Nottingham Road, 20 May 1992.

65. She said they earned one pound ten shillings in six months, although at ten shillings per month they would have earned three pounds in six months. Interview with Domby Phungula. The discrepancy probably resulted from a common confusion between the rand, the currency since the early 1960s, and the pound, the currency before then. A rand was worth ten shillings, half a pound, when it was introduced, so elderly informants assumed an ongoing two to one ratio in their accounts. However this change, combined with the vagaries of memory, often led to confusion and distortion. In this case, either figure is possible at the time and place she is describing.

66. Ibid.

67. Ibid.

68. Interview with Ntshaba, Mpofana, 27 Oct. 1992.

69. Ntshaba said he stopped wearing an *ibheshu* when he came to the reserve area where he now lives, approximately twelve years earlier. "I stopped as I was the only one, looking like an animal—they'd say 'you were born wearing an *ibheshu*, whereas we are clothed'—and then I stopped." Ibid.

70. Interview with Mchunu women, Mchunu-2, Weenen, 13 Aug. 1992.

71. Interview with Ntshaba.

72. Cf. Peter Delius, "Migrant Labour and the Pedi, 1840–80," in *Economy and Society in Pre-Industrial South Africa*, ed. by Shula Marks and Anthony Atmore (New York: Longman, 1980), 293–312.

73. Ibid.

74. Interview with Nokwabiwa Dladla, Mpofana, 28 Oct. 1992.

75. It is not possible to discern a consistent chronology from the events mentioned by Nokwabiwa Dladla. For instance, she says she was born during a locust invasion and that she remembers cattle dying in large numbers, both of which were recurring events. Her reference to the Great Flu could refer to the influenza of 1918, or perhaps to a later event such as the malaria epidemic of 1932, since at another point she says she was not married at the time of the Flu. Ibid.

76. The "time of GG" refers to the evictions beginning in the late 1960s. People were forcibly removed from their homesteads and relocated to the reserves in government trucks bearing license plates beginning with the letters GG. See Platzky and Walker, *The Surplus People*.

77. Interview with Nocolokololo Masoga, Mpofana, 28 Oct. 1992.

3

DEPRESSION, DROUGHT, AND THE "DRIFT OF NATIVES": CRISES OF CONTROL IN THE 1930S

[L]abour tenancy plays a large part directly and indirectly in causing the drift of Natives to the towns; directly, in so far as it compels the tenants or members of their families to go to the towns to earn the money they need . . . indirectly because the sons and daughters, who have to work for what is in effect their father's rent, seeing no return for their labour, run away to the towns, this in itself leading to eviction of the tenant who, because he has no children to work for the landowner, cannot get another tenancy and is also driven to the towns.[1]

I wrote to him and told him that I missed my periods. Until his father felt ashamed, not knowing what to say to me—he left to go and look for him—but never found him. . . . He then said we should go down to Nobamba [Weenen] and report the case, maybe the police may find him. They then sent me back and said they would go look for him. . . . And they said, even the government has failed to find him.[2]

A crisis of control gripped labor tenancy in the 1930s. A wave of rural discontent fueled by expansion of sheep and wattle production led to the rapid spread of the ICU in the late 1920s. The ICU caused white farmers and officials considerable nervousness as it took practical steps to help tenants fight eviction while spreading a millenarian message of return of land to Africans. Although the state successfully repressed the ICU and incipient rural radicalism in the late 1920s, multilayered tensions over the control of labor continued to strain social relations in the countryside. The Great Depression and a series of severe droughts led to considerable hardship for rural South Africans. In response, the state intervened with substantial aid for white farmers, eventually embracing wide-ranging marketing controls. At the same time, famine relief for rural Africans was grudging and intermittent. Post-Depression industrial upsurge combined with stagnation in farm prices and a further series of droughts to encourage increasing numbers of young African men and women to leave rural areas for the cities. Neither the state, white farmers, nor African heads of homesteads were able to stem this flow. At the same time, labor tenancy continued to offer advantages to land-hungry rural Africans and cash-strapped white farmers, and the institution easily survived criticisms of inefficiency and early calls for its abolition toward the end of the decade.

Three events important to labor tenancy occurred in the depths of depression in 1932. That year, the government took the decision to abandon the gold standard, leading in subsequent years to the greatest surge in secondary industry yet seen in the country, and bringing rapid urbanization in its wake. The NEC issued its report (discussed in the preceding chapter), including analysis of the contradictions in labor tenancy that were leading to a loss of parental control and instability in farm labor. Its recommendation for written labor tenant contracts had already been taken up in legislation passed that year as the Native Service Contract Act (NSCA). In its attempt to enable tighter control over farm labor, the NSCA also endorsed white farmers' demand that "*kraal* heads" be empowered to contract for their unmarried children, strengthened pass restrictions for labor tenants, and authorized whipping as a judicial punishment for breach of contract by labor tenants. Finally, in an attempt to control "*kaffir* farming," the act imposed minimum labor service requirements on farm tenants, who would otherwise face eviction. In the face of tenant resistance and the reality of lack of alternative land for rural Africans, however, both the NAD and white farmers were reluctant to enforce the provisions of the act, and it remained for the most part a dead letter.

By the latter half of the decade, the report of another national commission—the NFLC—made it clear that the NSCA had failed to achieve its aims. More young Africans than ever were leaving the farms for jobs and independence in the cities, leading to a farm labor shortage. Despite passage of the Natives Trust and Land Act (1936 Land Act), finally authorizing the expansion of native reserves that had been suggested in the 1913 Land Act, implementation was so slow, and the reserves and areas to be added to them already so over-crowded, that the state was still unable to implement laws limiting the number of tenants per farm. By the end of the decade, organized agriculture, representing "progressive" white farmers, was beginning to call for the abolition of the "inefficient" system of labor tenancy, a goal not realized until the 1960s. Until the widespread mechanization that began in the 1950s, the system continued to have advantages, both for tenants seeking access to land (although the grazing allotted to them was being progressively curtailed) and for farmers in need of cheap reliable sources of labor for expanding production that was now assisted by massive state subsidies.

This chapter provides the economic and social context of the crisis of control that is revealed more fully through the exploration of legal contests over tradition in subsequent chapters. We continue to trace the gender and generational tensions in labor tenancy that were ex-plored in chapter 2. Here those conflicts surface in an overall context of hardship: disease and famine resulting from depression and drought, and an increasing restriction of labor tenants' grazing rights on white farms. Farmers, encouraged by subsidies to expand production in the face of stagnant prices, urged officials to prevent hemorrhage of their labor supply through new controls and tighter enforcement. Politicians embraced this goal but proved unable to give it much substance in this pre-apartheid era. Although this is a story of loss for members of tenant homesteads, it is also clear that those seeking control—the state, white farmers, and African heads of homesteads—were unable to fully achieve their ends.

THE PRELUDE:
NATAL'S AGRICULTURAL ECONOMY IN THE 1920s

During the first half of the twentieth century, security of tenure and conditions of tenancy steadily declined, but labor tenancy re-mained the most important system of labor on white-owned farms and the dominant means for Africans to secure access to land outside the reserves. At the same time, the agricultural developments that began in the last part of the nineteenth century—wattle and dairy—contin-ued to dominate Midlands agriculture. There was a dramatic expan-sion in land cultivated by (white) commercial farmers after 1880, due mainly to increases in sugar and wattle farming.[3] Expansion contin-ued after the turn of the century: the area cultivated nearly doubled again between 1904 and 1921 (Figure 3.1), with World War I contrib-

Figure 3.1 Area Cultivated, Natal

Source: Adapted from Hurvitz, *Agriculture*, 25–26.

uting heavily to the growth. Farmers increased the area under cultivation another 45 percent by 1930, stimulated by good prices before the onset of depression.[4] The rate of growth then slowed, the cultivated area increasing only another 11 percent by 1946, as use of the most productive farmland appears to have reached its limit in the 1930s. Wattle cultivation, however (Figure 3.2), showed a 50 percent increase from 1921 to 1946, much of it in the districts we are concerned with, considerably reducing grazing land available to farm tenants.[5]

Both prices and rainfall patterns went through enormous swings from year to year, forcing commercial and subsistence producers to tailor their activities in response to these vicissitudes. A postwar depression hit agricultural commodity prices from 1920 to 1922. At the same time, good rains led to higher agricultural production. This triggered a paradox of farming in Natal: when rains were good, Africans as well as whites enjoyed good crops, reducing the need of both reserve dwellers and tenants of "labor farms" to take up work on Natal's commercial farms. The official analysis of this relationship was couched in discourses of native laziness and backwardness, wherein "work" meant wage labor for white farms or industries. "The natives, therefore, had surplus mealies for disposal, and this accentuated the labor difficulty, as the natives having plenty to eat and drink, were not compelled to work."[6] Officials also treated labor scarcity as a function of wages that were too high: "The native only works long enough to get sufficient money for his immediate wants and the higher the wages the quicker his wants are supplied and the smaller the avail-

Figure 3.2   Area Planted in Wattles, Natal

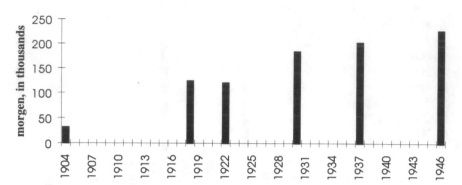

Source: Adapted from Hurvitz, *Agriculture*, 27.

able supply of labor."[7] White farmers struggling with the boom and bust cycle in Natal continued to agitate for tighter controls over workers, partly to ensure a steady supply of labor. They anticipated the controls introduced in 1932 by demanding that "natives residing on . . . farms" be treated as servants, not as tenants, and that "*kraal* heads" be allowed to make labor contracts for their minor children. The Natal Agricultural Union's (NAU) annual conference in 1924, for instance, demanded: (1) greater control of "lawlessness" among "natives"; (2) better control of "Native farm servants"; and (3) tighter pass controls, especially for labor tenants, including an increase in the pass renewal fee to defeat intentional "losing" of passes that showed employed status.[8]

By 1926, the Department of Agriculture boasted that agriculture was not only "the backbone of the country" but also "the chief industry of the Union of South Africa. The market value of its production is . . . considerably in excess of that of the country's next largest industry—mineral production."[9] However, this "chief industry" continued to be buffeted by the shifting winds of climate and markets. The Agricultural Census report for 1925–1926 led with these familiar words: "During the year under review a Severe Drought was experienced in almost every district of the Union."[10] The year brought a failure of the maize crop in Natal, where half the "normal" amount was reaped. This, however, had the effect of raising the price to thirteen shillings five pence per bag and had the usual "positive" effect on the supply of labor for white farmers. "Labour has been fairly plentiful during the year, both in Natal and

Zululand. This may be attributed to the fact that most of the natives reaped very little from their mealie crops and were compelled to seek work to maintain their families."[11]

By the late 1920s, the Land Bank began to show concern for the tremendous growth in cattle herds that was occurring in the Union, especially the growth of "native" cattle, meaning cattle owned by Africans, and this remained a subject of its concern for many years.[12] More than 1,300,000 head of "native" cattle were grazed on "European" farms in the Union, which meant that 6,500,000 morgen of "expensive European land" was "devoted to the maintenance of native cattle," the report claimed. "These figures are significant and should be remembered when the cost of native farm labour is being considered."[13] This too, would be a running theme of official reports, that the wage bill underestimated the true cost of labor tenancy.

> In 1923 the natives owned 74 head of cattle to every 100 of the Europeans; in 1927 this figure had risen to 91. Bearing in mind the fact that cattle owned by natives are generally of poor quality this state of affairs cannot be regarded as beneficial either to the native or to the European.[14]

Showing their lack of understanding of how and why Africans accumulated cattle, not to mention Africans' lack of access to good grazing, the compilers of the Agricultural Census went on to complain, "If the natives had concentrated, like many Europeans, on imported animals, they would have a real increase in wealth. As it is, increase in numbers of scrub animals only tends to depreciate the value of each animal."[15] Once again, this was to become a persistent theme in agricultural reports for the next several years.[16] Natal's farmers seemed to take to heart the advice about oversupply of cattle, as the trend toward increased production of sheep and wattles continued in 1928, encouraged by drought and high prices for wool and wattle.[17] "[O]wing to activity in the wattle-bark industry in Natal farmers in that Province are reported to be reducing the number of their cattle and converting their grazing lands into wattle plantations."[18] The growth of such plantations came at tenants' expense, helping to fuel the rural radicalism of the ICU.

THE RISE OF THE ICU

As we saw in chapter 2, the "red ticket" of the ICU was an important though vague memory for men and women who were raised in the 1920s. This section places those memories in the context of the movement's rise and the fears it aroused among white farmers and officialdom. The ICU, which began as a dockworkers' union in Cape Town in 1919, became in the second half of the 1920s a widespread social movement that gained a broad following in the rural areas of the Transkei, the Transvaal, and Natal. The union's leaders, young African teachers and clerks radicalized by their downward mobility, rallied a following in the countryside around (sometimes contradictory) messages of better wages, opposition to evictions, and land for Africans. These messages mixed in the countryside with Africanist and millennial ideologies that envisioned a removal of white settlers. Such ideas were especially appealing at a time when labor tenants and other farmworkers in Natal were under considerable stress as a result of the expansion of wattle cultivation and sheep farming.[19] In this atmosphere, many people bought the red ticket signifying membership in the ICU, seeking its protection both in the judicial world (against evictions and for better wages) and in the supernatural world. As one white farmer testified to the NEC:

> [T]wo kaffer [sic] girls, I did not actually see them myself, passed through our district and preached to the Natives that they should destroy all their pigs. . . . They said that if they did not destroy them the lightening [sic] would come and it would strike the pig and the pig would run about with fire in its mouth and burn all the kraals. These emissaries were really sent by the ICU.[20]

In 1992, more than ten years after Helen Bradford conducted her interviews, my informants remembered that their parents bought ICU cards, but they could not tell me why. Some, however, remembered that it represented a "fight" between blacks and whites. Domby MaButhelezi Phungula, born at the time of ICU, described the ICU as large white objects, like painted cement, that "attacked on the mountains" in some mystery connected with white men.[21] This blur of images makes sense if we recall from Bradford's work that ICU's appeal in the Natal countryside was related to sporadic calls for restoration of the land to Africans—and that whites in this period were staking out land ownership for commercial purposes.[22] The white objects were probably beacons (Domby said they were still there) that were being erected as whites asserted legal ownership at the time of the ICU threat. Domby's remembrance of the ICU as white pillars on the mountaintops is vague, but it carries a great deal of symbolic weight in reference to a time in which white owners and African tenants were contesting control of land and labor.

The wave of evictions that helped to spark enthusiasm for the ICU resulted primarily from the boom conditions in wattle and sheep farming in the mid- to late 1920s.[23] There was "great development" of wattle plantations and no fear of overproduction, as the price of bark had reached fifteen pounds a ton in London. The price of wattle-growing land had risen to six to eight pounds an acre. Sheep and wool production, encouraged by high wool prices, was also expanding into new districts.[24] Farmers who were bringing new land under cultivation were eliminating rent tenancies that had been grandfathered under the 1913 Land Act. A rent tenancy could be terminated (or converted into a labor tenancy) with one year's notice; three months' notice was to be given in the case of a tenant's breach of contract.[25]

The NAU's Executive Committee dealt with the ICU at length at its June 1927 meeting.[26] The president noted that ICU organizers, who were "being watched," were careful not to transgress the law but "were exceeding their rights in telling Natives that the latter were no longer under the same obligations to their employers as formerly." They were, he said, telling "natives" that their red membership card was the ticket to freedom from obligations to employers and restraint by police. Another committee member, Mr. Allsopp, confirmed that a "Native" had recently "shown him a red ticket and stated that he possessed with it all the privileges of the white man." Some present at the meeting warned that the ICU might mount a strike among farmworkers, and they argued that the government should outlaw agricultural strikes. Mr. Lymington reported that Parliament was considering a bill to "deal with persons stirring up troubles between Europeans and Natives."[27] There was also fear of impending violence. "Europeans" in Impendhle, where there was not yet much "agitation," had formed a Vigilance Committee, to protect each other on "isolated farms."[28] The Executive Committee passed a resolution to request its affiliated associations to consider binding members to evict tenants if they joined the ICU (as many were already doing), giving only one month's notice if they struck. They also resolved that living on a farm be considered sufficient evidence of the existence of a labor contract, and that magistrates' decisions concerning evictions be reviewed not by the Supreme Court but by the Native High Court, "who understand the Natives." Finally, the committee reiterated the NAU's position that *kraal* heads should have "complete control" to contract for unmarried and minor "inmates" of their homesteads.[29]

The NAU also began to promote standardized written contracts for labor tenants. The organization argued that written contracts would ensure better conditions and court enforcement of labor tenant obligations, hence enabling evictions of tenants who failed to work. Professor Burchell, an expert in "native" law, was brought in to advise the NAU on this point. Burchell recognized that "the Native also has his point of view," as there had been "bad masters *in the past,*" but that the ICU was the other principal cause of the prevailing "unrest." He found the ICU to have "communistic aims"; it was not representative of "the Natives" but "was a destructive organisation striking at the farmer through his labour." The answer was a uniform contract:

> The whole solution of the problem lay in the farmers' hands. All contracts in the past, whether fair or not, had been fixed by the white man without consulting the Native. There must be a uniform contract today throughout the Province.[30]

He believed the "Native Chiefs" would assist in dealing with "these alien agitators," as he called ICU organizers.

The belief that chiefs would help to repress the ICU was not unfounded. The NAU meeting noted a report from *Ilanga lase Natal* that Chief Solomon (the paramount chief) had "denounc[ed] the machinations of the ICU."[31] Mr. Wheelwright, the Chief Native Commissioner (CNC) for Natal, "had recently been round amongst the Chiefs and *Indunas* in the Umvoti and Weenen Counties and explained to them their responsibilities. . . . [A]s Natal was governed by the Tribal system Natives must be approached through their chiefs."[32] As the retired chief magistrate of Pietermaritzburg testified to the NEC:

> I must say that we are very much indebted indeed to Solomon and to these chiefs in regard to the attitude which they took up with reference to the ICU . . . were it not for them, the ICU would have got a tremendous hold upon the country and I feel that we are deeply indebted to them for their loyalty.[33]

By 1930, the ICU had collapsed under the weight of state repression, internal corruption, and unmet millennial expectations.[34] The issues raised by its appearance, however—evictions, land rights, labor contracts, and the authority of chiefs and patriarchs as a counterweight to radical movements—were to carry over into the next decade. These issues, especially those of authority and control, continued to surface in connection with struggles over implementation of the NSCA of 1932 and labor shortages, and more broadly in struggles over tradition and customary law. In the short run, the rapid agricultural expansion in mid-Natal that fueled the rise of the ICU ground to a halt with the collapse of agricultural commodity prices in the Great Depression, leading to a time of stress for tenants and to new forms of state intervention to ensure the economic viability of white-owned farms.

DEPRESSION, DROUGHT, AND MARKETING CONTROLS

The worldwide Depression that began in 1929 brought about severely reduced prices for agricultural commodities in South Africa, and the state began to intervene in the market in order to subsidize exports and minimize price swings. The continued stagnation of agricultural prices after 1932 led to expanded state intervention, culminating in the Marketing Act of 1936. The nadir of the Depression, in 1932, coincided with another round of drought, which contemporary observers called the worst of the century. Labor tenants, especially those in the thornveld, experienced this as a time of famine, aggravated by locusts and by malaria. It is remembered (along with other such years later in the 1930s and 1940s) as "the time of the queue," when state drought relief schemes provided tooth-grinding *bhokide* (yellow maize meal) to rural Africans. Drought and agricultural stagnation fueled the discontent of young farm tenants, contributing to the crisis of control that will be discussed in the last part of this chapter.[35]

Commodity Prices and Control Boards

The 1929 report of the Department of Agriculture, issued just after the October crash of the New York stock market, noted that South Africa had become a net exporter of agricultural products and argued that exports were the best hope for expansion. At the same time, there was likely to be increased competition, especially with the development of tropical agriculture in the African colonies. Therefore, the report continued, South African farmers must be prepared to compete in an environment of lower world prices.[36] With the arrival of the Depression, this proved to be quite the understatement. By 1930, reduced world purchasing power was ironically combined with a surge in production, putting further downward pressure on prices, especially for wool and maize, "two of our staple exports."[37] The report looked to the bright side: lower prices were having the salutary effect of making farmers think about the need for cooperation. To accelerate such thoughts, Parliament was beginning to impose cooperation on farmers through marketing boards and price controls, a trend that was to mark the development of agriculture in the 1930s.[38]

The first such legislation was the Dairy Industry Control Act of 1930. The act created a Control Board whose main power was to impose a levy on butter and cheese in order to subsidize the export of these products. The NAU, a proponent of amalgamation of dairies, greeted the act with enthusiasm, but it soon reported that the situation in the dairy industry, in view of the Depression, was grim, "in spite of the recent legislation."[39] The Depression continued to hurt agricultural markets in 1931, leading the Agriculture secretary to warn, "It cannot be expected that we will return to our era of high prices."[40] The secretary harped on two solutions: (1) lowering costs, including those incurred by "the employment of inefficient and slackly supervised labour," and (2) learning "the lesson of cooperation."[41] Officials continued through the decade to urge rationalization of the use of labor and government control of prices, coupled with subsidies for white farmers. Parliament continued to impose the latter solution, step by step. Following on the Dairy Industry Control Act of 1930, it passed the Maize Control Act in 1931, requiring that "surplus" maize be exported, with a subsidy. Thus South African consumers would subsidize both their own (white) farmers and world consumers of maize.[42]

South Africa began to climb out of depression after abandoning the gold standard in 1932. This had the effect of stimulating mining and led to a rapid increase in secondary industrialization, but there was no immediate effect on agricultural prices, which fell even further in the first half of 1932. Furthermore, the country fell into the grip of another severe drought, compounded in Natal by malaria and locusts. The continued depression proved the case for price controls and export subsidies.[43] Subsidies, adopted as temporary measures in the midst of depression, became permanent as commodity prices failed to recover in the 1930s.

Living through Depression, Drought, and Disease

In the early 1930s, labor tenants in Natal faced a plague of plagues: widespread malaria in 1932 and several years of drought and locusts resulted in misery, famine, and a huge loss of cattle. The Agriculture Department's annual report for 1933 painted a gloomy picture, blaming drought and depression for an agricultural climate that was the "most difficult that the agricultural industry of South Africa has had to cope with since the Anglo-Boer war" thirty years earlier. It called the drought "one of the worst . . . that has ever been experienced in the Union." As a result, farmers had "reaped practically no crops, while heavy losses in stock have been sustained."[44] However, sounding a note that was to become a common theme in colonial Africa in the 1930s and 1940s,[45] the report warned that the effects of drought were much worsened by "overstocking."[46] It emphasized two related themes that were to be hallmarks of South African agricultural policies well beyond the 1930s: (1) assistance to white farmers; and (2) restructuring agriculture to serve the most profitable export markets. It argued that given South Africa's production of a surplus of most agricultural products (in years of "normal" rainfall), its policies had to be attuned to export markets. As the decade wore on, the state entrenched subsidies for a wide range of agricultural products in order to aid exports at the expense of consumers.

Rural Africans experienced depression and drought much more directly, as processes acting on their bodies through famine and disease. Lower wages, higher prices, drought, and famine hit rural communities all at once. They saw a swift response to the suffering of poor whites and contended that assistance to whites was at the expense of Africans. In the words of Mkomeni, speaking at an Estcourt meeting:

> Starvation is facing us today. The work which was previously done by natives is now done by Europeans, and that I think is why there is so much unemployment. The work I am supposed to do is taken away from me and given to a European to do.[47]

The Weenen NC explained that the government was employing whites in public works such as road building (a traditional preserve of African labor) because "these men were starving whereas natives were not." He suggested that farm tenants could live on their "very much overstocked" goats, despite the total failure of their crops in 1931.[48] Tenants from the farm Onverwacht countered that "there would be deaths from starvation during the coming winter as men were returning from Johannesburg, Kimberly and Durban unable to obtain employment," and they therefore asked the NC for a tax extension and for the government to supply mealies on credit.[49] Africans in Central Natal were suspicious of government-arranged work for private employers, including mine labor. Chief Ndabayake said, "I have informed my people that they could get work through the NC, but they said they were afraid of the harsh treatment they receive at the mines and most of them die underground."[50] Others complained of the small wages paid by farmers, who, they noted, were able to buy motorcars as a result of low wage bills.[51] As Pondo Mazibuko argued wistfully, "What we really require is a native who could mint money."[52]

The year 1931 was the worst in a generation for Africans, according to the CNC's annual report. A falloff in remittances from the urban areas aggravated rural distress. "Chiefs complained that when grain was distributed the news went to the Rand and labourers there felt it was no longer necessary to send financial help."[53] Labor tenants were even worse off than Africans in the reserves, according to one official, as they had "suffered wholesale dismissals and serious cuts in wages."[54] Despite the dearth of employment, however, labor tenants and other rural Africans continued to be selective about the work they would take. In Umvoti, wattle growers still had to contract for migrant "Basuto labour," whereas the Kranztkop NC reported, "Mine labour does not appeal to the native of this area."[55] As one retired labor tenant told me, it was a "custom" that "Zulus never used to work in the mines."[56] By late 1931, the whole thornveld region was "completely drought-stricken," and many rural Africans could find neither work nor credit to stave off hunger as some farmers severely reduced their labor forces.[57] Farm tenants in Weenen complained that they got no help from their landlords, "as they [the landlords] say they have no money and have themselves had severe losses." Only one storekeeper there would supply mealies on credit, and he charged fifteen shillings a bag, the equivalent of six weeks' wages for an adult male labor tenant and about 25 percent above normal rates.[58] By December, there had been "only 11 inches of rain during the last 12 months and there [was] not a blade of grass in the district."[59] Toward the end of the year the state did distribute maize in the countryside, much to the displeasure of some farmers, who complained that the distribution was causing a shortage of labor. Africans in Kranztkop argued, reasonably, that they would return to work when wages returned to their pre-Depression levels.[60]

Despite the widespread hardship among Africans, the NAD continued to be more sensitive to the concerns of white employers than to hunger among unemployed rural Africans. In mid-December, it gave in to farmers' demands to stop the distribution of maize to "able-bodied natives who can procure work." Natal's CNC advised local officials instead to establish temporary labor bureaus "to bring employers requiring labour into touch with Natives," and the NAD established relief work projects in which African laborers were paid in grain. The roads and irrigation projects, however, were unable to employ all those who offered themselves. Rural unemployment was severe: "where three Natives are usually employed, only one is today." The maize crop in the relief area, including Weenen, Greytown, Kranskop, and most of Zululand and the north, had come to "nil."[61] By January 1932 the situation was more serious still. The Weenen NC advised the CNC of the need for continued relief:

> Cattle are dying by the thousand and those which are still alive are too thin to do ploughing. The stock inspector estimates the losses will amount to about 13,000 out of a total of 25,000. . . . In the circumstances I am of the opinion that natives will have to be assisted after February 1932 until next season.[62]

Nevertheless, the NC intended to help only old men and widows with children too young to work. Able-bodied men, in his view, "do not want work." Rumors were rife in this period of stress, and African men in Weenen apparently believed that the government would send them to the mines if debts for mealies supplied on credit were not repaid on time. As a result, Africans continued to be suspicious of work recommended by the NC.[63] African pleas for continued relief were ignored and in February 1932 the government discontinued supplying mealies, even to the unemployed. The NC concluded that men would have to take up undesirable work as "natives in search of employment in this district are far in excess of demand."[64] The Minister for Native Affairs advised that henceforth "limited rations of mealies should be issued solely for the relief of specific cases of actual starvation." The interests of rural employers were paramount to the department, and "[c]are should be exercised that no relief is extended to Natives who refuse work."[65]

To make matters even worse, Africans in several districts of Natal also suffered a severe outbreak of malaria from the end of 1931 through 1934. In May 1932 CNC J.M. Young reported that in some areas the fever was afflicting nearly every African homestead, leading to high rates of death and severe economic hardship. He noted that illness was preventing Africans from cultivating their fields or performing wage labor.[66] By late fall of 1932, officials in Estcourt called the malaria situation "serious" in the thornveld valleys of the Thukela, Blauwkraantz, and Bushman's Rivers. A farmer in Frere reported that he had nineteen cases on the farm and that work was "at a standstill."[67] The Weenen Magistrate agreed that "natives throughout the district" were suffering from malaria, but he noted a reluctance to take quinine that echoed resistance to dipping earlier in the century: "A rumour has got about that the Government is supplying quinine for the purpose of killing off the natives."[68] The malaria control policy dictated that while quinine was distributed free in the reserves (and apparently in labor farm areas such as Weenen), employers outside the reserves were required to provide quinine for their African employees. As one Greytown official noted, this often meant that employers charged for quinine "plus a little percentage added on for the trouble," so that many people were now "suffering rather than be put to this expense."[69] The Clan Syndicate, a wattle plantation in New Hanover, refused to provide its workers treatment for malaria "on the grounds that the natives have not the money to pay for visits from the doctor."[70]

The situation at Clan Syndicates explained the reluctance of Africans from Weenen to take up employment there. Depression and famine led the magistrate to secure an offer of work at the Clan Syndicate, "but not a single man from Weenen had applied for work there." There was also work for 1,200 men at the Pongola government irrigation works in subtropical northeastern Natal, but

> natives persisted that they could not get work. The pay was small for this class of work. . . . Natives complained that it was a fever district. It is true but Weenen was also a malaria district and a very large majority of the residents of Weenen had contracted malaria.[71]

Because these offers of work were available, "they have got to pay their taxes, and must not make excuses that they cannot get employment"[72]— even, apparently, if they were already sick and the offer of employment lay in a "fever district" at miserable wages, comparable to those on the farms.

THE NATIVE SERVICE CONTRACT ACT

In the midst of the Depression, the government introduced legislation aimed at satisfying farmers' demands for better control of tenant labor. The NSCA represented one prong in a broad state approach in this period to enhance social control and reform the economic conditions of rural Africans. In 1932, the NEC Report argued that the economic condition of "natives" in towns was intimately connected to economic and social conditions in the rural areas, especially the reserves, which it reported to be in a state of advanced deterioration. In deference to the political power of white farmers, the report was much less critical of the economic conditions of labor tenants, whom it found to be well off compared to "natives" in towns as a result of payments in kind, including rations, gardens, and grazing. The commissioners believed that the system was economically inefficient but that it persisted because it was too "deeply rooted in the special conditions of both European landholding and Native mentality [the supposed 'love of cattle'] to make possible any short cuts to its removal."[73] Nevertheless, the NEC was optimistic that this inefficient labor system was doomed to disappear in the long run, as a result of "agricultural progress." Rising land values and increasingly intensive use of the land were leading landlord-farmers to restrict the space available to tenants for ploughing and grazing. The disappearance of grazing privileges and the need for cash wages would drive Africans off the farms and lead farmers to the introduction of cash wages and full-time work for those who remained.[74] The commissioners believed that this trend should be accelerated. Furthermore, they argued that the introduction of more "progressive" and regular conditions for labor tenants would diminish complaints about the system by Africans such as those that had been submitted to the commission. Accordingly, the commission's principal call for reform of the labor tenant system was for the introduction of written contracts.[75]

This recommendation was anticipated by a few months in the Union parliament, which moved to tighten control of rural labor through a draconian new act, the NSCA. Underscoring the punitive nature of the act, it was introduced and administered by the Department of Justice, not the NAD, even though the latter was normally responsible for "native" legislation. The act called for effecting written contracts for labor tenants, but it went a good deal further in attempting to thoroughly restructure and bureaucratize the system of labor tenancy. It attempted to shore up the authority of the heads of labor tenant households while imposing tighter pass controls in order to stem "the drift of young natives to towns." The NSCA gave farmers and *abanumzane* the legal authority to retain the labor of young Africans while it provided the machinery for limiting tenancies to those providing "service" (as envisioned in the 1913 Land Act). Although the state failed to follow through on most aspects of the NSCA, the debates among whites and Africans over its provisions capture the developing concerns over the role of the state in shoring up the power and authority of white and African rural patriarchs.[76] These concerns would resurface in debates over the farm labor shortage a few years later.

The NSCA contained several essential provisions. First, it gave legal authority to an African "guardian" to bind his minor wards to labor tenant contracts.[77] Second, it imposed new restrictions, through pass controls, on the movements and "outside" employment of labor tenants.[78] Third, it required that labor tenant contracts be written and registered and have a maximum term of three years.[79] Fourth, it attempted to limit the number of homesteads on white-owned farms by authorizing the proclamation of districts where the government would impose a tax of five pounds on all able-bodied adult male Africans who did not render at least six months "service" to the landowner.[80] Finally, it authorized whipping as a judicial punishment of breaches of service contracts by African minors.[81]

The provision enabling *abanumzane* to contract on behalf of the minor "inmates" of their homesteads, contained in section 3 of the act, came in response to legal difficulties that white farmers had in enforcing labor tenant agreements in the courts. As we have seen, the basis of the labor tenant system was the agreement between white and African patriarchs for the provision of the labor of the latter's dependents for six months of the year. Since young men often resisted this bargain by overstaying (or remaining permanently) in urban areas after the six months "off," farmers attempted to enforce the agreement by threatening the *abanumzane* with eviction. Attempts to carry out these threats had been somewhat frustrated since the late 1920s, however, as the Natal courts had held that *kraal* heads lacked the power to bind the inmates of their *kraals* to labor tenant agreements. This ruling, as law Professor Burchell noted in his analysis of the NSCA, followed the "ordinary rules of the law of contract" that a person could not be bound by a contract to which that person was not a party.[82] The Masters and Servants Act had been amended to cover oral contracts (including almost all labor tenant agreements) in 1926, rendering breach of oral labor tenant contracts subject to criminal sanction. The courts had held, however, that this earlier legislation "did not affect inmates who refused to work in terms of such a contract unless an agreement was entered into between the landlord and the individual inmates."[83] Sons and daughters were therefore not liable for breach of agreements entered into by their fathers, purporting to bind their labor in return for a place on the farm. The NSCA attempted to close this loophole.

The legislation was therefore intended to counteract a prominent trend noted by contemporary observers, white and black:

> Kraal head's authority over the inmates is negligible to-day, and "Kraal head responsibility" of the old native family is fast disappearing. He has no power to compel his sons to fulfill the contract. This lack of authority is one of the main reasons why the labour contract cannot satisfactorily be fulfilled.[84]

Farming interests and others who wished to make labor tenancy more "efficient" believed that the answer to this problem lay not in requiring individual agreements between farmers and workers, but in legislation to secure the *kraal* head's right to contract on behalf of his minor children:

> The farmer . . . strongly feels that this form of labour contract is the only one which gives him a continuous and regular supply of labour, and it has failed in the past to do so because there is no machinery to compel inmates to work for the privilege of residing on the farm in their father's kraal.[85]

Having established the legal authority of the *umnumzane*, the NSCA went on to provide that a homestead could be evicted as a result of a breach by any one of its members.[86] The logic of this provision was to the detriment of homestead heads, however, as the act that purported to restore legal authority to the *umnumzane* now penalized him if he was unsuccessful in exercising it.

The act also sought to restrict the mobility of rural Africans by imposing new pass controls on both male and female Africans seeking work. Despite urban unemployment during the Depression, young Africans had continued to leave the even greater misery of the rural areas.[87] Under the NSCA, men were required to produce an identity document to the prospective employer. Males who "appear[ed] to be" under eighteen years old also had to produce a written statement, signed by their guardians and landlords, permitting them to be absent from the farm. An African male resident on white-owned land also had to produce a labor tenant agreement exempting him from service during the relevant time period. The act required African women (considered legal minors at any age) to produce written permission from their guardians (usually the father or husband) for them to "enter service."[88]

The most controversial provision of the act was Section 9, which provided for a five-pound tax on each able-bodied male African resident on a farm who did not render at least six months service.[89] (*Kraal* heads who had three or more "wards" working for the landlord would be exempt.)[90] It was obvious to contemporary observers that enforcement of this section would lead to massive evictions, as there were still large numbers of rent-paying tenants who did not render labor service or did so for less than six months per year. Rents were generally insufficient to cover the five-pound tax the section would impose for retaining rent tenants. Moreover, in the Transvaal, the customary service period was ninety days, only half the period required under the new legislation. (In Natal, six months had long been the customary length of labor service.) Once again, although the state was unable to implement the provision, it is revealing to examine why that was so.

After the NSCA was passed in May 1932, the Secretary for Justice instructed the magistrates, "bringing the Act into operation will not . . . automatically put the provisions of section 9 into force."[91] He ordered the magistrates to create local committees (composed of leading white male citizens) in each district to report on the customary periods of labor service on farms in their district and to "ascertain" what the probable effect of enforcement of Section 9 would be in terms of evictions.[92] Committees in Natal, whether they recommended for or against "proclamation" of their districts, made it clear that Section 9 would cause massive disruption of rural settlement patterns. In Umvoti, for instance, the committee (which voted 3–2 in favor of proclamation) concluded that enforcement would lead to eviction of 1,500 out of 5,000 "native laborers residing on farms." The government would therefore need to provide for about 6,000 (the 1,500 and their dependents) "natives" to "reside elsewhere." The Weenen committee (which recommended against proclamation) noted that the local farmers' associations opposed implementation and estimated that 4,000 to 5,000 tenants would be affected. All the local committees reported that existing reserves were overcrowded and that evicted African families would have "nowhere to go."[93]

On the basis of such reports, the Natal CNC concluded that implementing Section 9 would bring about a disaster in the countryside:

> [T]he enforcement of section nine . . . will be little short of calamitous. Out of a total Native population of about one and one half millions in Natal Province, there are, at a conservative estimate, between 600,000 and 700,000 residing in rural areas in Natal proper [i.e., not including Zululand] outside of scheduled areas [reserves] under labour tenant and rent-paying conditions. A reasonable estimate of rent-paying squatters or nonlabour tenants and their families in these areas would be from 200,000 to 300,000.[94]

The CNC estimated that 100,000 to 150,000 tenants would be liable to eviction under Section 9.[95] He also realized that labor tenants constituted for farmers an underemployed reserve army of labor. Not all labor tenants rendered six months service every year, far from it:

To this enormous number must be added the many labor tenants . . . in respect of whom the exemptive [sic] period of labour would not apply. These are they who might be termed the farmers' reserve labour force, for whom there is not sufficient work to keep them continuously employed for six months but whose services are nevertheless required on occasion.[96]

The bottom line was that probably 150,000 or more tenants and their "huge herds" of cattle and goats would need to be accommodated in the overcrowded reserves if Section 9 were implemented. The wave of evictions since the late 1920s as a result of agricultural development was already causing considerable difficulty "in introducing even small isolated groups of natives" into the reserves, and this made implementation even more difficult to contemplate.

Data gathered by local committees considering implementation of Section 9 provide us with a rich source of material on contemporary conditions of tenancy on the farms of the Natal Midlands and thornveld. In Weenen, for instance, the responses showed that there was still a large number of rent-paying tenants, who provided labor for town dwellers or left the district to work. The "reserve" aspect of labor tenancy was most evident in the case of labor farms. Commercial farmers kept labor farms in order to have a sure supply of labor when they needed it, located away from the valuable land of their productive farms. Some farms were owned by provincial industrial concerns, like the Natal Creameries, which enjoyed the flexibility of labor supply provided by the labor farm system, and therefore opposed the implementation of Section 9.[97] Wattle farmers and citrus growers also had irregular labor demands and depended on their labor farms for a regular but elastic supply.[98] They did not necessarily expect to get six months' service from all able-bodied males on the labor farms, as envisioned by the act. A farmer in Camperdown district (between Pietermaritzburg and Durban, in the mist belt) argued that having a labor farm was an "essential precaution" for dairy farms, worrying that enforcement of the act would result in the eviction of up to 75 percent of the African residents on white farms.[99] Farmers' correspondence with the committees showed how everyday acts of resistance to farm labor, especially on the part of young men, defeated farmers' strategy of having a regular supply of labor.[100] As Mungo Smythe reported:

I am in favour of clause 9. . . . I can never get enough labour . . . and I bought the farm Zyfferfontein trusting that I would be able to get a

regular supply . . . but I find that as soon as it is time for these natives
to come into work their six months they default with the consequence
that I have to give them notice to quit and they go on to other farms
close by who don't make them work.[101]

Smythe concluded the other farmers must have been getting rent "in cash
or kind." An Estcourt farmer agreed, "There is always great difficulty in
getting natives in to work." He continued, "They turn up [after working
"away"] overdue by months sometimes and would certainly not put in
six months with me annually."[102]

In part, debates over the NSCA represent manifestations of a
struggle between factions of the state.[103] The Department of Justice,
under Oswald Pirow, had introduced the NSCA and was responsible
for its administration. The NAD, on the other hand, would be forced
to deal with the consequences if "natives" were evicted on a massive
scale, and felt that cooperation with administration of some parts of
the act might compromise its ambivalently held role as "protector of
the natives."[104] The Weenen NC reported, "Our instructions from the
minister are that we must not recommend that Section 9 apply to any
area unless the natives who will be ejected can be found sites to reside elsewhere."[105] Because the government's land bill (which became
the Natives Trust and Land Act of 1936) had not yet passed, the NAD
would have had to accommodate displaced Africans on reserve lands
already deemed inadequate in 1913.[106] The NEC's 1932 report made it
clear to all that the reserves were overcrowded and in an advanced
state of decline.[107] SNA Herbst argued in 1933 that Section 9 should
be held in abeyance until Parliament had dealt with the "squatting
system" under the land bill.[108]

The NAD's views prevailed: Section 9 of the NSCA was never proclaimed in any district, and in late 1934 administration of the act was
transferred from Justice to Native Affairs.[109] Nevertheless, farmers used
the leverage provided to them by Section 9, as well as other parts of
the act, to carry out evictions. Farmers also used the evictions to in
effect confiscate tenants' cattle, as East Coast Fever (ECF) restrictions prevented evicted homesteads from removing their cattle, making evictees liable for grazing and dipping fees for cattle they could
no longer use.[110] As the 1933 NCs conference heard in Durban, the
NSCA provided landlords "[t]oo many easy ways of terminating contracts."[111] The conference passed a resolution opposing rigid enforcement of the act as "impracticable."[112]

That same year, Sabulawa Mkize provided an example of this to
his NC in Weenen. He said that his landlord, F.C. Rawlinson of

Estcourt, had given him and other tenants "notice to quit," telling them that he could not employ them all. Farmer Rawlinson had claimed, according to Mkize, that "he had no say in the matter of the eject-ments and really the government was ejecting us. We understood by that the government had taken over the farms." Mkize reported that this exchange had occurred despite the landlord's commitment to the NC to allow the *imizi* to remain on his farm pending a government decision on Section 9. In reply to Mkize at a public meeting, the NC, J.P. Rawlinson, stated: "[F.C.] Rawlinson is my cousin and he speaks Zulu very well. I am sure he did not tell you [that the government was taking over the farms]." This did not appease Mkize, whose re-ply, "The government should take away all the farms from the Euro-peans," was greeted with loud shouts of approval from the men assembled to meet with the NC.[113] The exchange is a vivid illustration of the close connections between officialdom and white farmers, as well as of the sharply divergent views of the state held by tenants and landlords. It also provides an interesting illustration of the possibili-ties of miscommunication and manipulation inherent in the compli-cated three-way lingual and cultural exchange among black tenants, white farmers, and officials.

The other provisions of the NSCA did go into force in 1933, but they proved difficult to enforce. Labor tenants resisted the NSCA by refusing to produce passes to their landlords. Landlords, however, took advantage of the act's provisions to evict homesteads if one member had failed to return to work, a common occurrence in the memory of many of my informants. As a result, Weenen NC Rawlinson knew of instances of "natives working six months in the year for nothing to avoid being evicted." When commissioners "explained" the provisions of the NSCA at public meetings in 1933, African tenants like Sabulawa Mkize made it clear that they opposed the act. They opposed written contracts, "as we do not trust the white man. If we sign we will not be allowed to leave the farm nor will they let us go and work else-where after we have completed our six months work."[114] NC Rawlinson advised them that the act did not require written contracts, but he admitted the catch that their landlords could evict them if they refused to sign written contracts. Labor tenants also opposed the NSCA's provision that *abanumzane* could be evicted because of the breach of members of their *imizi*. Bhekimbheko Mkize complained that his landlord, J. Cooke of Estcourt, "has ejected me because one of the inmates of my kraal would not work. I cannot get another site and am a wanderer."[115] Learning of the new restrictions imposed by the act emboldened Africans like Maminya Sitole of Tugela Estates in Weenen to argue, "The government should buy land for us as we are tired of working for farmers." Africans in Weenen recalled that farmers had only recently come to the district and that the government had been promising additional reserve areas since 1917. "The district was formerly all locations [Crown lands] but the government has now sold all the land to Europeans," one man commented—a reminder of the appeal of the ICU and the threatening manifestation of white encroachment in the form of boundary beacons. Dida Dhlamini of Muden said the act would result in a "fight between whites and blacks."[116] The authorities were becoming quite worried that this prediction would be borne out, and the forces of repression were called out to snuff out the embers of "hostility between Natives and Europeans," or at least to keep their low glow from flaring up. The Communist Party was circulating a pamphlet criticizing the NSCA, and a distributor in Pinetown (near Durban) was sentenced to a year in prison for "promoting hostility" and inciting the nonpayment of taxes.[117] The pamphlet contended (in Zulu and Xhosa) that a master could punish any African servant, including women, by tying her to a wagon wheel and thrashing her with a *sjambok* (ox-hide whip), concluding that the act meant "lasting slavery and famine in the land."[118] Similar arguments fueled opposition to the NSCA in Weenen.[119]

The stridency of African responses to the NSCA in 1933 showed that although rural radicalism had been effectively suppressed in the late 1920s, the ideas that underlay it had not died out. The anger also reflected a measure of desperation as Africans were squeezed between new attempts to repress rural labor and severe ecological hardship in the form of drought and famine in early 1930s, as well as a shortage of land.

URBANIZATION, RURAL DECLINE,
AND LEGISLATIVE RESPONSES

Ecological misfortune, including severe droughts and locust infestations, continued to afflict South Africa's farming areas through 1936. The branches of the state concerned with commercial agriculture persisted in offering large-scale aid to white farmers, while the NAD allowed only intermittent famine relief for rural Africans. The winter and early spring of 1933, June to October, "was the darkest and most difficult experienced by the farming community for the last thirty years, worse even than the [previous year]," with losses of more than 100,000 cattle and nearly as many sheep in Natal. In the Union as a whole there was "massive state aid" to keep (white) farmers from losing farms.[120] The year, hard by any measure, concluded with an intense infestation of red locusts, last seen at the time of the ECF epidemic of 1906 1908, as drought turned to heavy rainfall "just as sodden as the drought had been prolonged."[121]

Continuing this long chain of climatic disaster, another serious drought and famine hit the country in 1936. Farmers in the Natal Midlands, who were receiving subsidized supplies of maize to feed starving stock, made urgent appeals to the government for maize to feed "natives, pigs and poultry" (as they charmingly put it), as a hedge against a rise in stock theft and other crime.[122] Maize was eventually supplied for farm workers in several districts of Natal.[123] Famine relief was distributed in the countryside in the form of imported yellow maize, known in *isiZulu* as *bhokide*, a reference to its gritty tooth-grinding quality.[124] In Richmond, Chief Nxamalala "complain[ed] that yellow maize is unfit for human consumption and that it is unknown to and unwanted by the Natives."[125] There were calls in early 1936 to suspend the export quota and subsidies of the Maize Control Act in order to make more of the South African maize crop available locally at affordable prices. The plea of a Richmond mission superintendent reflected the desperate situation of African homesteads:

[The] plight into which we are fallen [is] owing to the ravages of drought and locusts. We cannot hope to reap any maize crops until the 1937 season, eighteen months ahead. Our crops of beans, potatoes, etc. have completely failed. Most of our available men are away at work trying to support their families. Their earnings are very small. The position of the women and children is becoming most desperate.[126]

Labor tenants in Natal had been unable to plant, due to drought, and therefore lacked the green mealies usually relied on in summer. If rains fell, tenants would be "called out by their landlords during the very short time in which any such ploughing can be done," and thus would still be unable to plant crops. Meanwhile farmers in Natal complained that "their supplies are exhausted and they cannot continue to supply their tenants any further"; indeed, they had "in most cases exceeded the advance allowance allowed" by the law regulating the provision of credit to tenants.[127] The Weenen NC reported that there would be no crops and that "natives" were already on the verge of starvation, but he promised his superiors that he would not supply maize to any able-bodied men.[128]

In hard-hit areas like Estcourt and Weenen, the drought and famine were beginning to expose cracks in the domestic structure, idealized as

Figure 3.3   Africans in Urban Areas, 1911–1936

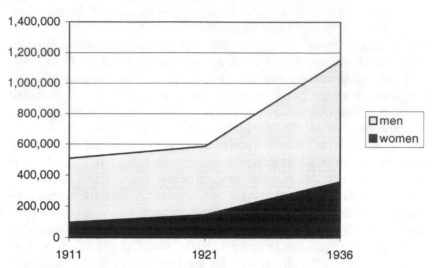

Source: 1936 Census.

harmonious and hierarchical, that underlay the ideology of "native" administration. In March 1936 the Weenen NC intervened with an employer
of a young African man to secure repayment of maize issued to his elderly father, to whom the son had failed to send funds during his twelve
months' employment on a sugar plantation. The NC stated that the maize
had been debited to the son at thirteen shillings per bag, "and unless he
remits money he will be prosecuted."[129] On the same day, he wrote to the
Pass Officer in Johannesburg to say that another young man, Sihlahla
Sikakane, would be prosecuted if he did not send money to his mother
and siblings, who were starving.[130]

    Census figures for the mid-1930s display the trends that were af-
fecting labor tenant households as well as the economic pressures on
their white landlords. The growth of urban employment, combined
with declining availability of land for farm tenants was making city
life increasingly attractive for young rural Africans. The 1936 census,
the first complete count since 1921, showed strong population growth
and considerable urbanization, even in the mainly rural districts. The
"urban Native population" had nearly doubled in those fifteen years
(Figure 3.3), and more than 17 percent of Africans were now urban-
ites.[131] Natal's cities and rural towns, like those of the Union as a

Table 3.1   Cattle Holdings in South Africa, 1923–1937

	Farms	*Tenants*	*Reserves*
1923	5,365,736	1,246,132	2,703,314
1929	5,264,340	1,508,430	3,878,584
1937	6,196,760	1,361,329	3,629,944

Source: Agricultural Census, U.G. 18-1939.

whole, showed considerable growth, though overall Natal's African population was still only 8.2 percent urban. The African populations of Durban and Pietermaritzburg each grew by about 50 percent.[132] Women were now 29 percent of Natal's urban Africans, and the rural African population was 54 percent female.[133]

One index of social age appears in the fact that 45 percent of African male workers in the Rand, and more than 50 percent in Durban, were reported as "never married."[134] While this partly reflects the abnormally high masculinity of the cities, it is also a reflection of the "youth" of migrant workers, many of whom were working in the cities precisely to earn money for bridewealth before returning to the countryside. A large majority of women in the cities, on the other hand, were reported to be married.[135]

The Agricultural Census for 1936–1937 (the first complete report since 1930) enables us to examine the state of agriculture in the Union and Natal after the Depression and a series of ecological hardships, showing the differential effects on white farmers and black tenants and reserve dwellers (Table 3.1).[136] African cattle holdings, both on white farms and in reserves, peaked around 1928–1929, and the devastating droughts and Depression caused a considerable decline. White farmers, meanwhile, experienced a trough in 1930 but significantly increased their holdings by 1936, whereas African tenants by 1936 held fewer cattle than they had at any time since 1925.[137] This was yet another reason for increased urban migration by young men hoping to marry. If they were to accumulate cattle for *lobola*, they would have to do so by earning cash.

The official data also provide a sense of the state of commercial farming in Central Natal in the 1930s. In Estcourt, 648 farms covered about 460,000 morgen, of which just over 9 percent was under crops and 1 percent in timber and wattles. The farms consumed 40 percent of the grain they produced, mainly for stock feed. Estcourt was still a prominent sheep district and had significant dairy farming operations as well as cattle for beef and hides. In Lions River, 215 farms were on 168,592 morgen, only 6 percent of which was devoted to agricultural crops and 1 percent to tree crops. Dairy farming led to consumption on farms of two-thirds of the grain grown in the district. There were increasing restrictions on tenants' small stock. New Hanover had 276 farms on 124,000 morgen. Agricultural crops were planted on 12 percent while timber and wattle plantations covered 31 percent. There were insignificant numbers of sheep in New Hanover, and landlords had nearly eliminated African-owned goats from the farms. Umvoti, the other principal wattle district in this area, had 278 farms on 171,000 morgen, of which only 7.7 percent was devoted to agricultural crops while 16.5 percent was in timber and wattles. Like Estcourt, but on a lesser scale, Umvoti was still a significant sheep district. In Weenen, a thornveld district primarily devoted to labor farms, with an irrigation scheme located around the district seat, 222 farms were on 119,000 morgen, of which only 3 percent was in agricultural crops and a negligible amount planted in timber. Farms retained half the grain produced there. The irrigated lands around Weenen town and in the citrus plantations covered 2 percent of the farmland. Deterioration of the labor farms was shown by the fact that Africans held twice as many goats as cattle.[138]

Besides continuing the string of drought, pestilence, and famine, the years 1936–1937 brought important legislation affecting agriculture and native policy. In 1936, the last of Hertzog's Native Bills were finally passed: the Natives Land and Trust Act and the Representation of Natives Act. The following year Parliament institutionalized the Depression-inspired subsidies and controls on agricultural markets under the central vehicle of the Marketing Act. The Natives Land and Trust Act (1936 Land Act), amending the 1913 Land Act finally established parameters for the expansion of the reserves ("Scheduled Areas") that had been envisioned in 1913.[139] The acquisition of the "released areas" by the trust was a long and slow process that was further delayed by South Africa's participation in World War II. The act placed no time limits on the acquisition of land, and the trust was dependent on appropriations by Parliament.[140] Like the NSCA, Chapter IV of the 1936 Land Act contained an antisquatting provision and extensive language enabling the regulation of labor tenancy. Chapter IV called for the registration of labor tenants and the establishment of labor tenant control boards in each district. The boards were empowered to determine the proper number of labor tenants for each farm, working from a presumption that five homesteads (including wives, children, and others "actually dependent") was sufficient.[141] As with the NSCA, however, because the regulation of labor tenants would result in massive evictions, Chapter IV was to be effected only upon proclamation of a district by the governor-general. The NAD explained that a district would be "proclaimed" only when doing so was favored by "European rural opinion" and there was adequate alternative land available for displaced "natives." The implementation of Chapter IV, then, was clearly dependent on the slow acquisition of new reserve land. In fact, before World War II only one district was ever proclaimed under Chapter IV. This was the brief disastrous experiment in Lydenburg, in the Eastern Transvaal, in 1938.[142]

The Marketing Act, passed in 1937, underscored the economic dilemma of South Africa's "progressive" farmers that was simultaneously being expressed in renewed cries of "labor shortage." Individual farmers attempted to maximize returns by continually increasing production. However, the weak and relatively small domestic market could not absorb that increase, turning producers ever more toward international markets, where prices had on the whole not recovered from the Depression. In order to "stabilize" the economic position of farmers (and ensure a profit for an important constituency) the state engaged in extensive marketing regulation that subsidized exports by raising domestic prices.[143] Officials described the Marketing Act as "a new milestone in the agricultural history of South Africa," which would once and for all eliminate the marketing problem of the disparity between world and domestic prices along with the erratic production resulting from the region's cycles of drought and pestilence.[144] Like legislation attempting to regulate tenancy, the Marketing Act was an enabling act that gave authorities the power to introduce and amend "marketing schemes" by proclamation, without further intervention by Parliament. The difference was that these powers were used regularly and extensively, substituting an interventionist state for "the market" as the determinant of prices.[145]

Subsidized production on the farms, however, faced a growing problem of labor shortage. As expanded and rationalized farming reduced the attractions of labor tenancy, especially to subordinated youth, urban jobs beckoned. These conditions brought the structural difficulties of labor tenancy to the attention of farmers, tenant fathers, and officials. The resulting official inquiries provide us with a retrospective window onto the generational conflicts that underlay rural labor shortage. The remainder of the chapter turns to this general issue as a prelude to the microhistories presented by litigation in the NC courts, discussed in subsequent chapters.

THE FARM LABOR SHORTAGE AND THE NFLC

The extent of African urbanization caused considerable alarm among white farmers and African homestead heads in the 1930s. The farmers' concern was vocal and organized, whereas that of African elders was more diffused. Organized agriculture, representing white "progressive" farmers, complained that the rapid industrialization that attended the Union's recovery from the Depression was draining necessary labor from farms, which could not pay wage rates high enough to compete with industry. Farmers' organizations, such as the NAU, called on government officials to enforce restrictions on the movements of rural Africans in order to ensure farmers' control of labor.[146] The secretary of the NAU Executive Committee capped a discussion on the causes of the farm labor shortage, in which some said "the Native would not work," with the unremarkable but oft-ignored proposition that "native labour" was going to where higher wages were paid.[147] Labor shortage, as Bundy noticed long ago, was a recurrent cry of South Africa's white farmers.[148] There was some substance to the cry in the late 1930s, however, and the reason for it was directly related to the country's overall economic recovery, which in other respects was good news for agriculture. The recovery made 1937 the "best year for the agricultural industry since 1931." Prices, though "still below the pre-depression level," were on the upswing. One reason for this was expansion in mining and industry, which was leading to increased purchasing power of South African consumers.[149]

In August 1937, the Cabinet appointed the NFLC to investigate the "shortage of native labour in farming industry."[150] Former Secretary for Native Affairs (SNA) Major J.E. Herbst chaired the seven-member committee, one of whose members was William Elliot, an Estcourt farmer and president of the NAU.[151] The NFLC was to consider the "economic condition of Native farm labourers, the rate of wages or other remuneration paid to them and generally the treatment they receive on the farms."[152] The labor shortage was not acute in central Natal; the perceived crisis was sharper on large capitalist farming enterprises in the Eastern Transvaal and the sugar plantations of the Natal coast.[153] Nevertheless, a certain hysteria began to build up in 1937 across wide swathes of white farmland, reflected and amplified by newspapers; appointing the committee was the government response. Thus, although the evidence presented to the NFLC does not suggest a real crisis in labor supply in the region of my study, evidence presented to the commission, and the public discourse around the issue of labor shortage, further reveals a crisis of control for farmers and labor tenant *abanumzane*. Young men and women, eschewing the restrictions, abuses, and low pay of work on the farms, the few benefits of which accrued mainly to their fathers, brought about the crisis as they trekked in ever greater numbers to South Africa's industrial centers.[154]

Natal's CNC disputed the notion of a generalized labor shortage. He argued that while "Industrial expansion has adversely affected the labour supply of many farmers . . . this state of affairs has not been general." He noted that wattle farmers were not experiencing a shortage, nor were the agricultural and pastoral farmers in the same region, concluding that if good pay and conditions were offered, no shortage would be experienced. Sugar farmers, however, were short of workers, due to "the absorption of labour for the Rand from old recruiting grounds in the Transkei."[155] Contradicting the report concerning implementation of the NSCA's Section 9, issued only three years earlier, he disputed the notion that the application of Chapter IV of the 1936 Land Act would have an appreciable effect on the supply of farm labor. "'Kaffir farming' does not exist to any extent in Natal," he said.[156] The CNC disparaged other proposed solutions to the farm labor shortage, such as providing a tax rebate for labor tenants, relieving them of the one-pound poll tax (per adult male) or part of it. He argued that the tax rebate would be unhelpful, as Africans would rather work in town for a good wage and pay the tax directly. Nor did the CNC support the institution of labor bureaus. He harkened back to the recent experience of the Depression, when the efforts of the department to secure employment for impoverished rural Africans had met with suspicion and "proved an absolute failure."

Despite the CNC's belief that there was sufficient labor in central Natal's agricultural belt, that was not the view of farmers in the region in the months just preceding the appointment of the commission. They attributed an "acute shortage of labour" to two causes: the "Natives' drift to [the] Rand" and a bumper harvest for Africans in 1937. As a result of the good harvest, "they have no need to go and work and foreseeing a plentiful supply of food over the winter do not force members of their family to work." The evidence in Estcourt and Greytown in the previous month, however, showed that farmers in those districts believed that they were suffering from a labor shortage, although most farmer witnesses agreed that those offering good wages and conditions were able to get sufficient labor. The farmers in Estcourt believed that an abundant harvest by "natives" was reducing the available labor supply, and they also complained that they could not compete with wages paid by the government at a research station in the district. Wattle growers in Greytown (Umvoti) said there had been a shortage for eighteen months, casing the wattle industry to suffer "as the bark could not be stripped in the dry season. . . . The Zulu is lazy."[157] Those who did not own labor farms bore the brunt of the shortage, according to farmers in Umvoti. "Farmers who do not own Native labour farms are finding the position very serious and despite willingness to pay the top scale of wages, have been unable to procure labour and in many instances have had to be content with Native women."[158]

Africans in the rural areas of Natal were more inclined to attribute the labor shortage to low wages on farms rather than to their own good harvests. Why should they work for ten, or at best thirty, shillings per month when they could earn three to six pounds per month in Johannesburg? As one "prominent Native" in the Drakensberg Location explained to a newspaper reporter:

> Some farmers . . . are *'ama-gentlemen.'* They pay us 25s or 30s. But many only offer 10s. Now that, sir, would be all right if it were not that so much which we have to buy has risen in price. Once I could buy a little pot, say a *'fif-gellen,'* for 5s. Now I have to pay 15s. And because of this a hundred or more men from hereabouts have gone to work in town. Most of them prefer Johannesburg. There they are paid more. Some get £3 a month. Others who are paid by the *'ma-hour'* may earn as much as £5 or £6.[159]

Tax regulations and gender dynamics apparently also played a role. Tax enforcement had led to labor shortages in some areas of "northern and central Natal" earlier in the year, as many had been arrested or had hidden in the hills "on hearing that the police have surrounded the farm." Africans were required to carry tax receipts, but white farmers argued that this was impossible, as "the majority of natives wear only shirts or just skins." The farmers argued that they should hold the receipts, which of course would give them greater control over the mobility of their workers.[160] In another incident that year, one farmer in the Midlands asked for workers to bring in the harvest. Only women claimed the work, but they reaped large quantities, and the farmer eventually noticed that when he went to the fields he found:

> [N]umbers of their men friends standing about, and I realised that the men, afraid to ask for work in case they might be asked (as the law requires) for their poll tax receipts which they had not got, had sent their womenfolk out as a vanguard and then came out them-

selves at quiet times to help and, on the sly, to claim a share of the [wages].[161]

The rigid enforcement of tax payments was apparently driving some of the male labor force underground while they continued to reap the benefits of the labor of wives and daughters.

Farmers who believed that labor was being drained away to the Rand for higher wages also believed that work *eGoli* was corrupting their labor force. In many cases, workers failed to return to complete their farm service. Those who did return often came back with new habits of mind and industry that made them, in the minds of their landlords, "bad servants."[162] Africans denied that work in town was corrupting, since they only went for short periods of time. They also defended their right to spend money in town:

> As you say, there is more on which to spend money in town. There are *'mabisikele'* [bicycles] and *'igramafone'* [gramophone]. But our people don't waste money like that. . . . But if their food and clothes do cost them more than on the farms they nevertheless get better food and clothes, and that is precisely what they earn their money to buy.[163]

In an attempt to diagnose the causes of labor shortage on the farms, the NFLC issued questionnaires asking farmers to describe their labor requirements, broken down by sex and seniority, and distinguishing between labor tenants and laborers. It also asked farmers to report wages in cash and kind, in addition to information concerning labor recruitment and cycles of labor use.[164] Several of the returned questionnaires from Estcourt farmers survive in the records of the NFLC and provide useful contemporary evidence concerning conditions of labor tenancy, albeit from the farmers' point of view. Mr. C. Haw of Willow Grange (whose heir I interviewed in 1992) submitted a response concerning his mixed farm, Woodleigh, and his labor farm, Moordkraal, each 3,000 acres. He reported that he employed sixteen labor tenants, including nine men, two women, and five youths. Two of the men and both women were employed as domestic servants. His labor tenants worked six months. He paid the men ten shillings a month and the women and boys five shillings a month, entirely in cash. During "off-seasons," he used only thirteen workers. He claimed to house the tenants in "good stone buildings with iron roof [sic]" when they were working and to give them daily rations of three pounds of mealie meal with bran and milk. Work hours were from 5

A.M. to 6:30 P.M. in summer and 7 A.M. to 5 P.M. in winter, with time allowed for breakfast and lunch. Labor tenant *imizi* were allowed five head of cattle, about twenty small stock and five acres of land for ploughing "for each working boy." He reported one labor tenant had failed to work *isithupa* during the previous year and that he had evicted that person (or homestead; it is not clear which). About twenty-five of his tenants had applied for permission to work elsewhere during their off time that year, and he had granted all such requests. His recommendations for "promoting the supply of farm labour or for procuring the equitable distribution of available supplies" were "Do away with *lobola*, don't allow kafir farming on European farms," and, despite the wages he reported—a maximum of ten shillings per month—"pay higher wages."[165]

F.W. Symons of Glenbella in Willow Grange (whose heir I also interviewed in 1992) submitted a response concerning his 2,300-acre farm on which he raised sheep, cattle, and poultry and grew grain as well as fruit. His report included three other farms of 1,200 to 2,000 acres, which were apparently labor and/or grazing farms. He reported that he employed twenty men in summer and twelve in winter, plus two female domestic servants. Six of the men were "labourers" and fourteen were labor tenants. The two women were labor tenants; he also employed an average of six female laborers. Two labor tenant boys were also employed. "Laborers housed on the farm" earned thirty shillings per month, whereas adult male labor tenants earned ten shillings to one pound; women and youths earned ten shillings. He paid wages entirely in cash, except that "during fruit picking some women prefer to be paid with fruit." He had experienced a labor shortage "[t]his year for the first time." He had sought twelve "outside men" for "silage making" but did not get any. He provided workers with three pounds of meal per day, some "wheaten bran for making fermented porridge" and an "[o]ld ewe" twice a month. The workday was thirteen hours in summer and ten in winter, with one hour for breakfast "after milking," and another for lunch. Workers were housed in "stone and iron" or "wood and iron" buildings. Labor tenant *imizi* were allowed fifteen head of cattle, and could plough "as much as they like on my thorn farm." He did not charge grazing or dipping fees. None of the *imizi* was supplying more than three boys. They worked six months service, then "rest at home for six months. After six months they can work for me @ 30/ per month if they wish." He too had one tenant who failed to show up for work during the previous year. He had not yet taken "disciplinary action" as the tenant was "still in Jo'burg." Twelve tenants had sought permission to work else-where during the year, and he had granted permission in each case.[166]

While "European" witnesses to the NFLC emphasized the adequacy of wages and conditions, "Natives" emphasized the problems of "long hours and small wages."

> Wages are so small natives cannot buy necessities. He is forced to buy food from his employer and spends his time working off the debt. Av-erage wage for [a] Labour tenant is 7/6. They get from 5/ to 10/ and have to work for 6 months. Boys and girls get average wage 5/ and are all required to work. A labour tenant has to give a number of his kraal inmates.[167]

Mr. Nzuza got to the heart of the matter of the "drift" of young Africans from the farms when he commented on the dim prospects for accumula-tion on the farms. "The children are all deserting their homes because they get no wages on the farm and they see the parents have no stock and they have nothing to look forward to.[168] African witnesses explicitly compared wages, treatment, and food in "town" to those on farms, say-ing conditions in town were far superior.[169] African witnesses also com-plained (counter the assertions of white farmers) that they had inadequate land for ploughing and, more important, inadequate time to cultivate it. Only Sundays were available for working their own land while they were in service.

> Land is not always given for ploughing and if it is natives have no time to work it. Owing to small amount of land allowed and the fact that they have no time to cultivate it, it is impossible for these labourers to keep their families without buying food.[170]

In addition, witnesses decried increasing restrictions on stock, mainly in the form of grazing and dipping fees. Chief Funizwe of Greytown said that dipping fees neutralized the earnings of the dependents of *ubunumzane*: "Kraalheads are only allowed 4 head of cattle and as dipping fees have to be paid these amount to more than the earnings of the children. No goats are allowed."[171] Greytown's Chief Zinti com-plained about dipping fees and claimed that in some cases farmers were using the same cattle for their own profit! "In many cases farm-ers take the milk from the natives' cows and the natives agree other-wise they would be driven off the farms. Farmers also use the natives' oxen for ploughing."[172]

Photo 3.1 Young boy milking a cow in homestead's cattle enclosure. A young girl faces the camera in the background. (Supplied and reproduced by kind permission of the Campbell Collections of the University of Natal [D10.115].)

Many farmers who employed labor tenants complained, ironically, that the system was a wasteful one, as it required them to keep a "double shift" on the farm. During the "free" months, "natives generally go to the towns . . . and do not come back in time to serve their obligations." They claimed that this was a leading reason for evictions.[173] Some farmers were beginning to guard against this attrition by requiring tenants to work full time. African workers received a labor tenant wage (if any) during the first six months, and an "outside" wage during the other six months, but were not allowed to work elsewhere.[174] The testimony of farmers to the NFLC also revealed strategies of resistance on the part of labor tenants.

> Contracts are broken by natives not observing the conditions, they steal, have frequent beer drinks and own too much stock. In that case they are given two or three months notice. Grazing and dipping fees are then charged as this is the only way to get the native to quit the farm.[175]

Farmers in Estcourt also complained of "weekend beer drinking." Africans, in turn, gave evidence of whites' counterresistance. "[The] Kraalhead is held responsible for the acts of the inmates and is given very short notice to quit. If he does not leave within the stipulated [time] he is ejected and his hut is burnt to the ground."[176] They also complained that low wages forced labor tenants to buy food "from their masters and as a result are always working off their debt to the master."

Other Perspectives

An economist in the Department of Agriculture ably analyzed the crisis that had led to the appointment of the NFLC, arguing that structural conditions precluded farmers from either reducing their dependence on labor or raising wages to competitive levels.[177] South Africa's twentieth-century transition to exporting agricultural commodities had unfortunately "coincided with the longest and severest decline in agricultural prices the world has known in recent times." He argued further that while people spoke of "native labour" as cheap, it was nevertheless "one of the major items of cost in our agriculture." He supported the view that the cost of labor also included the land, rations, and other "amenities" provided to farmworkers, and that farm wages were not so greatly different from urban wages if one considered the value of these benefits and their cost in urban areas. However, he understood that the benefits were conferred mainly on *abanumzane* and that it was no coincidence that it was young Africans who were leaving the farms.

> It is usually found that it is mostly the young and unmarried natives who leave farms for the urban areas. An important reason for this is probably due to the fact that such a large portion of the wage is in kind, most of which goes to the head of the family, with the result that there is little incentive for young natives to work with their families. Even where farmers are willing to pay good cash wages the bulk of it usually has to be handed over to the parent. . . . Consequently young natives strive continually to get well away from their relatives. . . . One important reason for the greater attractiveness of life in town to the young native, is believed to be the unrestricted freedom in the absence of control by the family.[178]

However, he recognized that higher wages were "the most important reason" for migration to towns. De Swardt summarized the reasons for "drift" to urban areas by farm tenants generally (not just the young) as follows: (1) larger cash wages; (2) crop failures which resulted in debt to the landlord; (3) the fact that the default of one family member affected all; (4) long and irregular hours on the farm compared to urban work; (5) lack of "proper agreements"; and (6) absence of farm schools.[179]

The De Swardt memorandum points up an important limitation of the commission—it failed to solicit directly the perspective of the young men who were at the crux of the labor shortage problem. Interviews eliciting early life histories provide a flavor of the options and strategies available to young African men on white farms in the 1930s and 1940s. Mzumeni Myaka, a former labor tenant with whom I spoke at his homestead in Keate's Drift, a town on the Mpofana River in Msinga to which many labor tenants were "removed" in the evictions of the late 1960s to the 1980s, adds some perspective to the stories presented in chapter 2.[180] Myaka was born on a farm in the early 1920s, after the Great Flu but before the ICU. His father, though not a Christian, had only one wife, who had ten children. His mother followed an "Ethiopian" church.[181] When he was young, men wore *amabheshu* and women wore *izidwaba* and *amabhayi*. Houses were still built of grass in the traditional "beehive" style. After white farmers came to the district, there was a shortage of grass, and they began to build in the modern style, with thatched roofs atop wattle and mud walls. The Myakas were allowed to have about sixty cattle and a hundred goats, but these restrictions varied from farm to farm. Eventually, at the time of the Nkonyane war, he was limited to four head of cattle and no goats. When he was young, his family had fields in which they grew "maize and sorghum, beans, pumpkins and watermelon and many other things, and *inzindlubu* (black beans)."

When Myaka was a child, his father worked *isithupa* on a maize farm, staying at home during the months "off," selling goats to raise cash. Once there were three or four brothers working *isithupa*, his father no longer worked. Myaka, however, after working *isithupa* on a Muden orange farm, worked *eGoli*, doing surface work at the mines. If a young man "did not come back from *eGoli* when he was expected to be back to start his *isithupa* . . . the whole family would be chased away." On the farm he got one pound a month; in *eGoli*, three pounds, enabling him to buy cattle. When he married, in 1945, his father paid the *lobola*. His sisters also worked *isithupa* on the farm, hoeing and working in the kitchen. They were paid ten shillings a month, with which he says they bought beads.

When asked to describe the difference between those days and now, Myaka says, "The difference is . . . the whites are no longer enslaving people, taking all the children to work." However, his memories bring mixed emotions. On the one hand he says, "They enslaved us, and did not give us food," just bland porridge. On the other hand, his concluding statement was, "What I want to say is that white farmers were a bit nice before, because they gave us [things], and also let us have any amount of stock we wanted to have." Like other informants, he draws a contrast between the oppression of his youth and the even worse conditions and ultimate evictions that came later.

The other obvious gap in the evidence "heard" by the NFLC (and the same criticism applies to the NEC and all other commissions of this era) was the lack of testimony by and about women. Indeed, all we learn about women from the evidence is that they did perform farm labor, both as labor tenants and as "outside" workers, and we get some idea of their rates of pay. Women were paid at about half the rate of men, about the same as boys. Girls were paid even less. Mrs. Rheinhallt Jones (wife of the Senator for "Natives") gave evidence to the NFLC on behalf of the South African Institute of Race Relations (SAIRR) concerning the conditions and complaints of African women on farms in the Transvaal and the Orange Free State. She summarized the complaints of female labor tenants as bad housing; lack of food, clothing, medical attention, schools, and churches; low or nonexistent pay; and unreasonable work hours. Her final points related to labor tenancy as a migrant labor institution, with attendant problems of disintegration of families, sexual danger for young female migrants, and lack of discipline for children left at the tenant homestead.[182] Jones's memorandum is, of course, the analysis of an outside (though sympathetic) observer. Interviews with women who were labor tenants at the time yield somewhat more complex views of women's situation within labor tenancy, though they lack any precision as to time.

Nomgqhigqho Mbata was born "during the Great Flu" of 1918 at Mkolombe farm (on the slopes of Mkolombe Mountain in Weenen), where her mother was also born.[183] Her family included six sisters and two brothers. Nozimpi ("with the wars") Sithole was born at Ntokozweni in Mngwenya (another area of Weenen district) "during the fight between the Thembus and the Chunus," the one known as Mabhaqa or Somathayi's. I estimated that she was born about 1924. She said, "Even my grandparents were born at Mngwenya." Sithole's family included seven brothers and three sisters. Both women were

born into nonpolygynous homesteads. In Sithole's case, this was perhaps related to her father's occasional church attendance. In the older
Mbata's memory, however, "No one was a Christian. Only my mother
was one when she was still a young woman. Afterwards she wore
isidwaba" (a hide skirt, worn by traditionalists).

In Mbata's childhood, her family lived on a farm owned by a minister, known therefore as *KwaMfundisi* (the place of the pastor). Mbata's
father paid rent and sent a girl and a boy to work in the kitchen; they
did not provide any other labor. Her father worked in Johannesburg,
perhaps at a laboratory or with an *inyanga* (herbalist). Sithole's brothers worked *isithupa* on the farm and then went to Durban or *eGoli* to
work. On the farm, the Mbatas and other families could keep as much
stock as they liked, even goats. As a result they weren't poor, even
though they had little money. Mbata herself never worked *isithupa*, as
Mfundisi only took a few girls to work in his household. In Sithole's
childhood, fathers worked *isithupa*; the mothers worked *togt*, "cultivating the fields and pulling out weeds." Sithole and her sisters, however,
did work *isithupa*. Tenants modified their cultural presuppositions of the
gender division of labor as a result of the exigencies of the absence of
male labor, just as reserve dwellers did. Although boys generally did
the ploughing at home in accordance with the belief that only men
should work with cattle, "girls did if there weren't enough boys—girls
were also supposed to know how to plough with oxen, be able to hold
the reins."[184] Working *isithupa*, Sithole worked in the garden, while her
sisters worked in the house. She earned three pounds (ten shillings a
month). Unlike her brothers, she did not work elsewhere during the "off"
months, as "It was a shame for a girl to leave home and work somewhere else . . . we weren't that poor," suggesting concerns related to
the appearance of poverty and perhaps chastity. Wages were turned over
to the father, who might return some to the child for discretionary spending. "He would take whatever amount he needed, and give some to
me—or would take it all if he wanted to." Sithole's brothers went to
school, but girls were not allowed to do so. As she explained, echoing
the narrator of the novel *Nervous Conditions*:

> During those days they said I should look after the cattle while the
> boys went to school. The school was quite near—and I would cry ev-
> ery day when they went to school, but would be told that a girl is not
> supposed to go to school, but look after the cattle and goats.[185]

Mbata was married about 1934 and Sithole about 1944, both in "traditional" ceremonies. In later years, "we took off our traditional wear,

went to the ministers and got baptized there." Mbata went to the *Wesli* (Methodist) church, Sithole to the Roman Catholic. Both had experience of their husbands staying away at work for a substantial period of time. As Sithole recounted, "He left after I was pregnant and the child didn't even know what his father looked like, but he came back afterwards," after the child was old enough to talk. Sithole said that her husband sent some money, "but that did not make me happy at all, because I didn't know whether he was with other women." Mbata's husband was missing for an even longer period. At first he sent money, but later "he just vanished."

I wrote to him and told him that I missed my periods. Until his father felt ashamed, not knowing what to say to me—he left to go and look for him—but never found him. . . . He then said we should go down to Nobamba [Weenen town] and report the case, maybe the police may find him. . . . They looked for him. . . . And they said, even the government has failed to find him.

While he was away, she managed by growing crops and selling stock. Eventually Mbata's husband returned, because he was ill.

Despite these experiences, both women looked back fondly on the days of *isithupa* and rent paying (compared to later conditions of full-time work), as it enabled the men to earn good money *eGoli.* "It was wonderful, because they brought the money home. But we would tell the kids not to do any wrong as their father would come back, and he doesn't like it. At least there was money *eGoli,* unlike here in the farms."

Rationalization and Inaction

In 1939, after hearings around the country, the NFLC issued a report that analyzed the reasons for farm labor shortages but offered little hope of relief in the short run.[186] Only higher wages and better conditions, which could be slowly induced by bureaucratic oversight, would ensure farmers the labor they needed. Like the NEC, the NFLC discounted many of the complaints it had heard about conditions of farm labor by noting that the "Native witnesses" who had made them "were as a rule educated urban dwellers who appeared as spokesmen for farm labourers. They could only speak from hearsay."[187] On the other hand, the committee report also discounted the call of farmers for yet more legal restrictions on the movements of farm laborers. It noted that most of the restrictions called for already existed and that force was a futile means of inducing Africans to accept a type of work that they did not want.[188] Instead, the report argued that the key to securing sufficient supplies of farm labor was the establishment of better conditions, including better wages, in combination with tighter enforcement of pass restrictions.[189] The NFLC accepted the premise that there was "a general shortage of Native farm labourers," attributing the shortage to several factors. Among them, it placed heaviest emphasis on the "inefficient" nature of the labor tenant system, to which it devoted considerable analysis. It also pointed to the "loss of former parental control over young Natives."[190] The NFLC understood correctly the attraction of labor tenancy for both farmers and tenants. For farmers, the system provided a "reservoir of labour on farms" while enabling them to compensate workers mostly or entirely in the form of land and grazing. For tenants, it provided a means to keep cattle and raise crops. The committee accepted the evidence, however, that these benefits accrued mainly to "older Natives."[191]

Despite its inherent advantages, the system was now economically unsound in the eyes of the NFLC.

> From evidence submitted it is apparent that the system has served its time; that it is now economically unsound; that it is out of place in areas where land values have risen and farming has become more intensive; and that it forms a wasteful distribution of labour.[192]

Its inefficiency resulted from the part-time nature of the contract, which meant that for a large part of the year tenants were either "idle" or seeking employment in other centers. In addition, farmers were becoming disenchanted with the system because tenants were unreliable and inefficient workers who occupied increasingly valuable land and failed to appreciate the value of the land and other in-kind benefits. Furthermore, "the young Natives, who form the main source of the farmers' labour supply, have no longer any inclination to work on farms," and were "deserting" and moving to urban areas, leaving farmers with "the old, infirm, sickly and inefficient Native workers." Tenants, on the other hand, were dissatisfied because of low cash wages. They resented being evicted "because younger Natives fail to carry out the contractual obligations entered into by their parents." Younger tenants objected to the contractual powers of the "kraalhead" over all. Finally, tenants complained that stock was unduly restricted and insufficient land was given for cultivation and insufficient time allowed to attend to that land. The NFLC concluded that "the labour tenant system, in its present form, is not only uneconomical and wasteful, but also . . . no longer satisfies either party." It noted that this was not a new conclusion and that indeed the NSCA had been designed to counteract the disintegration of labor tenancy. Despite the regulations of the NSCA, the system had continued to disintegrate, and the NFLC believed that further restrictions designed to shore up labor tenancy would not work.[193]

Recognizing, however, that the "uneconomical and wasteful" system of labor tenancy was likely to persist for some time despite tendencies toward disintegration, the NFLC made recommendations designed to rationalize the system in order to make it more efficient. The committee accepted that much of the rapid urbanization in the country was the result of the "drift" of young Africans from the farms.[194] It therefore recommended the appointment of "labour advisory boards" in each district, to be composed of representatives of farmers' associations and chaired by the district magistrate. "Even" chiefs could occasionally provide advice to the boards. There was no mention, however, of seeking the advice of tenants or other workers themselves. The boards would collect and disseminate information to bring about the nationwide implementation of Chapter IV of the 1936 Land Act, which in turn would ensure the rational distribution of farm labor.[195] They would provide guidelines (without legal force) on the setting of wages, rations, housing, and other conditions of employment. The moral authority of these boards would "bring influences to bear which would surely lead to betterment of relations and more satisfactory workmen."[196] The NFLC declined to require the "revolutionary" step of requiring written contracts (already theoretically required by the NSCA), but it did recommend registration of contracts in districts where that was agreeable to a majority of tenants and farmers.[197]

CONCLUSION

The Depression and droughts of the 1930s imposed real hardships on rural South Africans. For Africans on farms and in reserves, these included recurring famine, loss of cattle, epidemics, wage cuts, and unemployment. White farmers were of course afflicted by the same economic and environmental forces but faced them with the support of sympathetic state structures, which came to their aid with loans, subsidies, and regulation of markets. The Departments of Justice and Native Affairs also tried to respond to the complaints of farmers about the "drift" of young Africans away from farms and to the cities. Parliament enacted the draconian NSCA, an act that gave homestead heads the power to contract for their children, authorized evictions of surplus tenants, and proposed whipping as a punishment for breach of labor tenant obligations. The harsh provisions of the act showed the lengths to which some branches of the state were prepared to go in asserting control over rural Africans in the wake of the ICU-encouraged radicalism of the late 1920s. Ironically, however, the nonenforcement of the act demonstrated the limits of state power. The NAD was unwilling to incur the disruption that would be engendered by the massive evictions resulting from full-scale implementation of the act's Section 9. While farmers used the existence of the act as leverage against tenants, they too were inconsistent and restrained in their reliance on it.

By the late 1930s, the resurgence of urban economies, combined with diminished opportunities for accumulation or even security for young farm tenants, led increasing numbers of them to seek new opportunities in urban areas, either temporarily or permanently. This process, ongoing since the previous decade, led to perceived shortages of farm labor, prompting appointment of the NFLC. Evidence presented to the committee shows that while there was not a severe labor shortage in Central Natal (although the shortage was severe in some other regions and agricultural sectors), farmer-landlords and African elders were increasingly anxious over their inability to secure the obedience of the rising generation, whose labor was critical to ongoing production for farmers and security of tenure for *abanumzane*. The state, farmers, and patriarchs were all caught in the bind that although law and tradition were on their side, a tidal shift in economic and social forces was pulling young rural Africans to ignore those laws and challenge elders' versions of tradition.

In the following chapters, we explore more deeply the conflicts and struggles within labor tenant households in the 1920s through the 1940s, ironically exposed in the context of customary law litigation, despite that system's endorsement of "traditional" hierarchies. The migration of sons to the cities provoked increased anxieties on the part of the state to ensure social control by promoting rural traditional hierarchy, and on the part of farmers to limit mobility of labor tenants in order to guarantee an adequate supply of labor for state-subsidized production. The increasing movement of young African men and women to the cities also provoked debate within African society, including labor tenant homesteads. Labor tenant *abanumzane* were increasingly anxious about their loss of control over the young and over women. Youths and women continued to assert their independence, through migration and by challenging the rights of fathers and husbands to command their labor. In the next chapter we delve into the construction of the period's customary law regime and examine litigation in the NC Courts in order to look specifically at generational conflict over issues of control, labor, and tradition.

NOTES

1. *NEC Report*, addendum by Mr. F.A.W. Lucas, 203.

2. Interview with Nomgqhigqho Mbata, Weenen, 12 Mar. 1992.

3. Hurwitz, *Agriculture*, 25–27.

4. World War I also stimulated the industrialization of the Durban-Pinetown area, which had begun as a result of the mineral discoveries. This in turn catalyzed agricultural production in the Natal interior, supported by new local processing plants for dairy, meat, and wattles. Ibid., 17. It also provided new openings for tenants in migrant labor.

5. Ibid., 25–26. The most densely farmed area was in the Midlands and along the line of rail extending from Durban to the Rand. In the Midlands, where intensive and semi-intensive farming prevailed, farms averaged from 554 morgen on owner-occupied farms to 728 morgen on managed farms, as of 1946. Farms about 50 percent larger prevailed in the extensive farming areas in the north.

6. *Report of the Land and Agricultural Bank of South Africa for the Year Ended 31st December, 1920*, U.G. 9-1921, 12.

7. Ibid., 6.

8. When speaking of "lawlessness," the Natal Agricultural Union (NAU) was primarily concerned with stock theft and "faction fights" associated with drinking at large gatherings such as weddings. NAU Resolutions, 1924, 1925.

9. *Annual Departmental Reports, No. 6, Department of Agriculture, Year Ended 30th June 1926*, U.G. 6-1927, 198.

10. *Report on the Agricultural and Pastoral Production of the Union of South Africa, Agricultural Census 1925–26*, U.G. 24-1928, 6.

11. *Fifteenth Yearly Report of the Central Board of the Land and Agricultural Bank of South Africa for the Year Ended 31st December, 1926*, U.G. 12-1927, 32–33. Production of "*kaffir* corn," 82.55 percent of which was grown by "natives," was down 69 percent. *Agricultural Census 1925–26*, U.G. 24-1928, 15.

12. *Report of the Central Board of the Land and Agricultural Bank of South Africa for the year ending 31st December, 1927*, U.G. 18-1928, 20. See also *Department of Agriculture Annual Report 1926*, U.G. 6-1927, 206.

13. "A Year's Work. Annual Report of the Secretary for Agriculture. Year Ended 30th June, 1927," *Farming in South Africa*, 2, no. 20 (Nov. 1927), 373. Three years earlier, the Department of Agriculture had sounded a similar note of warning: "There are probably close on nine million cattle in the Union to-day [sic]. . . . These are increasing at a very much greater rate than is probably thought possible, due largely to the reduction of disease brought about by the extended use of the dipping tank." *Department of Agriculture Annual Report 1923*, U.G. 9-1924, 377–78. Perhaps not coincidentally, the East Coast Fever situation in Natal improved in 1928, according to reports, with only forty new outbreaks, half of them in Kranskop and Richmond districts. "The Year's Work. Annual Report of the Secretary for Agriculture. Year Ended 30th June, 1928," *Farming in South Africa*, 3, no. 32 (Nov. 1928): 1052.

14. Ibid.

15. Ibid.

16. Exporting beef was one of the recommended solutions. The bank noted that only 5 percent of the country's total herd was slaughtered each year, against more than 18 percent in the United States, a deficiency attributed to Africans' failure to slaughter their stock. *Land Bank Annual Report 1926*, U.G. 12-1927, 18; *Agricultural Census 1923–24*, U.G. 4-1926, 17. In Natal, as of 1927 "Europeans" had 773,210 head of cattle and "natives" on "European" farms had 410,218 head. Africans by this time were already much more likely than whites to own goats, an indication of their relative poverty. Africans on white-owned farms had 441,189 goats, slightly exceeding the number of their cattle. (Reserve-dwellers had 836,642 goats.) *Agricultural Census 1926–27*, U.G. 37-1928, 29–30.

17. Agriculture Annual Report 1928, 1054.

18. *Land Bank Annual Report 1928*, U.G. 18-1929, 36. Bark fetched up to twelve pounds a ton in Durban, and usually ran from six pounds to eight pounds. Again the Bank reported that considerable acreage was being planted. In Natal, 135,000 morgen of the total 285,454 morgen was planted with trees under three years old, whereas only 46,000 morgen had trees over seven years old. Natal as a whole had 77 percent of the morgenage planted in wattles. *Agricultural Census 1927–28*, U.G. 41-1929, 33.

19. See Bradford, *Taste of Freedom*, esp. 186–212; Beinart and Bundy, *Hidden Struggles*, 270–320.

20. Central Archives (CA), K 26, vol. 4, NEC Evidence, 6585, testimony of Robert Spiers, Pietermaritzburg, 8 April 1931.

21. Interview with Domby MaButhelezi Phungula, Nottingham Road, 20 May 1992.

22. Bradford, *A Taste of Freedom*, esp. 186–212.

23. Ibid. Concerning evictions, see also testimony of Charles Wheelwright, Mtubatuba, 25 Sept. 1930, CA, K 26, NEC Evidence, Vol. 4, 1744.

24. *Land Bank Annual Report 1926*, U.G. 12-1927, 37–38.

25. The NAU was agitating for three months' notice of eviction under the Land Act. Notice would be given in March and the eviction carried out in June, enforced by the government without cost to the farmer. NAU Resolutions 1927, 6; NAU Resolutions 1928, 17-18; NAU Resolutions 1929, 36. The Secretary for Justice replied that the Natives Land Amendment Bill then before Parliament provided a "summary and inexpensive method" of evicting "native squatters" from farms. NAU Minutes, 4 Dec. 1929.

26. NAU Minutes, 2 Jun. 1927. At the annual congress earlier in the year, the NAU had referred to the South African Agricultural Union (SAAU) a resolution that the government assert stronger control over the ICU "with a view to preventing seditious propaganda being spread." ICU branches should be registered with the NAD; its meetings should be approved by the magistrate and attended by "two European Native Linguists"; the tribal system should be more strictly adhered to. NAU Resolutions, 1928.

27. NAU Minutes, 2 Jun. 1927. He added that "One of the chief agitators—a native by the name of Butelese [Wellington Buthelezi] held letters of exemption and was therefore not subject to the Native Law." The bill being discussed was the Riotous Assemblies Act, passed in 1929.

28. NAU Minutes, 2 Jun. 1927.

29. Ibid. This power was granted in the Native Service Contract Act (NSCA) in 1932, discussed below. In an apparently unrelated item, the Executive Committee rejected the report of the Native Welfare Society concerning the need for a "more balanced diet" for farm laborers, noting that the society apparently didn't understand the different standard of living for farm natives compared to "Europeans."

30. NAU Minutes, 17 Aug. 1927.

31. Ibid.

32. NAU Minutes, 2 Jun. 1927. Three months later the Weenen magistrate noted that some defendants in eviction cases were being represented by the ICU, "which seems to have terrified the farmers all over Natal." PAR, 1 WEN 3/3/1/1, 2/6, Weenen Mag. to Sec. for Justice, 31 Aug. 1927.

33. CA, K 26, NEC Evidence, Vol. 4, 6622, testimony of Col. Frank Foxon, Pietermaritzburg, 9 Apr. 1931. Chief Nxamalala Mkize of Richmond also testified in a local proceeding that he had stopped ICU meetings from taking place, under the orders of Magistrate Lugg, later the CNC of Natal. PAR, 1 RMD 3/3/1/4, N1/1/3/8, Interview: Members of Church of England: Complaint against Acting Chief Nxamalala: Embo Tribe, 27 Nov. 1929. Some chiefs, however, used the ICU in order to advance their own land claims. See PAR, CNC 82A, 2/73/59, Estcourt Mag. to CNC, 3 Sept. 1928.

34. Bradford, *Taste of Freedom.*

35. The Depression is unfortunately something of a black hole in terms of reports and statistics from the Union government, as reporting was diminished and publication temporarily stopped to save funds. *Report of the Agricultural and Pastoral Production of the Union of South Africa, 1929–30, Agricultural Census No. 13, 1930,* U.G. 12-1932, 11. When the Land Bank resumed publication of its reports in 1931, it no longer contained the provincial reports or analysis of production and prices for the year that were so informative in the reports issued in the 1920s. See, e.g., *Land Bank Annual Report 1930,* U.G. 12-1931. The Department of Agriculture, however, continued to issue its annual reports in *Farming in South Africa.*

36. *Farming in South Africa 1929,* 365.

37. "The Year's Work. Annual Report of the Secretary for Agriculture. Year Ended 30th June, 1930," *Farming in South Africa,* 5, no. 56 (Nov. 1930): 357. Wool exports were up by 24 million pounds, but their value was down 5.12 million pounds. Ibid., 361.

38. Ibid.

39. NAU Minutes, 20 Nov. 1930 and 11 Dec. 1930.

40. "Fostering our Farming Interests. Annual Report of the Secretary for Agriculture. Year Ended 30th June, 1931." *Farming in South Africa,* 6, no. 68 (Nov. 1931): 287.

41. Ibid.

42. Ibid., 302. The NAU's delegates to a national Maize Conference endorsed the principles of the act. NAU Minutes, 28 May 1931.

43. "The Union's Agricultural Outlook. Annual Report for the Year ending 30th June, 1931," *Farming in South Africa,* 7, no. 80 (Nov. 1932).

44. "Review of the Union's Agricultural Industry. Activities of the Department of Agriculture. Annual Report for the Year ended June 30, 1933" (Agriculture Annual

Report 1933), *Farming in South Africa*, vol. VIII, no. 93 (Dec. 1933), 447. Drought resulted in the maize crop being only half of "normal," coming in at 8.6 million bags. The Mealie Control Act was therefore suspended; no export quota was fixed. Due to drought there was a "serious scarcity of pasture," and much of the maize crop was being devoted to stock feed. Ibid., 452.

45. See, e.g., David Anderson, "Depression, Dust Bowl, Demography and Drought: The Colonial State and Soil Conservation in East Africa during the 1930s," *African Affairs*, 83, no. 332 (Jul. 1984): 321–44; William Beinart, "Soil Erosion, Conservationism and Ideas about Development: A Southern African Exploration, 1900–1960," *Journal of Southern African Studies*, 11, no. 1 (Oct. 1984): 52–83.

46. *Agriculture Annual Report 1933*, 447. As the secretary noted, droughts are a recurrent fact of life in South Africa, but the droughts of the early 1930s were particularly severe. Although there was a tendency among farmers to believe that rains were diminishing over time, and to blame overstocking and soil erosion, there was no evidence to support this belief. In 1951, a government commission concluded that "probably 95 per cent" of the country's rainfall comes from adjacent oceans and cannot be affected by actions in the interior such as afforestation. *Report of the Desert Encroachment Committee*, U.G. 59-1951, 22–23. See also *Interim Report of the Drought Investigation Commission*, U.G. 20-1922, 4. Many parts of the country are subject to drought even when average rainfall is good, and "[a]s thunderstorms are characteristic, a disproportionate percentage of the total annual precipitation may occur in torrential downpours giving a heavy loss in run-off." *Third Interim Report of the Industrial and Agricultural Requirements Commission*, U.G. 40-1941, 7. This pattern of recurrent drought and torrential rains is characteristic of Natal's thornveld.

47. PAR, 1 EST 3/1/2/6, 2/16/3, Minutes of Quarterly Meeting of Natives at Loskop, 10 Feb. 1932.

48. PAR, 1 WEN 3/3/1/1, 2/3/10, Weenen NC to CNC, 5 May 1931. In Weenen, the drought still had not broken in June 1933 when the NC reported, "For the last five years natives in this district have not had one good crop." PAR, 1 WEN 3/3/1/ 1, 2/3/10A, Weenen NC to CNC, 13 Jun. 1933.

49. Ibid. The request for general tax relief was denied, but the acting CNC said that requests could be considered on an individual basis (acting CNC to Weenen NC, 8 May 1931). The tenants had reported the prevailing price of maize as twelve shillings a bag. NAD, 1 WEN 3/3/1/1, 2/3/10, Weenen NC to CNC, 5 May 1931.

50. PAR, 1 EST 3/1/2/6, 2/16/3, Minutes of Quarterly Meeting of Natives at Tabamhlope, 26 May 1932.

51. PAR, 1 EST 3/1/2/6, 2/16/3, Minutes of Quarterly Meeting of Natives at Loskop, 22 Oct. 1930, comments of Nathan Mobongwe, Induna to Chief Tatazela, reporting wage of 4 pence per day.

52. PAR, 1 EST 3/1/2/6, 2/16/3, Minutes of Quarterly Meeting of Natives at Loskop, 6 Jun. 1932.

53. CA, NTS Evidence, 1750, 45/276(28), Annual Report for 1931, Natal CNC to SNA, 5 Feb. 1932.

54. CA, NTS Evidence, 1750, 45/276(28), Annual Report for 1931, New Hanover NC to CNC, 2 Feb 1932.

55. CA, NTS Evidence, 1750, 45/276(28), Annual Report for 1931, Greytown NC to CNC, 11 Jan. 1932; Kranskop Mag. to CNC, 26 Jan. 1932.

56. Interview with Disemba Zamisa, Malanspruit, 18 Feb. 1992. Some Zulu-speakers did of course work on the mines, but my informants agreed that mine work was rare among labor tenants from Mid-Natal in this period.

57. PAR, 1 WEN 3/3/1/5, 2/23, O.L. Nel, farm "Middleton," Greytown, to Major Herbst, SNA, 11 Oct. 1931.

58. PAR, 1 WEN 3/3/1/5, 2/23, Weenen NC to CNC, 27 Oct. 1931, referring to comments of Nkuku Mvelase at Quarterly Meeting of Natives, 26 Oct. 1931.

59. PAR, 1 WEN 3/3/1/5, 2/23, Weenen NC to manager, Clan Syndicate, 11 Dec. 1931.

60. "Free Maize for the Natives," *Natal Mercury*, 28 Dec. 1931. See also NAD, CNC 94A, 68/1, N&/8/2(X), O.R. Nel, Greytown, to Minister of Native Affairs, 9 Dec. 1931. Nel complained that the maize distribution was causing a shortage of labor on Umvoti wattle plantations, and that it undermined the farmers' market selling maize to Africans in the "locations" at thirteen shillings a bag.

61. PAR, CNC 94A, 68/1, N7/8/2(X). Malcolm, NAD engineer, to CNC, 29 Dec. 1931. See also "Zululand Mealie Dole to Be Abandoned," *Natal Witness*, 22 Jan. 1932.

62. PAR, 1 WEN 3/3/1/5, 2/23, Weenen NC to CNC, 5 Jan. 1932.

63. PAR, 1 WEN 3/3/1/5, 2/23, Weenen NC to manager, Clan Syndicate, 22 Feb. 1932.

64. PAR, 1 WEN 3/3/1/5, 2/23, Weenen NC to CNC, 18 Feb. 1932. The NC later reported that he had distributed 1,350 bags of grain in 1931–1932. NAD, 1 WEN 3/3/1/5, 2/23, NC Weenen to SNA, 7 Feb. 1934. The outstanding debts from famine relief in 1931–1932 and 1935–36, which ranged from thirteen shillings to four pounds six shillings, were finally written off in 1947 as unrecoverable. Most of the debts had been repaid. NAD, 1 WEN 3/3/2/1, 2/33/2, 1936–1949.

65. PAR, CNC 94A, 68/1, N7/8/2(X), SNA to CNC, 23 Feb. 1932.

66. PAR, CNC 16A, 4/1, CNC to SNA, 25 May 1932. See also PAR, CNC 16A, 4/1, 13/2/6(20), Kranskop Mag. to CNC, 13 May 1932.

67. PAR, CNC 16A, 4/1, 13/2/6(10), B.J. Brewitt, district surgeon, to CNC, 12 May 1932 and H.G. Winter, farm "Powana," Frere to CNC. The paradox of malaria in a time of drought is explained by the fact that the outbreak was most severe in the low-lying river valleys.

68. PAR, CNC 16A, 4/1, 13/2/6(47), Weenen Mag. to CNC, 16 May 1932. The NC reported distributing 124,000 quinine tablets in 1933 and 47,500 in 1934. PAR, 1 WEN 3/3/1/11, 17/2/7, Annual Reports—Justice, Weenen Mag. to Sec. for Justice, 30 Jan. 1935. From late 1931 to mid-1932, officials reported 500 malaria deaths in Greytown (Umvoti), 199 in New Hanover, 410 in Estcourt, 204 in Weenen, and 1,423 in Msinga, a reserve district bordering on Weenen along the Thukela River. This amounted to about 1 percent of the African population in each district. Some districts had losses of nearly 5 percent. See NAD, CNC 17A, 13/4/2, "Mortality as Estimated by Magistrates during Period November, 1931, to June, 1932." The Weenen NC estimated 333 malaria deaths at the end of 1932, "but these do not reflect all the deaths," as the rates of infection had been as high as 90 percent. NAD, 1 WEN 3/3/1/2, 2/15/2, Annual Report on Native Affairs 1932, Weenen NC to CNC, 10 Jan.

1933. Concerning resistance to dipping, see Beinart and Bundy, *Hidden Struggles*, 191–221.

69. PAR, CNC 16A, 4/1, 13/2/6(11), town clerk, Greytown, to CNC, 21 March 1932.

70. PAR, CNC 16A, 4/1, 13/2/6(3), Asst. Health Officer Ross to Magistrate, New Hanover, 17 Mar. 1932. Chief Mguquka of Camperdown complained in 1934 that "though farmers were doing what they could for their native servants they could not be expected to treat the families of their employees, and as natives on private lands were in a worse plight than those living in Native areas he could not understand why anti-malaria assistance was withheld from them." PAR, CNC 16A, 4/1, Minutes of Meeting of Chiefs and Headmen held and office of Camperdown NC, 11 May 1934.

71. PAR, 1 WEN 3/3/1/1, 2/3/10, "Minutes of Quarterly Meeting of Natives," 8 Nov. 1932. The work at Clan Syndicate was "tasked work and the rate of pay is 1/ 4 [one shilling four pence] and rations per completed shift. . . . Since the arrival of frosts, malaria is no longer the menace that it has been during the past few months." The company's manager noted that it was trying to do away with migrant Pondo labor in favor of "local sources," but that "we fear that the Natal Native is too indolent to help himself." PAR, 1 WEN 3/3/1/5, manager, Clan Syndicate, to Weenen Mag., 30 May 1932.

72. Ibid. The previous year, African tenants in Weenen asking the NC for tax relief had been advised that they could get employment on the sugarcane plantations, but they had replied that they "were afraid of malaria." PAR, 1 WEN 3/3/1/1, 2/3/10, Weenen NC to CNC, 5 May 1931.

73. *NEC Report*, 57.

74. Ibid., 55.

75. Ibid., 57. The NEC recommended that such uniform written contracts be executed before and recorded by the district magistrate. It also suggested an experiment whereby the written contract would separately reflect cash and in-kind payments and deductions for cultivated land and grazing. The commission believed that this system would enable all parties to know the value of what they were exchanging and would "assist the transition [on the part of Africans] to the purely economic outlook on cattle." *NEC Report*, 58.

76. The political background to the NSCA is discussed more fully in Dubow, *Racial Segregation*. For a "fractions of capital" approach, see Marian Lacey, *Working for Boroko: The Origins of a Coercive Labour System in South Africa* (Johannesburg: Ravan Press, 1981).

77. NSCA (Act No. 24 of 1932), Section 3. South African Institute of Race Relations (SAIRR), Univ. of the Witwatersrand, Historical Documents. AD843; B46.3. The act applied only in the Transvaal and Natal, except for sections 1 (definitions); 7 (enforcement of 1913 Land Act prohibition of rent tenancy); 8 (requirement to supply information concerning "natives" residing on white owner's land); and 10 (penalties for noncompliance: a ten-pound fine or two months' imprisonment), which applied throughout the Union. Ibid., Section 13.

78. Ibid., Section 2.

79. Ibid., Section 4, 5.

80. Ibid., Section 9.

81. Ibid., Section 11. The NSCA also repealed the Natal Master and Servants Act (40 of 1894), which had previously governed written service contracts in Natal. Prof. F.B. Burchell, "Relationship between Landlord and Native Tenant in Natal," SAIRR, AD 843; B46.1.2. No date; probably 1932.

82. Burchell, "Relationship between Landlord and Native Tenant in Natal."

83. Ibid.

84. Ibid.

85. Ibid.

86. NSCA 1932, Section 5 (11).

87. David W.M. Edley, "Population, Poverty and Politics: A Study of Some Aspects of the Depression in Greater Durban," (M.A. thesis, University of Natal, Durban, 1983), 6–7.

88. NSCA 1932, Section 2. White farmers were prohibited from refusing permission during a period in which the tenant was not required to render service on the farm. Ibid. Section 2 (5). This amounted to a first step toward a nationwide system of pass controls for rural African women, a goal not realized for three more decades.

89. Ibid., Section 9.

90. PAR, 1 WEN 3/3/1/11, 17/33, Weenen Mag. to J. Kerr, Rochmount, Estcourt, 13 Jan. 1933.

91. CA, NTS, 8632, 61/362, Sec. for Justice to Transvaal and Natal Mags. 5 Nov. 1932.

92. Ibid.

93. CA, NTS, 8633, 61/362, Summary of Committees' reports, 1933.

94. CA, NTS, 8633, 61/362, Natal CNC to SNA, 18 Sept. 1933.

95. Ibid. The largest proportion of rent-paying tenants (and labor tenants who did not actually render service) were in the less commercially viable, arid areas of northern Natal, where extensive farming coexisted with "*kaffir* farming," but farmers' labor requirements were low. See V.S. Harris, *Land, Labour and Ideology: Government Land Policy and the Relations between Africans and Whites on the Land in Northern Natal, 1910–1936* (Pretoria: Archives Yearbook 1, 1991). However, this practice was still common even in the heart of the Midlands. The vice-president of the Maritzburg Farmers' association objected to the enforcement of Section 9 on the grounds that "many farms were quite unsuited to agriculture, and derived their principal revenue from native tenants." "Farm Labour for Natives," clipping from SAIRR, no cite, probably *Natal Mercury*, 1933.

96. CA, NTS, 8633, 61/362, Natal CNC to SNA, 18 Sept. 1933.

97. PAR, 1 WEN 3/3/1/11, 17/33, Minutes of Local Committee appointed under Act 24 of 1932, comments of R.M. Buchan, 1 Mar. 1933. Buchan was chairman of the Weenen Town Board and an attorney who represented the Geekie Estate. Geekie owned the Onverwacht farm, occupied mainly by rent tenants, and also the Natal Creameries, which owned the Doornvlakte farm and had "factories all over the country."

98. PAR, 1 WEN 3/3/1/11, 17/33, J.E. Scheuer, Mooiplaats, New Hanover to Weenen Mag., 14 Jan. 1933, and Golden Valley Citrus Estates to Weenen Mag., 12 Jan. 1933.

99. "Native Contract Hardships," *Natal Mercury*, 8 Feb. 1933. See also the similar views of the Mooi River Farmers' Association, presented to the local committee in Estcourt, "Native Service Contract Act," *Natal Mercury*, 14 Jan. 1933.

100. Cf. Scott, *Weapons of the Weak.*

101. PAR, 1 WEN 3/3/1/11, 17/33, Mungo Smythe to chairman of Comm. on NSCA, Weenen, 27 Feb. 1933.

102. PAR, 1 WEN 3/3/1/11, 17/33, M.R. Heath, Runnymeade, Estcourt to Weenen Mag., 14 Jan. 1933.

103. See Dubow, *Racial Segregation,* 121–22. Cf. Bruce Berman and John Lonsdale, *Unhappy Valley: Conflict in Kenya and Africa. Book One: State and Class* (London: James Currey, 1992), 77–126.

104. For the NAD's sense of itself as "protector of the natives," see *Report of the Native Affairs Department for the Years 1922 to 1926 (NAD Report),* U.G. 14-1927, 14. The report stated that this role limited the department's involvement in recruiting schemes, as it had to "guarantee proper treatment and fair and reasonable conditions." See Dubow, *Racial Segregation,* 117–27; cf. Berman and Lonsdale, *Unhappy Valley,* 77–126. For a contrary view of the NAD's role in recruitment for agricultural labor, see Helen Bradford, "Getting Away with Murder: 'Mealie Kings', the State and Foreigners in the Eastern Transvaal, c.1918–1950," in *Apartheid's Genesis: 1935–1962,* ed. by Philip Bonner, Peter Delius and Deborah Posel, 96–125 (Johannesburg: Ravan Press, 1993).

105. PAR, 1 WEN 3/3/1/11, 17/33, Weenen Mag. to Thomas E. Turner, J.P., Oldland, Lowlands, 18 Jan. 1933.

106. CA, NTS, 8633, 61/362, D.L. Smit, Under Sec. of Justice to Minister, 15 Sept. 1933. See also analysis of NSCA bill by Edgar Brookes, "The Amazing Bill of Mr. Pirow," *Rand Daily Mail,* (date unknown) Mar. 1932. Brookes noted the discrepancy between the three pound squatter tax proposed in the land bill and the five-pound tax in the NSCA. He argued that the NSCA was being rushed through Parliament in advance of the report of the NEC and without submitting it to the Native Affairs Commission.

107. *NEC Report.*

108. CA, NTS, 8636, 61/362(1), SNA to Sec. for Justice, 12 May 1933.

109. CA, NTS, 8634, 61/362, 19 Oct. 1934.

110. CA, NTS, 8633, 61/362, Natal CNC to SNA, 18 Sept. 1933.

111. PAR, CNC 109A, 94/9,N1/15/5, Minutes of NCs' Conference, 15–17 Nov. 1933.

112. PAR, CNC 109A, 94/9,N1/15/5, Minutes of NCs' Conference, 15–17 Nov. 1933.

113. PAR, 1 WEN 3/3/1/1, 2/3/10, Minutes of Quarterly Meeting of Natives, 9 Jun. 1933. The NC's memo to the CNC noted that the meeting was large and that "feeling was, at times, running high." Ibid., 13 Jun. 1933. "Europeans," meanwhile, demanded that Section 9 be applied to "organisations of a semi-religious nature . . . and Native owned farms in European areas," hoping to reduce numbers of Africans in the "white" countryside who did not provide them with labor. NAU Resolution 31, Apr. 1933.

114. PAR, 1 WEN 3/3/1/1, 2/3/10, Minutes of Quarterly Meeting of Natives, 9 Jun. 1933, remarks of Sabulawa Mkize.

115. PAR, 1 WEN 3/3/1/1, 2/3/10, Minutes of Quarterly Meeting of Natives, 9 Jun. 1933.

116. Ibid. The NC severely reprimanded Dhlamini for his remark, reminding him that it could subject him to penalties under the Riotous Assemblies Act and

telling him: "You Cunus [people of the Chunu chiefdom] may have fought amongst yourselves but you will never be able to fight the white man." Dhlamini said that he merely meant the act would cause "ill feeling" between landlords and tenants.

117. "Native Promotes Hostility," *Natal Mercury*, 26 Jul. 1933.

118. Ibid.

119. PAR, 1 WEN 3/3/1/1, 2/3/10A, Weenen Mag. to Pinetown Mag., 27 Jul. 1933.

120. This aid had amounted to 7.5 million pounds; another 9 million pounds had been budgeted for rehabilitation for the following year, while 3.5 million pounds in debts had been written off by the Land Bank. "Progress and Future of our Agricultural Industry. Activities and Policy of the Department of Agriculture. Annual Report for the Year ended 31 August, 1934" (Agriculture Annual Report 1934), *Farming in South Africa*, 9, no. 105, Dec. 1934, 469–70.

121. *Agriculture Annual Report 1934*, 469.

122. PAR, CNC 96A, 68/1D, N7/8/2(x), Part 5, "Resolution. Purchasing of Maize for the Feeding of Natives, Pigs and Poultry," Pietermaritzburg and District Farmers Association, 17 Jan. 1936.

123. The districts included New Hanover, Umvoti, Kranskop, Estcourt, and Weenen. "Progress in Agriculture. A Review of Farming Conditions and Problems. Annual Report of the Department of Agriculture and Forestry for the Year Ended 31 August 1936" (Agriculture Annual Report 1936), *Farming in South Africa*, 11, no. 129, Dec. 1936, 522.

124. Church Agricultural Project (CAP) newsletter (Sept. 1992), 2. *Bhokide* was again distributed in the drought of 1992, which the press called the worst in a century. My informants in the Weenen-Msinga area asserted that they had never seen its like, though many remembered "the time of *bhokide*" or "the time of the queue" from their youth.

125. PAR, CNC 17A, 13/4/3(39), Richmond NC to CNC, 16 Mar. 1936.

126. PAR, CNC 96A, 68/1D, N7/8/2(X), Part 5, S. Le Grove Smith, superintendent minister and resident missionary of the Indaleni Mission Reserve to Richmond NC, 14 Jan. 1936.

127. PAR, CNC 96A, 68/1D, N7/8/2(X), Part 5, CNC to SNA, 9 Jan. 1936; ibid., Richmond NC to CNC, 4 Jan. 1936.

128. PAR, CNC 96A, 68/1D, N7/8/2(X), Part 5, Weenen NC to CNC, 7 Jan. 1936. He also reported that only four inches of rain had fallen in the previous nine months, but later in the month he reported good rains in January, leaving drought conditions "decidedly improved." He requested five hundred bags of maize for relief as "Natives [are] too prone to look to government to supply mealies and many [are] too lazy to work," and traders would sell mealies only for cash. Ibid., 21 Jan. 1936.

129. PAR, 1 WEN 3/3/1/5, 2/23, Weenen Mag. to manager, Avoca Estates, 19 Mar. 1936. The employer replied that the son, Mashangana, had been injured on the job and that he would be "in funds shortly," from worker's compensation. Manager, Avoca Estates to Weenen Mag., 21 Mar. 1936. Avoca Estates was a sugar grower that owned a labor farm in Weenen, and it was the highest-paying employer of labor from the district, at thirty shillings a month. Three citrus growers in the district paid twenty shillings per month, as did H.W. Meyer of

Wartburg, a wattle farmer. The Natal Creamery, another labor farm owner, had reduced its wages from twenty to fifteen shillings. "The rest of the farmers pay from 5/ to 10/ per month." CA, NTS, 1914, 147/278, Annual Report 1935, Weenen NC to Natal CNC, 17 Jan. 1936.

130. PAR, 1 WEN 3/3/1/5, 2/23, Weenen Mag. to Pass Officer, Johannesburg, 19 Mar. 1936.

131. *Report of the Native Farm Labour Committee, 1937–1939 (NFLC Report)*, par. 435–36, 76–77.

132. *Census of Population, 5th May, 1936, Preliminary Report*, 16–17.

133. There was a masculinity ratio of .95 in Natal (excluding Zululand) and .81 in Zululand, which suffered greater rates of male migrancy. Union of South Africa. *Sixth Census. 5th May, 1936, Vol. 9, Natives (Bantu) and other Non-European Races*, U.G. 12-1942, (*1936 Census, Vol. 9*), ix. Cf. R.H. Smith, "Native Farm Labour in Natal," *South African Journal of Economics*, 9 (1941): 154–75.

134. *1936 Census, Vol. 9*, xvii. Only those ten years and older were counted.

135. Ibid., 86–87. In Durban, for instance, 51 percent of women were married and 9 percent widowed. Only 38 percent were "never married," and less than 1 percent were reported as divorced.

136. *Agricultural Census 1936–37*, U.G. 18-1939. The census compared production and stock holding from 1923 through 1937.

137. *Agricultural Census 1936–37*, 7–8.

138. Ibid., 14–15; 25; 47–48; 60; 66; 72, 92; 108. The figures are based on "returns received," meaning that not all farms in the district are necessarily included. Natal still had nearly half of the total morgenage of private timber and wattle plantations, with 202,543 morgen, more than half of which was planted with trees less than five years old. Almost 47 percent of the wattle and timberland was in New Hanover and Umvoti combined.

139. *NAD Report 1935–36*, U.G. 41-1937, 10. KCAL, KCM 3408, Natives Land and Trust Act No. 18, 1936. It also established the South African Native Trust (which would subsume the Natal Native Trust and other such bodies), as "trustee" of the reserve lands. The trust was empowered to purchase "released" land for addition to the reserves, mainly in the Transvaal, where the Act authorized the purchase of more than five million morgen. In Natal, up to 526,000 morgen of released areas could be purchased, mainly near Natal's southern boundary. In the intervening twenty years since the Beaumont Commission, the areas recommended by it for addition to the reserves (contiguous with existing reserves) were designated "Released Areas," within which the government would normally give consent for the purchase of land by "Natives" from "non-Natives." In practice even this exception was limited by the government's deference to the wishes of neighboring white landowners. The effect of the 1936 Act was to make this consent unnecessary. See also Lacey, *Working for Boroko*.

140. *NAD Report 1935–36*, U.G. 41-1937, 22. The Native Affairs Commission was delegated to "visit released areas to investigate the need for land and needs for adjustments" to the boundaries of released areas. At the end of World War II, the NAD reported that purchases were commenced in Natal in 1940 and that by 1945 about 50,000 morgen had been acquired, much of it already "fully settled with Na-

tives" at the time of purchase and therefore providing no outlet for existing over-crowded reserves. Furthermore the government undertook to provide Crown land for "returned European soldiers," resulting in the eviction of "surplus" Africans from Crown land. *NAD Report 1944–45*, U. G. 44-1946, 111.

141. KCAL, KCM 3408, Natives Land and Trust Act No. 18, 1936.

142. SAIRR, AD 843, B53.5.1, "Application of Provisions of Chapter IV of Act 18 of 1936 to District of Lydenburg," Proclamation 264 of 1937. Those who did not perform adequate labor service to be registered as labor tenants were to be registered as "squatters," and, as under the NSCA, to be taxed. The rate was ten shillings per year for the first two years, graduating up to five pounds per year from the tenth year onward. "The Effects of the Application of Chapter IV of the Native Trust and Land Act 1936 to the Lydenburg District of the Transvaal," SAIRR, AD 843, B101.27, para. II, 21 Mar. 1938. See Stefan Schirmer, "Land, Legislation and Labor Tenants: Resistance in Lydenburg, 1938," in *White Farms, Black Labor: The State and Agrarian Change in Southern Africa, 1910–50*, ed. by Alan Jeeves and Jonathan Crush (Portsmouth: Heinemann Press, 1997), 46–60.

143. G.D. Alexander, Agricultural Editor, "Administration of Agriculture," *Natal Mercury*, 15 Mar. 1938. Although wool and wattle exports (both important to mid Natal) were profitable, sugar, maize, and butter (the latter also forming an important export sector in central Natal) were exported at a loss.

144. "Strengthening Agriculture: Improved Agricultural Conditions in the Union. Annual Report of the Secretary of Agriculture and Forestry for the Year ended 31 August 1937" (Agriculture Annual Report 1937). *Farming in South Africa*, 12, no. 141 (Dec. 1937), 471–506.

145. *Report of the Marketing Act Commission* (1947), U.G. 48-1949, 3. The Marketing Act covered twenty-five primary products, including cereals, industrial dairy products, and meat. Timber was not included, nor was sugar, which was covered by separate legislation. The marketing boards for each product covered by a "scheme" were required to be made up of producers, who would constitute a majority, and an official of the Department of Agriculture. Consumers were not represented, nor, of course, were workers. Ibid., 3, 5.

146. NAU Resolutions, 1–2 May 1935, 34; 29–30 Apr. 1936, 30/54/37; 31/55A/37; 32/55A/37.

147. NAU Minutes, Jan. 1936 to Oct. 1939 and 24 Apr. 1937. The number of "Natives" from Natal and Zululand recruited for the mines, for instance, had zoomed from 789 in 1935 to 2,840 in 1936, according to the Director of Native Labour in Johannesburg. Ibid.

148. See Bundy, *Rise and Fall*.

149. *Agriculture Annual Report 1937*, 473.

150. It is not clear why the NFLC was named a "committee" rather than a "commission," as normal. It seems to have operated in much the same way as the NEC, for instance.

151. PAR, CNC 121A, 102/3.N3/13/4(X), Natives to Usutu (telegram), 31 Aug. 1937. *NFLC Report*. The committee consisted of Major J.F. Herbst, former SNA (chairman); H.S. Cooke, former CNC for the Witwatersrand; W. Elliot; J.P. Jooste, former member of Parliament (MP) and now chairman of the Diamond Control

Board; Colonel S.J. Lendrum, retired deputy commissioner of Police; J.H. Viljoen, MP, and R.A. Hockley, formerly an MP. "Natives' Need of Better Food," *Rand Daily Mail*, 23 Aug. 1939.

152. *NFLC Report*, 5. Like the NEC, the NFLC traveled the country taking evidence at various centers. In Natal these included Estcourt, Greytown, and Richmond in the Midlands area. NCs in these districts were advised to secure the attendance of "not more than one labour tenant and one farm labourer" at their district centers, in addition to chiefs and "leading Natives." African witnesses other than "specifically invited" chiefs and headmen were to attend "at their own expense," a consideration that would have limited enthusiasm because the committee did not appear in all districts, by any means. PAR, CNC 121A, 102/3.N3/13/4(X), CNC to Port Shepstone, Vryheid, Richmond, Greytown, Empangeni, Ladysmith, Estcourt, and Umzinto NCs, 5 Oct. 1937; SNA to CNC, 26 Oct. 1937; CNC to Natal and Zululand NCs, 27 Sept. 1937. It appears that "labour tenant" witnesses were in fact literate town-dwelling spokesmen, such as A. Gumede in Estcourt, who was the "native interpreter" in the magistrate and NC's office.

153. See Bradford, "Getting Away with Murder."

154. Cf. Adam Ashforth, *The Politics of Official Discourse in Twentieth-Century South Africa* (Oxford: Clarendon Press, 1990).

155. PAR, CNC 121A, 120/3. N3/13/4(X), CNC to SNA, 30 Dec. 1937.

156. PAR, CNC 121A, 120/3. N3/13/4(X), CNC to SNA, 30 Dec. 1937.

157. CA, K356, Box 4, summary of evidence, Greytown, 1 Nov. 1937.

158. "Serious Shortage of Farm Labour," *Natal Mercury*, 11 Jun. 1937.

159. "Labour Shortage on the Farms," *Natal Mercury*, 27 Sept. 1937.

160. "Native Arrests Lead to Shortage of Farm Labourers," *Sunday Times*, 18 April 1937.

161. "Labour Shortage on the Farms," *Natal Mercury*, 27 Sept. 1937.

162. "Serious Shortage of Farm Labour," *Natal Mercury*, 11 June 1937.

163. Ibid., comments of "prominent Native."

164. CA, MVE 538/79/97S, 354/280. NFLC. Questionnaire Nos. 1 and 2. The questionnaires defined labor tenants as "any Native or a member of his family, who has to render service for a minimum period of 90 days in return for rights to lands for residence, grazing and/or ploughing."

165. CA, K356, Box 7, NFLC, Questionnaire No. 1, C. Haw, 20 Nov. 1937.

166. Ibid., F.W. Symons, 22 Nov. 1937.

167. CA, K356, Box 4, comments of Mr. Gumede, Estcourt, 2 Nov. 1937. Summaries of the testimony of witnesses appearing before the NFLC in mid-Natal show that wages ranged from nil to twenty-five shillings a month for adult male labor tenants and thirty shillings or two pounds for contract workers, who were in some cases labor tenants "staying on" during their six months "off." Girls, if paid, got five shillings a month. Workers on wattle plantations were generally paid on a task basis, about one shilling for 400 pounds of stripping. "If they strip more they are credited with so many days work, so that it is possible to complete 6 mths [sic] in 5 months; but this is not a general practice. Natives working right thro [sic] year get 30/—p.m." Ibid., comments of Mr. Slatter, Greytown, 1 Nov. 1937. A written submission by wattle growers in Greytown stated that labor tenants doing *togt*, after completion of six months service, were paid a "fairly uniform" wage of three pence

per 100 pounds of Green Bark stripped "where it is estimated that 800 lbs. can conveniently be stripped." The growers said that workers could complete more than one "task" in a day but instead chose to "finish their task calculated at say 2/ per day [800 lbs.] and go off to their homes on a Thursday or Friday when they have completed 6 tasks equivalent to a week's work." Women were also paid on a task basis for hoeing in the plantations, as were other workers performing "dry bark tying," sawing, and carrying wood.

168. CA, K356, Box 4, comments of Mr. Nzuza, Estcourt, 2 Nov. 1937.

169. Ibid., comments of Mr. Gumede, Estcourt, 2 Nov. 1937.

170. Ibid.

171. Ibid., comments of Chief Funizwe, Greytown, 1 Nov. 1937.

172. Ibid., comments of Mr. Gumede, Estcourt, 2 Nov. 1937. Cf. Charles Van Onselen, "Race and Class in the South African Countryside: Cultural Osmosis and Social Relations in the Sharecropping Economy of the South-Western Transvaal, 1900–1950," *American Historical Review*, 95, no. 1 (Feb. 1990): 99–123." Keegan, *Rural Transformations*.

173. CA, K356, Box 4, comments of a Mr. Newmarch, Greytown, 1 Nov. 1937; a Mr. Schiever, Estcourt, 2 Nov. 1937.

174. Ibid., see comments of a Mr. Hill and Chief Funizwe, Greytown, 1 Nov. 1937.

175. Ibid., summary of evidence, Greytown, 1 Nov. 1937.

176. Ibid., Estcourt, 2 Nov. 1937.

177. CA, K356, Box 5, Memorandum on Native Labour for Committee to Investigate Farm Native Labour Problems, S. J. de Swardt, senior professional officer, Division of Economics and Markets, Department of Agriculture and Forestry (de Swardt Memorandum), 6 Sept. 1938.

178. Ibid.

179. Ibid.

180. Interview with Mzumeni Myaka, Keate's Drift, 26 Oct. 1992.

181. "Ethiopian" churches were African separatist churches that had broken away from mission churches, while "Zionist" churches were established by African prophets and based on Old Testament narratives with greater sympathy for African cultural practices, especially those associated with healing. See Jean Comaroff, *Body of Power, Spirit of Resistance: The Culture and History of a South African People* (Chicago: University of Chicago Press, 1985); Bengt Sundkler, *Bantu Prophets in South Africa*, 2nd ed. (London: Oxford University Press, 1961).

182. CA, K356, Box 3, SAIRR, "Native Farm Labour."

183. Interview with Nomgqhigqho Mbata and with Nozimpi Sithole, Weenen, 12 Mar. 1992. Reflecting the ongoing intersection of patriarchies, my interview with these two women was mediated by two men: the white farm owner (who lived miles away on another farm and was not present but had arranged for me to conduct the interviews at Mkolombe) and the senior male labor tenant on the farm, Kotayi Mkhize, who insisted on being present during the interview, which was conducted one day after my interview with him. Although the women did not seem uncomfortable with his presence—and indeed, it may have been reassuring, as he was their contemporary and neighbor—Mkhize was a strong presence who intervened with his own comments a few times during the interview.

184. Many historians and anthropologists of southern Africa have noted that the introduction of the ox-drawn plough altered notions of the sexual division of labor. Males, as custodians of cattle, were drawn into cultivation, primarily the province of women, to do the ploughing. See, e.g., John Comaroff and Jean Comaroff, *Ethnography*, 145–46; Bundy, *Rise and Fall*, 95–96. Dependence on ploughing and a cultural construction of the activity as a male preserve created difficulties for women left behind for increasing periods of time by male migrants. See interview with Shupu Mchunu, Mpofana, 29 Oct. 1992. Cf. Colin Murray, *Families Divided: The Impact of Migrant Labour in Lesotho* (Cambridge, UK: Cambridge University Press, 1981), 75–85.

185. Tsitsi Dangarembga, *Nervous Conditions: A Novel* (Seattle: Seal Press, 1996).

186. *NFLC Report*. Although the report was published, it was not given a U.G. number like most government reports. The report is consequently difficult to locate now, especially in the government archives, despite the archives' collection of the records of the committee. I eventually found copies of the report at the University of Cape Town and the University of Natal, Durban, and I added a copy to the library of the University of Natal, Pietermaritzburg. The speculation that the report was suppressed does not appear to be correct. See Judith Streak, "Perceptions and Conflict: White Farmers, Labour Shortages, Tenancy and Labour Control in Northern and Mid-Natal during the Late 1930s" (B.A. honors thesis, University of Natal, Pietermaritzburg, 1990).

187. *NFLC Report*, para. 10–11, 6.

188. Ibid., para. 12, 6–7. The NAD issued a circular in 1938 reiterating the pass requirements of the NSCA applicable to labor tenants. The circular stated that a labor tenant could not obtain a traveling pass or permit to seek work without the written permission of his landlord. The traveling pass or permission to seek work was to be endorsed, "Farm Labour tenant, not to be employed after _____." CA, MKB 48/2, 354/280, General Circular No. 22 of 1938, 9 Jul. 1938.

189. Cf. Smith, "Native Farm Labour."

190. *NFLC Report*, para. 28, 10–11.

191. Ibid., para. 31, 11.

192. Ibid., para. 33, 11.

193. Ibid., para. 34–45, 12–13. Legislative restrictions on the movement of farm laborers noted by the committee included pass laws, master and servant laws, and the NSCA. The committee was "satisfied that both the Pass Laws and the Native Service Contract Act contain such strict provisions to prevent the issue or possession or [sic] illegal documents . . . that further restrictive measures will serve no useful purpose." The NSCA, for instance, prohibited employment of a male "native" over eighteen unless he had a "document of identification," normally the tax receipt. If the "native" were not from a reserve the identification was to be endorsed by the farm owner where he resided giving him leave for a specific period. The tax receipt in effect functioned as a general pass document which showed "also the name and address of the Native, name of his chief, name of his employer, his age, tribe and all particulars required by the Native Service Contract Act." Ibid., para. 56–70, 16–18. The NFLC found that the system's failures were largely due to farmers "failing to make the necessary endorsements" and inability to supply tax identity numbers of missing employees.

Ibid., para. 73, 18. There was also considerable testimony about evasion of the system by Africans who "lost" tax receipts and applied for new ones that then did not contain restrictive endorsements. The NFLC believed that better enforcement of the NSCA and other pass restrictions by farmers and state officials would meet the concerns of farmers about "loss of control by Native parents and guardians over their minor children and wards." Ibid., para. 87–95, 20–21.

194. Ibid., para. 441, 78.
195. Ibid., para. 46–54, 13–15.
196. Ibid., para. 469–79, 81–82.
197. Ibid., para. 83–86, 20.

4

Kufanele Ukusebenza Isithupa: FATHERS, SONS, AND BRIDEWEALTH, 1927–1944[1]

All fathers pay all the *lobolo* for all their sons. When a boy marries it is right that his father should find the *lobolo*. . . . That is the duty of the father.[2]

I refused to pay over this cattle because Zigebendu has failed to support me and he has failed to render farm service. . . . My son . . . refused to work for me even before his marriage. I promised to pay Zigebendu's *lobolo* with the hope that he might turn over a new leaf.[3]

If you can control our children so that we can teach them wholesome doctrine such as we and our fathers were taught from the beginning, it would be well and good; but our children have become like wildcats. You can no more catch a wildcat than a flash of lightning; it disappears and runs away from you, and so do our children nowadays.[4]

When white farmers complained about labor shortages resulting from the hemorrhage of youth from rural areas, as described in the last chapter, they reflected the decade's wider crisis of control revolving around labor and rural social order. The state and patriarchal authorities in the countryside were increasingly anxious to exert control over rural youths and women. They attempted to do so through segregation policy, including retribalization and the hardening of customary law under the 1927 Native Administration Act, through labor repression like that contained in the NSCA, and through restrictions on African mobility. With respect to farm labor, fathers, farmers, and administrators were especially concerned with the movement of young men, whose labor was in demand both in the cities and on the farms. When they failed to return in a timely fashion from urban centers to work *isithupa*, they threatened their fathers' security of tenure on the farms. At the same time, sons were disinclined to stake their futures on farmwork, as wages were low and in any case tended to benefit their fathers more than themselves. Moreover, continued agricultural expansion (encouraged by state subsidies, despite stagnant market prices) meant more commercial use of farmland, resulting in a loss of privileges for farm tenants, especially with respect to grazing rights. The erosion of grazing rights in turn threatened the ability of tenants to accumulate the cattle necessary for *lobola*.[5] Young Africans from the white-owned farms continued, in the late 1930s and 1940s, to express their distaste for farm labor and rural authority by leaving or overstaying their "off" months in the cities.

The conflict between fathers and sons over the changing benefits and burdens of labor tenancy was also expressed in other contexts. In particular, the NC Courts were sites of domestic struggle despite the apparently unchallengeable patriarchal hierarchy expressed in the Natal Code of Native Law (Natal Code). The NC Courts were forums for struggle over the meaning and content of tradition, in spite of the Natal Code's endorsement of a uniform and unyielding version of tradition. Although NC Courts tended to endorse the hardened version of custom suggested by the code, litigants showed that custom was a focus of debate, not something with fixed content. This meant that while the NAD sought to use traditional hierarchies to suppress social change, conflict and change nevertheless formed an essential part of the fabric of NC Court litigation. In this chapter and the next, I use records of such litigation to look at relations of gender and generation in the vortex of customary law. I look at the generational divide particularly in the form of conflict over claims that sons were obliged to work *isithupa* for their fathers, and fathers in turn were obliged to provide *lobola* for their sons. The cases demonstrate a general sense of mutual obligation, but they also show that reciprocity between fathers and sons was under strain as a result of the forces reshaping labor tenancy in central Natal. Many sons were no longer willing to work for fathers who could not ensure the accumulation of cattle necessary to establish the sons' marriages; fathers were no longer willing to provide bridewealth to sons whose recalcitrance endangered their own security and chances for accumulation.

THE NATIVE ADMINISTRATION ACT

The Native Administration Act of 1927 (1927 Act) was truly a draconian piece of legislation, despite a transparent transition from the old regime in Natal. The 1927 Act signaled a new mood coalescing around increasingly conservative conceptions of segregation under the Hertzog administration. The harshness of the 1927 Act was also a response to the militancy and unrest that had affected both urban and rural areas of the country since the end of World War I, including the rapid spread of the ICU.[6] The most radical effect of the 1927 Act was to give the NAD the power to legislate and govern over natives and in native areas by proclamation.[7] In this sense, the 1927 Act was a sharp departure from practice in late colonial Natal, where the legislature had enacted and amended the code. Government by proclamation was a return to Shepstonian practice, with the significant difference that it was in the hands of an industrial-era bureaucracy rather than a paternalistic Victorian autocrat. The 1927 Act vastly expanded the administrative powers of the NAD. It gave the department the power to define tribal boundaries and to remove tribes or individual natives to internal exile if it deemed this "expedient." Those who defied removal orders were liable to criminal prosecution.[8] It specifically made it an offense, punishable by imprisonment or banishment, to make any statement or do any act "with intent to promote any feeling of hostility between Natives and Europeans."[9] The NAD had further special powers to regulate the lives and conduct of Africans in the reserves by the issuance of regulations concerning, for instance, weapons, "assemblies of Natives," and the carrying of passes.[10] The NAD had authority to appoint and to depose chiefs and headmen and to define their powers and responsibilities.[11] Although he argued that segregation drew on practices from every province, Saul Dubow placed great emphasis on Transkei as the model for administration in the segregation era; as opposed to David Welsh, he downplayed the precedential value of Natal. The administrative structure established across the Union by the 1927 Act, however, was congruent in every important respect with the system established by Shepstone. Furthermore, I find no evidence in the districts I have looked at, nor at the provincial level of the CNC of Natal, that the Shepstonian system of indirect rule had fallen into disuse nor that the Natal Code was being ignored, as Dubow suggested.[12]

The 1891 Natal Code established a hierarchy headed by the "Supreme Chief." While Natal was a separate colony, its governor was Supreme Chief; after Union, the Supreme Chief was the governor-general of South Africa. The powers of the Supreme Chief were delegated to Natal's NAD, headed by a CNC. After Union, the Natal department was subordinated to the national NAD, and Natal's CNC became its provincial head.[13] The 1891 Natal Code was administered by magistrates acting as "Administrators of Native Law." Magistrates were officers of the Department of Justice, but in respect of native administration were subject to the authority of the CNC and the NAD generally. The 1927 Act established the position of NC to administer native affairs and hear litigation among Africans in each magisterial district, but as before, the NC was often the same person as the magistrate. In busier magistracies, an assistant NC, who was subordinated to the magistrate, handled native administration. In districts dominated by African reserves, such as several in Zululand, the NC was an officer of the NAD and was the prime government official in the district. These jurisdictional differences do not seem to have resulted in divergent views or actions at the district level, however.

Cope and Marks have demonstrated that in 1920s Natal a constellation of agribusiness interests (like the segregationist ideologue George Heaton Nicholls), African leaders of various political stripes and ambiguous motivation, and the Zulu royal family formed a coalition in favor of "retribalisation," a central tenet of the segregation project.[14] The 1927 Act vigorously embraced this goal and gave it administrative shape. The judicial segregation that was part of the package introduced (or in the case of Natal, continued) by the 1927 Act vividly shows this turn to retribalization and a corollary ossification of "native law." Examination of litigation in the NC Courts, however, shows that many African litigants, even if they embraced "tradition," rejected the unitary and rigid version of it represented by the Natal Code and now increasingly supported by the NAD at all levels.[15]

CONTESTS OVER TRADITION IN THE NC COURTS

The 1927 Act established NC Courts to hear civil cases "between Native and Native only," and made the application of "native law" and "customs followed by Natives" discretionary with the NC Courts. It contained a repugnancy clause, stating that "native law" could be applied as long as it was not "opposed to the principles of public policy or natural justice," but it explicitly certified the nonrepugnance of *lobola* and "similar custom[s]."[16] The 1927 Act also authorized courts of chiefs and headmen to try cases between Natives under "native law and custom." It gave parallel original jurisdiction to chiefs and NCs in civil cases among African litigants, but cases tried by chiefs or headmen could be "appealed" to the NC. In practice, these appeals resulted in trials de novo, although the chief or headman would sometimes testify as to the rationale of his judgment.[17] Litigants could appeal from the NC to the Native Appeals Court (NAC).[18]

There is little popular memory of NC Courts. When asked about these courts, informants responded that one would go to the white court in a case concerned with fighting (that is, so-called faction fights), referring to criminal cases in the magistrates' courts.[19] Because the magistrate and the NC were often the same person, and their courts were in the same place, there was no reason for non-English speakers to distinguish between these technically separate arenas: both were theaters of white state authority. When questioned directly, however, informants admitted that divorces (technically, dissolutions of customary unions) were litigated in the white court. They explained this as a matter of "rendering unto Caesar": Because one was married at the court (i.e., customary unions were registered there), one was also divorced at the court. One man described the difference between divorce of Christian and customary marriage as follows: "Some, with respect to the [wedding] ring, want to break it, and others, with respect to the [marriage] certificate, want to tear it."[20]

Although divorces had to be taken to the NC Court, other disputes could be litigated first before an *induna*, or chief, and could then be appealed to the NC. In practice, cases were first heard (formally) by an *induna*. "If the *induna* was not fair enough and the person lost, he may decide to go to the chief, and he might win the case there." From there, it was possible to appeal to the NC, but one informant who recalled this option believed that such an appeal inevitably failed: "if the case failed at the chief's court, it will fail again at the 'Bantu Affairs.'"[21] If such a perception were widespread, it would certainly have affected the willingness of litigants to appeal to a distant and alien court. On the other hand, the alien nature of the NC Court was part of its attraction for those who were denied justice by chiefs and headmen; the alien court might afford an "equal" hearing to those of lower status in the traditional order.[22]

Another dispute-settling authority, not recognized in law, was the white farmer, who was sometimes called on to settle minor disputes. "No, Mr. Blauwini [Brown] was in command, he usually sorted out all the misunderstandings—hence there was no need to take cases to the magistrate—no divorces took place in this farm."[23] Farmer informants agreed that tenants sometimes came to them to settle disputes. One, however, said that when women came to complain that their men had beaten them, he told them to "bugger off and settle their own problems."[24] Finally, farm *indunas* (the foremen appointed by the farmer) also heard cases brought by farm tenants, although like the farmers they had no legal status. Farm *indunas* heard cases about who was entitled to garden land, and perhaps other cases.[25]

Although NC courts purported to administer customary law, the NCs were white, and the procedure and practice in the courts was derived from British law and flavored with the theatrics of colonial power.[26] For instance, the code specifically required that Africans entering or leaving the court were to greet the NC "with uplifted right hand and uncovered head," and forbade anyone to interrupt a "judge or officer of the Government or chief."[27] Trials were held indoors and presided over by the NC, assisted by an interpreter. Litigants were entitled to appear without counsel, but it was common for one or both parties to be assisted by a lawyer, invariably white. Proceedings were therefore conducted in a mixture of *isiZulu* and English. The NC or a clerk produced a handwritten English record of the proceedings, which gave a partial transcript of testimony, and noted by whom the witness was being questioned or cross-examined but did not directly record questions posed by lawyers, litigants, or the NC. Witnesses appeared one at a time, usually waiting outside until called to testify. Cases often took more than one session to complete, sometimes resulting in an interruption of several days or weeks. There was to be no further discussion after the NC pronounced judgment, although parties could appeal to the NAC. At the conclusion of a case the losing party was required to pay the costs of the other party, including attorney's fees, and these costs were quite substantial in relation to rural wages.[28]

A 1929 case from the NC's court in Estcourt, *Mazibuko v. Mazibuko*, demonstrates several elements of this discussion about customary law and provides a fascinating glimpse of the system's multi-layered contradictions. [29] First, it shows the intersection of Western notions of law with the divergent conceptions of African litigants. Second, the case shows how the customary law system embodied a hardened concept of custom, in which the colonial process had privileged some features of traditional social practice over others. Third, it shows that despite that hardening, and despite its reinforcement by the state in the late 1920s as a result of the rise of segregation doctrine, African litigants continued to debate the meaning and content of custom and tradition.

The conflict pitted brother against brother over inheritance of the considerable cattle holdings of the younger brother's deceased twin. The dispute revolved around customary practices concerning twins, and whether those practices were in conflict with the "ancient custom" of primogeniture, one of the main pillars of "native" law as conceived by the colonially shaped code. The case of the Mazibuko twins arrived in the NC court of appeal from the court of Chief Peni Mabaso, who denied the plaintiff elder brother's claim for the deceased twin's thirty-eight cattle and eighteen goats, over which the surviving twin had assumed control. Bringing his appeal, the elder brother complained, "The Chief in giving his judgment stated that he was trying the case under the old Zulu custom which I am ignorant of myself."[30] Kula, the surviving twin, argued that "our customs" consider twins to be one person, so that on the death of an heirless twin, the surviving twin inherits all his property.[31] Absent the complicating factor of twinship, all (including the code) were agreed that the estate of the deceased brother (who had no children) would go to the eldest brother (plaintiff), their father's "general" heir.[32] Kula claimed that his eldest brother, Dhlozi, recognized Kula's status as the heir of his deceased twin (Nyovana) at the time of the latter's death and burial. On Dhlozi's orders, Kula's personal effects, including sticks, "prepuce cover" (sheath worn over penis), and other clothing, were buried with the deceased twin, while the similar effects of the deceased twin were turned over to Kula. As further evidence of the twins' perceived unity, Kula and his witnesses pointed out that Kula now planned to marry the fiancée of the deceased twin, and they claimed that the elder brother had arranged this. Kula intended to marry her with cattle already pointed out from his deceased twin's estate. Dhlozi, the elder brother, argued simply that twin succession was not the custom. He did not deny having handed over the deceased twin's personal effects, but he denied arranging for the fiancée to marry Kula and argued that this might have happened in any case even had they not been twins, as brothers often married their widowed sisters-in-law under the *ukungena* (levirate) practice. No other witnesses appeared for Dhlozi.

What turned out to be the crucial strategic error in Kula's case was an admission that this practice regarding twins had not been the practice "from time immemorial." Kula, being questioned by the NC, stated: "*Originally* the native custom was to kill one of the twins as it was thought that if one was not put out of the way both would die and it was also said that if one was not put out of the way the parents would not have more children" (emphasis added). Chief Peni, testifying more or less as an expert witness, agreed, *"In the old days* it used to be the custom to put one of the twins out of existence" (emphasis added).[33] He claimed that the then current custom was for the twins to be separated and brought up in separate *kraals*, although this apparently had not been done in the case of Kula and his twin, a discrepancy that seemed to worry the white judge more than it did the black litigants. Chief Peni and another witness cited some relatively recent instances of twins succeeding to estates of deceased wombmates. Kula's supporting witnesses presented facts to show that the twins were treated as one "person." They said that a "native"—probably *umuntu munsundu* (brown man) in the witnesses' original words—would not normally wear the clothes of a deceased man, as Kula had done. They claimed that Dhlozi had stated that no mourning period or "cleansing" for the fiancée was necessary. These facts were said to show that no "real" death had occurred—the deceased twin lived on in the surviving twin. As Chief Peni concluded, "I therefore gave judgment for the defendant (Kula) . . . [as he] and the deceased were looked upon as only one person and not two different persons."

The NC and Native Appeals Court (NAC) rejected these arguments and reversed the judgment of Chief Peni, finding in Dhlozi's favor.[34] The NC's judgment held that the "custom" of twin succession did not have sufficient longevity to overcome the code's fundamental principle of primogeniture because "it only originated within the last fifty or so years while the law of primogeniture has been observed by the natives from time immemorial." The NC viewed the evidence as establishing merely the following:

> *Within the last 50 or 60 years a custom has sprung up, amongst the natives of this district*, of treating twins as a single entity . . . thereby ousting the eldest son of the "house" from his right to succeed . . . by the law of primogeniture. [Emphasis added]

This "springing up" of a new custom was not sufficient to overcome the principle of primogeniture under the standard applied by the NC and upheld by the appeals court:

> Is the alleged custom . . . [one] that can be regarded as a well-established custom having the authority of Law? Van der Linden on custom says (1) it must be based upon sound reason; (2) it must be satisfactorily proved (a) by a great number of witnesses; (b) by an unbroken chain of decisions; (c) by living usage. Holland in his Elements of Jurisprudence says [of custom as law], "It is characteristic that it is a

long and generally observed course of conduct . . . *no one was ever present at the commencement of such a course of conduct.*" [Emphasis added]

Because the twin succession "custom" was of recent origin (as far as the evidence showed), it did not meet this standard. Furthermore, as a result of an offhand remark by Chief Peni, the courts found the claimed custom in conflict with the "present acknowledged custom of rearing twins in separate kraals [which] seems to me to negative [sic] the fiction of one entity for the two persons."

The NAC enthusiastically endorsed the NC's reasoning and went on to carefully smother this "twin custom" to ensure that it did not cause the death of the elder brother's primogeniture. It is instructive to note the stridency of the court's language:

[I]t would indeed be a *dangerous doctrine* to hold that because such is the modern development within a tribal entity in a given area, a law which has its genesis in the ancient polity of the founders of the race and has been universally recognised and generally applied down through the ages to the present time, a law which is embodied and receives its further sanction and reaffirmation in the Code of Native Law, Sections 101, 106 and 115, is ousted thereby. [Emphasis added]

As further proof of the invalidity of the "new" twin succession custom, the NAC cited evidence of "certain leading tribes," including the Venda and Thonga as well as Zulu, all of which were claimed to kill either one or both twins or at least to severely disfavor them, regarding them as "bad characters." The court looked to A.T. Bryant as an authority on Zulu practice, while the judge cited his own experience among the Venda. The court concluded that "the disabilities of twins in the general make up of Native family life" were decisive and conclusive compared with a "comparatively modern innovation" in the district of Estcourt. "[I]t does not lie with this Court to allow these attempts at impingement upon institutions of Law entrenched, sacrosanct"—that is, the institution of primogeniture.

The courts therefore approached the issue as one of whether the alleged "custom" of twin succession was of sufficient antiquity and universality to overcome the "sacrosanct" principle of primogeniture, claimed by the authors of the code to be one of the main principles—along with the subjugation of women—of native law. Once the issue was framed this way, it was clear that Kula would lose. The twin succession rule was not explicitly admitted to be recent, but the cases cited by the witnesses were within living memory. More crucially, Chief Peni admitted that "in the old days it used to be the custom to put one of the twins out of existence," implicitly admitting that the twin succession was an innovation at some stage. Innovation, especially one deemed to be in conflict with one of the fundamental principles of "native customary law," was not to be permitted. As Peni was forced to admit on cross-examination, "*Shepstone* laid down that all the property in a kraal belonged to the head of the kraal" (emphasis added). Peni's ironic citation of Shepstone as the white, nineteenth-century lawgiver seems to have made no impression on the courts. The concept of innovation was in conflict with the colonial conception of customary law as that which emanated from "time immemorial" and was therefore "sacrosanct."[35]

The case record shows that most of the African participants in 1929 had a very different conception of custom and "customary law" from the colonial conception. Rather than something fixed and immutable, they were satisfied that although one practice had been followed "in the old days," another practice might be followed now. Thus, if twins, or one of them, were no longer killed, "twin succession" might emerge as a limited exception to the general rule of primogeniture. This flexibility may also reflect other interests at work in the historical context of the case. The parties were, at the time of the deceased twin's death, residents of a white-owned farm in the Estcourt district. After the chief heard the case, Dhlozi had moved away, leaving behind the deceased twin's cattle. Kula mentioned that whites had only recently been present on the farm where he lived and that he had sold some cattle to pay dipping fees. The elder brother had been evicted for reasons not stated in the record. The deceased twin had been working in Johannesburg for several years and had sent accumulated funds to Kula, a widower with one surviving child, to purchase cattle. It appears that the Mazibukos, who were probably former rent-paying tenants on land owned by absentee landlords, were in the late 1920s being drawn into relations of labor tenancy. Dhlozi may have been ejected for refusing to enter into a labor tenancy contract or for refusing to pay dipping fees to the newly resident landlord. Alternatively, he may have planned a move to Klip River in order to maintain the herd he believed he had inherited from the deceased twin, as it may have exceeded the number allowed by the landlord. If Kula inherited the cattle, on the other hand, he would immediately turn over eleven head to his in-laws and begin again to build up a family.

Under the powers granted by the 1927 Act, the NAD proclaimed a wholesale revision of the Natal Code of Native Law in 1932. However, the Code was not substantially changed; rather, it was modified in order to make it better organized, to make it consistent with the 1927 Act, to bring some provisions into accord with court decisions since the enactment of the 1891 Code, and to a very small degree to take account of social change among Africans.[36] A committee appointed by the NAD, consisting of two Midlands NCs (one of whom later became CNC) and a law professor, drafted the revised Code between 1928 and 1931.[37] Consistent with the aim of bringing the Code into line with the 1927 Act, the new Code gave NAD officers in Natal virtually unlimited powers. The most notable provision was the prohibition of judicial review of the "validity or legality of any act done, direction or order given, or punishment inflicted by the Supreme Chief" or his deputies.[38] This amounted to the imposition of a permanent state of emergency over Africans. The Code also contained provisions for group liability, detention without trial, and summary punishment of defiance of NAD orders.[39] In addition, the revised Code made some small steps in the direction of taking account of social change that had occurred since 1891. For instance, males became legal majors, capable of entering into contracts, on marriage or at age twenty-one. Females, however, remained legal minors throughout their lives (with limited exceptions discussed in chapter 5). All remained subject to the authority of the *kraal* head so long as they remained living in the *kraal*, even if they had attained majority.[40] On the whole, however, the 1932 Code's view of "native law and custom" was little changed from that reflected in the 1878 and 1891 Codes. As another scholar put it: "Though purporting to update customary law, the 1932 Code had the effect of embalming it."[41]

The Code was prepared without consultation of those who would be affected by it. In fact, the NAD continued to refuse to even translate the code into *isiZulu*!

> I regret to say that, on the grounds of expense, the department would not be induced to have the revised code translated into Zulu officially, and the translation of legal enactments by unofficial, non-legal persons is obviously not desirable.[42]

When its provisions were outlined at public meetings just after the draft proclamation, however, African elder men reacted strongly to some of the limited changes introduced by the new code, especially the provision enabling women to seek divorce on the grounds of "accusations of witchcraft."[43] The provision was not altered.

In short, the ossified view of custom and tradition represented by the Mazibuko case in 1929 was in no way remedied by the 1932 Code; instead it was reinforced and entrenched. Nor, as we shall see, did the NC Courts alter their hierarchical approach to questions of gender and generation. On the contrary, in tune with the stridency of 1930s segregation, the cases tended (although there were exceptions) to reflect a hardened attitude toward the propriety of order, authority, and hierarchy. Meanwhile, women, sons, younger brothers, and others who were not empowered by the Code or tradition continued to use the strange hybrid court, the NC Court, to challenge and sometimes to usurp that authority. These challenges reflected, as the Code did not, the broader social processes at work in a country in the throes of rapid industrialization and the social tensions that reverberated in the countryside but did not reach a resolution.

THE LABOR TENANT CONTRACT
AND THE FILIAL CONTRACT

The central issue surrounding labor tenancy in Natal from the late 1920s through the 1940s was the ability of African fathers to command the labor of their sons.[44] In various ways, this issue was bound up with diverse conceptions of contracts (state-imposed, private, and informal) and attempts to enforce, evade, or alter those contracts. First, as we have seen, labor tenancy was itself bound up in a multilevel contract among white farmers, African heads of homesteads, and their dependents. A homestead head secured his place on a farm (which gave him access to grazing and fields) by promising the labor of various dependents, especially his young sons. In the 1930s, the South African state attempted to secure this system—in danger of breaking down due to the recalcitrance of sons—by granting homestead heads the legal right to contract for their minor dependents.[45] At the same time, labor tenant fathers and sons implicitly agreed that fathers would provide *lobola* for sons (especially firstborn sons) who both faithfully fulfilled the labor tenant contract by working *isithupa* on the farm and remitted wages from urban jobs in the free months. I call this implicit sense of mutual obligation the *filial contract*. In the 1930s, the parties to each of these contracts were breaching or dissolving them as sons failed to return to farms from urban jobs, tenant fathers and their families were evicted by farmers, and fathers sometimes refused or failed to provide *lobola* for sons.[46] Sons who worked *isithupa* very often also migrated to work in the cities during the six months

Photo 4.1   Wedding procession near Eshowe in Zululand region of Natal province, 1928. (Supplied and reproduced by kind permission of the Campbell Collections of the University of Natal [D7.146].)

"off" in order to earn money needed for taxes, supplemental food, and for their own bridewealth payments. If they failed to work *isithupa* or to return on time (or at all) from the cities, their fathers' homesteads were at risk of eviction. Sons who worked *isithupa* for their fathers believed that their fathers should in return provide *lobola* so that they could get married and establish their own homesteads. In a sense, this formed a filial contract between fathers and sons, analogous to the marriage contract that has been discussed by many writers.[47] Sons agreed to work for their fathers—both on the farm and in the city—in the expectation that fathers would provide them with bridewealth. Fathers or sons who failed to carry out their side of this "bargain" were seen by some labor tenants to be failing in their paternal or filial duties.[48]

Disemba Zamisa, a retired Estcourt labor tenant, provided a useful perspective on the labor tenant contract.[49] Zamisa was born in 1918 on a thornveld farm. He began working *isithupa* as a small boy, then as he "grew up," he began "working with the other laborers, leading oxen and sowing." The brothers did not all work *isithupa* at the same time because the farmer wanted one son from each "house" (a wife and her children) at a time. He and his brothers also went away to work in the cities, working three times, for instance, in a construction firm *eGoli*, mixing cement. His father paid his *lobola* because "if you worked *isithupa*, your father would pay *lobola* for you." He and his brothers sent wages earned in migrant labor to their father. Perhaps his father used these funds to acquire cattle, but Zamisa, reflecting the normative account of sharing *lobola* transfers in brother-sister pairs, says his father used cattle acquired from his sisters' *lobola* to pay *lobola* for the brothers.[50] After he married and fathered his first child, Zamisa went to work in Port Elizabeth (P.E.). He worked in a flourmill and earned a good wage, but he spent it all there. He worked for one and a half years, until he was arrested and brought back home. "I wasn't intending to go back home," he recalled, as P.E. was "very nice." Nevertheless, he was arrested at the behest of his parents and their white farmer-landlord.[51] Zamisa's story provides a sense both of the filial contract and of the stresses that were affecting it as sons sought out new opportunities in the cities. Fathers and authorities reacted by attempting to reassert control over sons through a variety of legal means and domestic pressures.

LOSING CONTROL

From the late 1920s through the 1940s, African fathers in rural Natal (including the "native reserves" as well as white-owned farms) were expressing more general concerns about a growing loss of control of their sons. Like farmers' complaints about labor shortages, these complaints were perennial, reflecting the structural antagonism between fathers and sons in southern African homesteads.[52] The complaints reached a new crescendo from the late 1920s, however. As rural land tenure became less secure and sons reacted to new opportunities, the preexisting structural antagonisms were exacerbated by economic and social change that undermined reciprocity between fathers and sons. These concerns were expressed as a general complaint against the younger generation for its lack of respect, and sometimes in specific complaints against recalcitrant sons.

In 1928, Chief Vuta of Estcourt district sought to disinherit his son, Njingani, because the son had left the chief's *umuzi* without permission and had established his own homestead on a farm near Mooi River.[53] The chief complained that his son

> left my kraal and took his two wives and six children away without authority from me and is now living with them on the farm Briar

Mains, the property of John Whittaker in the Mooi River District. Being the eldest son of my chief and first wife I looked upon [him] as my chief son and general heir but owing to his misconduct and refusal to be controlled by me, I now wish to disinherit him.[54]

Njingani, the respondent, claimed that he had left his father's *umuzi* because of a dispute with his father's third wife, Matebeni.[55] He said that he left because he had been falsely accused of "smelling out" (*nuka*) Matebeni as a witch. Njingani therefore asked his father to permit him to leave and build his own *umuzi*. Because his father "had no place that he could give me to build on," Njingani left and got a place on Whittaker's farm.[56] Njingani therefore denied that he had defied his father's authority, instead suggesting that he was a victim of intrigue on the part of one of his father's wives. He also intimated that his father could not provide land and therefore did not deserve his respect; Njingani had therefore *khonza*'d the white farmer instead.[57]

Chief Vuta portrayed these events in a considerably different light. He said that Njingani had refused beer from Matebeni. Such an act would constitute a serious breach of etiquette. Matebeni had complained to an *induna*, and when Njingani was questioned by the elders he stated that he had not refused Matebeni's beer but had refused his father's beer, indicating an unwillingness to accept his father's hospitality and hence his authority. Later, Chief Vuta said, Njingani had struck his sister and Matebeni when they interfered with him beating a drunken man. Finally, addressing his son directly in court, Vuta argued that the crux of the issue was that "you will not listen to me or be controlled by me. You have left my kraal in defiance of me and have gone out and established a kraal of your own." He said that his son had demanded that he should disinherit him. Njingani, of course, denied that he had refused beer or had asked to be disinherited. A minor official of Vuta's court testified that the elders, discussing the matter of the beer, "came to the conclusion that both father and son were to blame, the father because he did not consult with his son on business matters and the son because he wished his father to disinherit him." After discussion with the elders, the father and son were briefly reconciled. Later, Njingani again came into conflict with Matebeni and asked to establish his own *umuzi*. Vuta refused permission, and the minor official declined to find fault with Njingani's decision to move away.[58] An underlying issue was the loss of labor represented by Njingani's move away from the *umuzi*. Matebeni complained, "Respondent does not plough for us as he should do—he used to plough for his father but now that he has a place of his own he does not."[59] Njingani apparently complained that he was unable to plough without oxen, again challenging his father's right to command respect by suggesting that his father lacked the normal proprietary attributes of a respectable man—cattle.[60] Njingani thereby implicitly impugned the ability of his father to provide the necessary means of reproduction, just as he had allegedly been unable to provide Njingani with a (separate) site for an *umuzi*.

The NC refused Chief Vuta's application to disinherit his son on the ground that "as . . . Respondent has moved away from his father's kraal there is no reason why they should not become reconciled to each other."[61] The NC therefore failed to understand that there was no basis for reconciliation, as Chief Vuta no longer had any direct authority over his son. The NC thus refused to endorse the chief's attempt to control his son, presenting us with an anomaly in the overall picture of state backing for rural patriarchy in the segregation era. However, the case shows that there were additional forces at work in 1928. An NC was an upstanding member of the rural white community and was unlikely to discourage a prominent young African man from taking up residence on a white farm inevitably owned by someone of the NC's acquaintance.[62] Furthermore, the NC may have favored Njingani as the best candidate to succeed his father, whereas disinheritance would have scuttled such a plan. The other sons of Vuta did not appear in the case, leaving us with an unreadable silence.[63] It is clear, however, that multiple interests were at work in the attempt to resolve a dispute between an elite rural father and his son, and that the dispute remained unresolved.

A few years later, witnesses before the NEC also expressed considerable concern about loss of control and the lack of respect on the part of youth. The Native Commissioner of Ixopo, for instance, noted:

> The young native of today has not the respect for his elders that was so noticeable a few years ago. The young man of today very often thinks of himself and has very [little] regard for his elders. . . . These natives very often are the ones who compose the *laita* gangs.[64]

These comments were echoed by some chiefs who testified to the commission about a loss of control and a diminution of respect.[65] Chief Gebeweni attributed this loss of control to the influence of "white" religion and education. Chief Majozi, of Richmond, complained of a decline in youthful respect and blamed the interference of courts, in which juniors might lodge complaints, as well as the poll tax, which gave juniors the impression of independence. By contrast, he claimed,

Photo 4.2 Young man in urban attire, including military-style coat, holding *sjambok*. (Courtesy of the Pietermaritzburg Archives Repository [Frame 28].)

"Persons in authority in the old days exercised unlimited power over their dependents, and that is how the *hlonipha* system worked, it included shewing [sic] respect in all manner of ways."[66] Such complaints were perennial in public testimony to commissions inquiring into "native affairs" in Natal, pointing to the structural divides between generations, but the social and economic change accelerated by the colonial and capitalist context did in fact exacerbate such tensions. The stridency and frequency of the complaints in the segregation era suggests that this was a time of particularly sharp generational tension, engendered by the intersection of new opportunities and new frustrations for African youth.

Administrators, rural elders, and farmers also pointed to the growing incidence of so-called "faction fights" in the 1930s and 1940s as a worrisome sign of elders' loss of control of youth. White journalists and officials used the expression *faction fight* to refer to a range of conflicts, from fights that broke out at wedding feasts or "beer drinks" to "wars" lasting for a period of weeks or months between districts or chiefdoms.[67] Faction fights were (and are) especially frequent in Weenen district and other sections of the thornveld. A major "war" broke out between Chunus and Thembus on the farms of Weenen and Estcourt in 1934 after serious disturbances in 1926 and 1928 and a Chunu "civil war" over the chieftainship in 1932.[68] In the mid-1930s, the NAD began to take a more active interest in quelling these fights, especially because of their potential to "disorganise labour" on the farms. "Farmers cannot get their servants to leave their farms nor can they get their cattle out of the thorns. Natives leave their work to join up with the *impis* [war parties]."[69] Authorities proved unable to end the disputes, however; indeed, the NAD's tinkering with succession and residency probably played a major role in catalyzing the disputes. *Ngongolo*, the war between the Chunu and Thembu chiefdoms analyzed by Clegg, took place in Weenen in September 1944, culminating in a battle on a labor farm where several of my interviews took place fifty years later. The war resulted in the deaths of sixty-five men and "extensive cattle killing, looting and hut burning." *Ngongolo* was significant enough to serve as a major marker of time, as in "I was married about the time of *Ngongolo*." This "war" and other faction fights of the time led the department to once again plan for the demarcation of "tribal" boundaries, a recurring idea.

Ten years earlier, in the wake of the 1934 war, Weenen NC J.P. Rawlinson expressed his concern that the "younger men have got out of hand. They are now introducing the tactics of the "Sigebenga and Lieta [*sic*; gangs] of Maritzburg and Durban, to the countryside."[70] Thus the

gangs of urban men employed as houseboys, who expressed their soli-
darity in a rural idiom of warriors, now carried the infection of "disorder" back to the countryside.[71] In a report to the CNC, a Weenen farmer
agreed that the problem was lack of respect for authority on the part of
young men, not, as the popular white interpretation had it, an instance of
"tribal" war:

> In my opinion, it has very little to do with tribal ancestral hatreds, as
> the responsible sections of these tribes do not take part, but is purely
> local and concerns only the farming area above mentioned and has been
> brought about by a too lenient administration of the laws. Through le-
> niency and neglect the young boys of 18 to 25, say, have no respect
> for authority, for it has been non-existent and the old fear instilled into
> the older generations no longer exists and nothing has been put into its
> place.[72]

Authorities worried not only about the disorder created by the clashes
but also about the increasingly prominent role of *amagosa* (dance-company leaders). *Amagosa*, also known as "leaders of the young men," were
captains both of martial dance competitions as well as tactical and hierarchical leaders of battles between rural neighborhoods, districts, and
chiefdoms. In his 1931 report to the NEC, NC Rawlinson worried that
the "*gosos*" [*sic*] were undermining the authority of chiefs and hence were
undermining "tribal authority" in general.

> Another factor . . . is the extraordinary power in [sic] the leaders of
> young men (*Gosos*) have over the young men under their command.
> The *Gosos* according to Zulu custom are appointed by the young
> men themselves for the purposes of leading them at dances. In the
> Estcourt and Weenen districts . . . they have more power than the
> chiefs. The *Gosos* have constituted themselves as generals and lead
> the men at fights. The *Gosos* are undermining all authority of the
> chiefs.[73]

Despite such pleas by officials, *amagosa* continued to exercise extralegal
authority in the Estcourt-Weenen area. In 1938, the Estcourt NC found it
necessary to decry the practice of according fifteen *lobola* cattle to the
daughter of an *igoso* (dance-company leader), as if he were an official
induna.

> These men are in no sense "*indunas*" within the meaning of section 87
> of the Natal Code. . . . If the Chiefs desired to appoint "*Gosos*" the

Native Affairs Department has no objection, but it must be clearly understood that there was no such rank recognized by the Government.[74]

Officials were concerned about the rise in prominence of *amagosa*, therefore, not only because of their potential to disrupt order physically
through "wars" that interrupted rural labor, but also because of their character as unrecognized nodes of authority outside the official ideology of
top-down structures and gerontocracy. Their concern, and that of "responsible" elder Africans, may in turn have reflected a fear of the independence gained and asserted by youths who migrated to urban jobs, where
they earned relatively high wages out of the direct control of fathers and
chiefs.[75]

Generational tensions were fueled by the fears of disintegration of
the structures of respect and control that ensured the reproduction of
authority. Elders' complaints about loss of control over youths also
concerned the more directly material issue of labor on the farms, essential to ensure the elders' continued tenure and potential to prosper.
The refusal of youths to submit to parental discipline concerning
farmwork, and fathers' consequent insecurity, exacerbated tensions and
spurred renegotiation of the filial contract. Both fathers and sons
sought guarantees that the other generation would uphold its part of
the implicit exchange of labor and bridewealth. In some instances,
fathers and sons made these claims explicit in the realm of tradition,
domestic struggle, and law: the NC courts.

RENEGOTIATING THE FILIAL CONTRACT

By the late 1930s, the filial bonds that held the labor tenant contract in place were stretching to the breaking point. As we have seen,
the agricultural boom of the late 1920s, which had drawn many rent
tenants into relations of labor tenancy and which had squeezed farm
resources (grazing and gardens) available to labor tenants, came to an
abrupt end with the Depression, and farm prices did not substantially
recover until the onset of World War II. In the 1930s, however, the
state stepped in with subsidies and credit for white farmers, encourag-
ing farmers to maintain full production, so there was continuing pressure on tenant access to farmland. Devastating droughts seared Natal
through most of the early 1930s, with minimal relief for farm tenants.
While industry and mining expanded rapidly in the mid-1930s, meaning that there were more jobs at better pay in the cities, rural wages
stagnated. Farm wages and benefits in any case accrued to the
abanumzane, not to the young men and women who provided most of

the labor. Under these conditions, migrancy from the farms and re-serves soared; young men stayed longer and, in many cases, settled in the cities.[76]

Prior to this industrial expansion, the South African government had moved to control the loss of farm labor, to shore up the authority of *abanumzane*, and to fill a hole in the legal remedies available to farmers, when it passed the NSCA in 1932.[77] The NSCA gave *abanumzane* the legal power to contract for their minor dependents. The act therefore as-sumed that *abanumzane* had paternal authority over their sons, and it sought to strengthen and legitimate that authority. The NSCA was, in this sense, not only a reflection of the state's attempts to ensure farm labor for its white farmer constituents but also a part of the process of retribalization and refurbishing traditionalism that the state undertook in the 1920s and 1930s. The NSCA's assumptions and goals therefore re-flected those in the Natal Code of Native Law. However, by the late 1930s it was clear that the NSCA (and other tools of policy) had failed in the goal of retaining labor tenant sons on the farms, although it had given farmers greater leverage to discipline or evict their tenants. This situation brought about renegotiations of the filial contract concerning labor and bridewealth.

The Natal Code was structured on the basis of Western preconceptions about "primitive law," including Maine's dictum: "The movement of the progressive societies has hitherto been a movement from Status to Con-tract."[78] The code therefore conceived customary law as mired in an un-changing world where rights and obligations were a function of status. Chapter V of the Code, for instance, was entitled "Personal Status" and began by stating, "Every Native is either a kraal head or a kraal inmate subject to the kraal head in all kraal matters."[79] The *kraal* head was the fulcrum of authority under the Code, at the lower end of a hierarchy extending down from the "Supreme Chief" (the governor-general). The *kraal* head had, according to the Code, absolute authority in the *kraal*. His dependents (called *kraal* inmates) "irrespective of sex or age are . . . under the control and owe obedience to the kraal head."[80] A *kraal* head was also "entitled to the earnings of his minor children and to a reason-able share of the earnings" of other dependents, such as wives and mar-ried sons.[81]

Under the Code, there was no quid pro quo for the duties owed by sons to fathers. On this point, however, the Code began to recognize the "movement" from status to contract, to which Martin Chanock directs our attention in Maine's formulation.[82] The Code provided in Section 91 that "Younger sons are usually assisted by the kraal head in paying *lobola* for their first wife." The section went on to emphasize the precatory nature of this provision by stating that it was "not enforceable as law" unless the son or younger brother could demonstrate an agreement that he would be provided with *lobola* in return for contributions to the support of his "house."[83] A contemporary NC and commentator on customary law advised that the "obligation is entirely a moral one" but noted that such an agreement could arise, because under the "changed circumstances" of wage labor, sons or other "inmates" could "become practically the bread winners of the family." In such circumstances, the courts might infer an agreement between father and son that the father should provide *lobola* for the son who contributed an ill-defined extra amount to the *umuzi*.

> Where a son has done no more than his duty to help the kraal head by contributing from his earnings . . . and has been maintained by the kraal head, he could not expect repayment as of right, either in the form of *lobolo* or a refund in cash. Where, however, he has done more than that he is entitled to some compensation. Although the obligation is stated to rest on an agreement, the courts will probably infer an implied agreement when considerable contributions have been made and the inmate has relied on *lobolo* being provided.[84]

In contemporary court records, and in interviews two generations later, African fathers and sons articulated a wider range of opinion of the question of the obligation of fathers to assist their sons. This suggests (as the Code comes close to admitting) that fathers and sons, as well as older and younger brothers, contested the question of obligation and whether it was to rest on agreement or on status within the household.[85]

"It is customary for the kraal head to supply *lobola* for a son from kraal property for his [the son's] first wife," according to Gideon Mude, an *umnumzane* who sought transfer of *lobola* cattle from his daughter's father-in-law.[86] In another case, an "Official Witness" gave an improbably broad reading of the *umnumzane*'s responsibility.

> All fathers pay all the *lobolo* for all their sons. When a boy marries it is right that his father should find the *lobolo*. It is recorded in every customary union that the father is to complete the *lobolo*. . . . In no case is the balance of the [unpaid] *lobolo* to be delivered by the son [bridegroom]. That is the duty of the father.[87]

Few contemporary actors or recent informants agreed with this all-encompassing reading, but most agreed that a father had some degree of responsibility in connection with the bridewealth payments of his sons. There were indications that many rural Africans, especially labor tenants, saw the father's obligation as relative to the son's performance or nonperformance of his filial duties, especially the duty to work *isithupa*. Bettina Dladla, for instance, recalled that her brothers gave their wages to their father and that he paid *lobola* for them. "Yes they did [give their wages to the father] as it was according to customary law, the father was supposed to pay *lobola* for them."[88] Kotayi Mkhize asserted, "*Lobola* was paid for those who worked for six months only; the others would pay for themselves."[89] In the 1930s and 1940s, the sense of mutual obligation—that fathers would provide bridewealth (at least for a first wife) for sons who worked *isithupa* on the farm and who remitted wages from migrant labor in the cities— was taking on the character of an enforceable legal contract in the context of disputes they brought to the NC courts. Renegotiations of paternal and filial obligations concerning work and bridewealth, centering on filial performance of the labor tenant contract, played out in disputes between fathers and sons in the NC courts. The fragility of rural tenure and the loosening of sons' ties to farms that gave them little reward resulted in a hardening of positions around the filial contract. Cases from Central Natal in the late 1930s and early 1940s provide evidence of these new strains in the filial contract.

Zuma v. Ntombela[90]

Ngolodo Ntombela sued Gcina Zuma in the Lions River NC Court in 1943. He demanded five head of cattle as outstanding bridewealth debt in respect of the marriage of his daughter Mary Jane to Pawula, the son of Zuma. Ntombela testified that Zuma "agreed he was responsible. [Zuma] said he would furnish the balance of *lobola* from the *lobola* that would accrue to him on the marriage of his daughter, whom he pointed out." Zuma's daughter subsequently married, but Zuma failed to transfer the *lobola* to Ntombela. On cross-examination by Zuma's attorney (a Mr. Howard), Ntombela reiterated the point that the *lobola* was to come from Zuma, not his son Pawula, the bridegroom, emphasizing that he could get no satisfaction from the son and that "custom" demanded that payment come from the father. "The man Pawula, my son-in-law, has nothing. . . . It is the custom for the kraal head to deliver the *lobola* on behalf of his son." He expressed surprise that the official record of the marriage indicated that the balance of the *lobola* was to come from the bridegroom-son, Pawula.

Further testimony, however, indicated that *lobola* was not purely a question of obligation based on status but was related to the question of working *isithupa*. Both litigants agreed that some time after the marriage, Pawula left the farm where his father lived and went to live on the farm where his father-in-law was a tenant. Ntombela claimed that this was because Pawula had been evicted from his father's farm. Zuma, however, claimed that he had given his son eight of the necessary eleven head of cattle and that Pawula was performing a form of brideservice to earn the rest.[91] "My son went after the marriage to live at his father in law's. He did so of his own accord . . . in order to earn the balance of three head *lobola* after I had helped him with seven head and the *nqutu*.[92] I had four sons and I said I would help them all." He noted that when his son had lived with him, the son "had to work six months a year for Mr. Morton [the farm owner]."

The NC ruled that the marriage record was "conclusive." The NAC disagreed, and it decided the case based on the evidence presented to the NC. The appeals court's ruling concurred with Stafford's suggestion of a variable obligation on the part of fathers.

> Here we have a man with four sons who has contributed 7 head of cattle towards the *lobolo* of one of them. He has done as much as he can reasonably be expected to do and it would require much stronger evidence than is available in this case to prove that he had undertaken liability for the payment of the balance of three head of cattle.

The Native Appeals Court therefore held in effect that Ntombela would have to seek satisfaction from the son. It took the view that the filial contract was relative, depending on the extent of a father's potential obligations, explicit undertakings, and sacrifices made on his behalf by a son.

Ngema v. Ngema[93]

A more direct view of the filial contract emerged in a more complex factual setting in a 1936 New Hanover case. Multiple lines of obligation and authority intersect in the case. Fanyama, the second son of a junior wife, sued his father, Mahobe, to enforce a promise to provide six head of cattle for *lobola* for the son's wife. The father's eviction left the son residing on the original farm with his mother; the father refused to supply *lobola* if his son would not join him and labor for him at the new farm. Chief Velapi Ngubane recounted the proceedings in his own court, saying that the father, Mahobe, "admitted that he had promised to help . . . with six head . . . but that as his son had refused to come and live with him on the same farm he would not lend him the cattle." The Chief ruled for the son, Fanyama.

In the NC Court, Fanyama again explained that his father had withdrawn his offer to supply the *lobola* cattle because he, the son, would not return to live on the farm where his father resided after the father had been evicted by his landlord (Wortmann) for reasons that were not stated in the record.

> When the wedding was being arranged my father withdrew his promise of the cattle, saying that I should go and live with him on the farm of Heine Lundanda (Hellermann). I am with my mother on the farm of Wortmann. My mother refuses to go and live with my father on the farm of Heine. As my mother refuses to live with my father I told my father that I would not live with him and in consequence of that he refuses to let me have the cattle.[94]

From the father's point of view, his offer to provide *lobola* for his estranged second wife's second son was dependent on the son remaining with him and working *isithupa* on the father's account. Mahobe, the father, also hoped to use his son to get his wife to rejoin him:[95]

> [H]e ordered me off his farm and I left but [Fanyama] and his mother remained on Wortmann's. . . . [Fanyama] is the cause of his mother refusing to come to me. . . . If [my son] had come with me I would certainly have helped him with part of the *lobola* but he and his mother have thrown me over.[96]

The NC court reversed the chief's ruling and gave judgment for the father.[97] The ruling implicitly supported the notion of a filial contract of mutual obligation, with labor being the necessary quid pro quo for paternally provided *lobola*.

Mfusi v. Mfusi[98]

The ruling was not explained, but in a 1940 Estcourt case the NC Court apparently accepted the father-defendant's plea that under "native custom" a son could not sue his father. In that case, Joel Mfusi sued his father, Josiah, for cattle he had left with the father, apparently as a loan, to be returned from the marriage payments in respect of one of Joel's younger sisters. The son decided to call the debt in early, as his father was claiming ownership of the cattle. The father denied his son's claim, but in the main he rested his defense on the "customary law" claim that "it is contrary under native custom for a son to sue his father," a "custom" of which his son, Joel, denied knowledge. The father claimed that he was still Joel's guardian even though he had ejected Joel from his *kraal* for adultery with the wife of Joel's deceased brother. Two of Joel's brothers, apparently still living with their father, claimed that the cattle had come as a gift from the deceased brother. They agreed with their father against the exiled brother, "It is not our custom for a son to sue his father." The NC apparently agreed with this argument, as he entered judgment for the father-defendant without comment.

Majola v. Mcunu[99]

The filial contract was asserted more starkly still in a 1943 case in Weenen district. Majola sued to recover bridewealth in respect of his daughter, Zahlope, who had married Mcunu's son, Zigebendu. The marriage register recorded that Mcunu promised to pay from the prospective *lobola* of his daughter, as in *Zuma v. Ntombela*. Five years later, however, Mcunu refused to pay because his son had failed to work *isithupa* for him.

> I refused to pay over this cattle because Zigebendu has failed to support me and he has failed to render farm service. . . . My son . . . refused to work for me even before his marriage. I promised to pay Zigebendu's *lobolo* with the hope that he might turn over a new leaf.[100]

In court, however, Mcunu renewed his promise by agreeing to pay the *lobola* out of the bridewealth of the first marriage of one of Zigebendu's daughters. The court gave judgment for the plaintiff, Majola. It is notable that Majola was represented by an attorney whereas Mcunu, the loser, was not.

Vilagazi v. Vilagazi[101]

A final case implicating the filial contract comes from Estcourt district in 1936. Mlazalozi sued his half-brother Mtateni over the inheritance from their father, Matshana Vilagazi. On the surface the case was about which man's mother had been Matshana's chief wife, and this revolved around an announcement Matshana had allegedly made shortly after his marriage to Mlalozi's mother in the year after the battle of Isandhlwana (1880).[102] A concurrent issue, however, was Mlalozi's contention that he had worked *isithupa* for his father, whereas his brother Mtateni had not. "My father was a farm tenant living on private lands in Weenen district. I was employed on the farm. [Mtateni] never worked on the farm."[103] Mtateni agreed that he had not entered farm service for his father's landlord (Mr. Green), but he argued that it was because he left, with his father's permission, to live on an African-owned farm:

> At one time Mr. Green was my landlord. I did not enter into farm service with Mr. Green although my father was staying on Mr. Green's farm. . . . I had my father's consent to go to Cornfields and I did not move because of any quarrel. I deny that I left rather than work for Mr. Green.

Mtateni acknowledged, however, that Mlalozi "remained on Mr. Green's farm and rendered service until he left to go on the adjoining farm belonging to Geekies [an adjoining farm in Weenen]."[104]

This last case provides further evidence of multiple lines of obligation and expectation in labor tenant households. Fathers expected that sons would work *isithupa* (and in migrant labor, although that issue does not tend to arise explicitly in the cases) for their fathers. Sons expected that if they did so they were entitled to help in making bridewealth transfers to in-laws. Brothers in some cases argued (in combination with other factors) that having worked *isithupa* gave them a prior claim to inheritance.[105] The courts sought to enforce "tradition" but did so in the context of wage labor obligations, private property, and concurrent concerns about labor shortages and close relations with white farmers. The outcomes of such cases, therefore, were not easy to predict, although the courts did seem to endorse the notion of a filial contract.

CONCLUSION

Generational tension, inherent in the structure of rural African homesteads, was exacerbated by social and economic change from the 1920s through the 1940s, especially in the context of labor tenancy. In this period, fathers and sons argued over the ownership of cattle following the breakup of fathers' homesteads. Their arguments sometimes led to legal disputes, and in some cases fathers sought to disinherit their sons.[106] The complaints of administrators, chiefs, and elders—about youths' lack of respect and the growing incidence of "faction fights," representing independent and violent action on the part of youth and their extralegal-leaders, the *amagosa*—also revealed widespread tension and anxiety about the slippage of fixed hierarchies. The filial contract cases reflect a growing estrangement between elders and juniors in the late 1930s and early 1940s, concentrated on the issues of bridewealth and labor.

The crisis of control in the 1930s had profound effects on the institution of labor tenancy and brought about a renegotiation of the filial contract. The incipient political and social movements of the late 1920s had disintegrated as a result of internal disorganization, inability to demonstrate progress toward radical goals, and deliberate repression by the South African state. The state, however, continued to worry about authority, urbanization, and ensuring a labor supply for its white farmer constituents. Parliament passed legislation to tighten political and ideological control of Africans through the policy of retribalization, in the form of the 1927 Act, which authorized the continuation of the customary law regime in Natal. The failure of the NSCA also exposed a breakdown of the filial contract. Labor tenant fathers continued to expect their sons to work *isithupa* and in migrant labor, but as a result of a squeeze on labor tenants' access to resources, they were unable to ensure the accumulation of cattle that would enable sons to establish their own homesteads. Under these conditions, combined with new opportunities in the cities, many sons refused to work *isithupa* or overstayed in urban jobs.

The renegotiation of the filial contract is revealed in a variety of cases in the NC Courts. Despite the official ideology embodied in the Natal Code, the cases show that members of the labor tenant household contested paternal authority and filial obligation. Rather than reflecting a movement from "Status to Contract," the cases show that "contracts" within the household were subject to constant renegotiation in the context of changing social and economic conditions. These expectations and arguments show the ways in which the customary law system, conceived as timeless and unchanging, became the site of struggles generated out of changes in South African economic and social structures. The expectation under customary law that sons would be obedient and deferential was difficult to sustain in light of the growing realities of sons' frequent stints of migrant labor and fathers' inability to engender security and prosperity for their sons on the farms. As a result, at least in the context of NC litigation, relations between labor tenant fathers and sons became more contractual and contingent in nature. The customary law regime, intended as a bulwark against change, ironically became a vehicle for reworking familial relationships under the new circumstances of the 1930s and 1940s.

Marriage and other formal relationships between men and women also came under increased strain in the 1930s and 1940s. In the next chapter we turn to cases of marriage and divorce that reveal struggles over sexuality, mobility, and tradition in the context of the crisis of control surrounding migrancy, the rural order, and labor tenancy. Once again, we find that a system devoted to preserving tradition was in fact the site of furious struggles over obligations and loyalties, as periodically absent husbands struggled through fathers, brothers—and, when necessary, *amakhosi* and NCs—to discipline their wives. For women, the period was one of social pressures to obey and maintain homestead production combined with new ways to evade or dispute the demands of husbands, fathers, and brothers-in-law. In some cases, women were able to make their claims in a forum that in many ways conspired to silence them: the NC Court. Once again, the records reveal indecisive struggles that speak to the exacerbation of tensions within labor tenant (and other rural) households under the changing economic conditions of the 1920s through 1940s.

NOTES

1. *Kufanele ukusebenza isithupa* means "it is necessary to work six months," in *isiZulu*.

2. PAR, 1 HWK 2/1/2/1, Case 3/1943, *Zuma v. Ntombela*, testimony of Ndava Zuma.

3. PAR, 1 WEN 2/1/2/2, Case 60/1943, *Majola v. Mcunu*, testimony of Sikopoli Mcunu.

4. CA, K 26, NEC Evidence, Vol. 4, 6191, testimony of Acting Chief Gebemeweni, Durban, 1 Apr. 1931.

5. The noun for bridewealth is *ilobolo*, while the verb is *ukulobola*; in English the noun is variously rendered as *lobolo* or *lobola*. To avoid confusion, I use *lobola* both as noun and verb, except in direct quotes.

6. Concerning the 1927 Act, see Dubow, *Racial Segregation*, 111–19. Ironically, the NAD continued to view itself as "protector of the natives" even while it embraced this more repressive role. Ibid.

7. Native Administration Act, Act No. 38 of 1927, Chapter VI. Proclamations under the act came into effect one month after publication of a draft in the *Gazette* and after a further fourteen-day period during which Parliament had the power to reject or modify the proclamation. Ibid., Sections 24–26.

8. Ibid., Chapter II. The authorities used this provision to remove political figures such as A.W.G. Champion, leader of the ICU in Natal, and to remove "troublemakers" who were not directly involved in politics, such as leaders of "faction fights" in Weenen.

9. Ibid., Section 29.

10. Ibid., Chapter VII. Zulu-style spears and sticks became infamous as "traditional weapons" after President De Klerk suddenly unbanned the carrying of them during the violent conflict of the early 1990s. African men in rural Natal almost always carry an *isagila* (knobkerrie).

11. Native Administration Act, Act No. 38 of 1927, Chapter I.

12. Dubow, *Racial Segregation*, 104–5. According to Dubow, the NAD pushed for the Act as part of its struggle to rebuild and expand its influence after losing both size and jurisdiction to the Justice Department in an administrative reshuffle in the early 1920s. Ibid., 117–27.

13. See, generally, W.G. Stafford, *Native Law As Practised in Natal* (Johannesburg: Witwatersrand University Press, 1935), especially 22–23.

14. Ibid.; Nicholas Cope, *To Bind the Nation: Solomon kaDinuzulu and Zulu Nationalism 1913–1933* (Pietermaritzburg: University of Natal Press, 1993); Nicolas Cope, "The Zulu Petit Bourgeoisie and Zulu Nationalism in the 1920s: Origins of Inkatha" in *Journal of Southern African Studies*, 16, no. 3 (1990): 431–51; Shula Marks, "Patriotism, Patriarchy and Purity: Natal and the Politics of Zulu Ethnic Consciousness," in *The Creation of Tribalism in Southern Africa*, ed. by Leroy Vail (Berkeley: University of California Press, 1989), 215–40.

15. Litigants whose interests were supported by the Code, of course, embraced its version of "tradition."

16. Native Administration Act, Section 11. This confirmed existing law in Natal.

17. Divorce cases, however, had to be brought to the NC in the first instance. The NC Courts, however, lacked jurisdiction over divorce in the case of "Christian" or "civil" marriage. Ibid., Chapter IV, Section 10. The NC Courts were also precluded from jurisdiction over wills. The venue of NC Court cases was the district where the defendant resided, and the law prevailing in the defendant's district was to be applied in the case of conflict. Ibid., Sections 10 and 11.

18. Ibid., Section 12. One Native Appeals Court was for the Cape and Orange Free State; the other, for Natal and the Transvaal. The Natal and Transvaal appeals courts superseded the Natal Native High Court with respect to civil matters; the latter court's criminal jurisdiction devolved to the Natal Provincial Division of the Supreme Court. Ibid., Section 17.

19. See, e.g., interview with Nokwabiwa Dladla.

20. Interview with Boy Ndlovu, Nottingham Road, 18 May 1992. See also interview with Mzumeni Myaka.

21. Interview with Nozimpi Sithole. The NAD was known as "Bantu Affairs" in the 1950s and 1960s.

22. Cf. Robert Kidder, "Western Law in India: External law and local response," in *Social System and Legal Process*, ed. by Harry M. Johnson (San Francisco: Jossey-Bass, 1978), 155–80.

23. Interview with John Dladla.

24. Interview with Godfrey Symons. See also Isak Dinesen, *Out of Africa* (New York: Vintage International, 1989), 94–104.

25. Interview with Nocokololo Masoga.

26. On courtrooms as theaters of power and authority, and on the limitations of trial records, see Clifford, *Predicament of Culture*, 277–346.

27. *Natal Code of Native Law* (Johannesburg: University of Witwatersrand Press, 1945), Section 145.

28. The losing party's responsibility for the winner's legal bill is a normal part of the British judicial system.

29. PAR, 1 EST 2/1/2/1; Case 60/1929, *Mazibuko v. Mazibuko*. The appeal record, included with the trial record, is Native Appeals Court Case No. 8/3/30. See discussion of the case in Thomas McClendon, "'A Dangerous Doctrine': Twins, Ethnography, and Inheritance in Colonial Africa," *Journal of Legal Pluralism*, 39 (1997): 121–40.

30. Both brothers were assisted by counsel. It was common, but not universal, for one or both parties to have lawyers in the NC Court. The lawyers were white, in all the court records I have examined.

31. A father of twins in Msinga, near Estcourt, confirmed that this is still customary among "traditionalists." Twins count as one "person" and cannot be considered dead until both have died. Interview with Mashiya Dladla, Keate's Drift, 10 Aug. 1994. Another informant, a *kholwa* mother of twins, stated: "I was told they were one person, but still knew they were two." Interview with Domby Phungula.

32. In this case, the deceased father of the litigants had only one wife, so there was no complicating factor of a separate inheritance for each "house" (the property allocated to a wife and her children).

33. The Code made no distinction between expert and percipient witnesses, nor did it bar hearsay. It also contained no statute of limitations.

34. The NC structured his judgment, however, so that the eleven cattle stipulated for the fiancée of the twins could still come from the deceased twin's estate, being "regarded as *lobolo* given by the elder brother for the younger brother's wife"—that is, a gift that the court required the elder brother to make.

35. Three years later, in the neighboring district of Weenen, the NC gave the following assessment of the customs concerning twins: "I have not heard of a case of the killing of one or more of plural born children. . . . I have spoken to a number of natives who inform me that it was an old Zulu custom but was discontinued many years ago. . . . The present custom amongst some . . . is to separate the children but the majority do not do so." PAR, 1 WEN 3/3/1/2, 2/5/5, Weenen NC to CNC, 31 Oct. 1932.

36. Dubow, *Racial Segregation*, 117–18.

37. The NCs were H.C. Lugg of Richmond and "a Mr. Farrer" of Estcourt. The law professor was F.C. Burchell, an expert on native law. PAR, CNC 20A, 14/1, N1/12/3, CNC to SNA, 2 May 1928; Johannesburg Joint Council of Europeans and Natives, "Criticisms of Draft Proclamation Amending the Natal Code of Native Law of 1891," SAIRR, AD843, B72.3, n.d., but response to proclamation of 6 Nov. 1931. Dubow, *Racial Segregation*, 117–18.

38. Natal Code of Native Law (1932), Section 10.

39. Ibid., Sections 5, 6, 8.

40. Ibid., Sections 27–28, 35, 38.

41. Dubow, *Racial Segregation*, 117.

42. PAR, 1 WEN 3/3/1/2, 2/5/5, CNC to Weenen NC, 14 Dec. 1932; CNC 18A, 14/1, 2/7/5, Eshowe NC to CNC, 25 Jan. 1933. The department also refused to distribute free copies in English even though they were available from the government

printer for one shilling. Ibid., CNC to Bulwer NC, 16 Mar. 1933; 14/1, CNC to Harding NC, 22 Apr. 1937. The 1891 Code had been translated and printed in both English and Zulu, but the CNC's office had exhausted its supply by 1919, although it still distributed English versions "in handbook form." PAR, CNC 86, 16/0/1912, Umzinto Mag. to CNC, 20 Aug. 1912; 2294/1919, CNC to Helpmakaar Mag., 23 Aug. 1919.

43. Ibid., 2/5/3, Weenen NC to CNC, 11 Nov. 1932. See *Natal Code*, Section 76(2)(b). The relationship of witchcraft to marital tension is discussed in chapter 5.

44. I am concentrating here on a particular gendered generational divide: the relation between fathers and sons. There are, of course, other gendered generational dynamics: relations between fathers and daughters, mothers and sons, and mothers and daughters.

45. See discussion of the NSCA in chapter 3.

46. Keegan, *Rural Transformations*, 121–40, has described a similar sense of mutual obligation between tenant fathers and sons. Beinart analyzes generational tensions, also focusing on household dynamics and bridewealth, in the context of a reserve economy. See Beinart, *Political Economy of Pondoland*.

47. For the marriage contract, see, e.g., Richard Roberts, "Women's Work and Women's Property: Household Social Relations in the Maraka Textile Industry of the Nineteenth Century," *Comparative Studies in Society and History*, 26, no. 2 (1984), 229–50.

48. My conception of the filial contract also resembles the idea of moral economy, which Glassman, *Feasts and Riot*, uses extensively and for which he provides a historiographical analysis.

49. Interview with Disemba Zamisa.

50. Cf. Krige, *Social System of the Zulus*.

51. Zamisa had remained in his father's homestead after he married, but later they separated the homestead due to some quarrel "and divided the cattle amongst ourselves." He established another homestead on the same farm.

52. See, e.g., Carton, *"Blood from Your Children;"* Lambert, *Betrayed Trust*; Keegan, *Rural Transformations*; Beinart, *Political Economy of Pondoland*. For earlier complaints about the younger generation's lack of respect, see, e.g., evidence presented to the Natal Native Commission of 1906–1907.

53. PAR, 1 EST 2/1/2/1, Case 28/1928, *Mkwanana v. Mkwanasi*. Mooi River was then a section of the Estcourt district but is now a separate magisterial district.

54. Ibid., testimony of Vuta Mkwanana.

55. Chief Vuta had four wives. The first wife, mother of Njingani, was dead. The third wife, Matebeni, was the only one remaining in Vuta's *umuzi*.

56. Ibid., testimony of Njingani.

57. It is unclear whether Chief Vuta was also a tenant, as many chiefs were, or if he was a chief with responsibility for a section of reserve land.

58. Ibid., testimony of Gobeyana Ranyile.

59. Ibid., testimony of Matebeni Ndaba.

60. Ibid., testimony of Gobeyana Ranyile.

61. Ibid., judgment.

62. For an analysis of the place of magistrates in rural white towns, see Mazower, "Agriculture, Farm Labour and the State;" see also the turn-of-the-

twentieth-century satirical novel, Douglas Blackburn, *Leaven: A Black and White Story* (Pietermaritzburg: University of Natal Press, 1991).

63. For the problem of silence in the archives, see Frederick Cooper and Ann Stoler, "Introduction: Tensions of Empire: Colonial Control and Visions of Rule," *American Ethnologist*, 16 (1989): 619; Donald Moore and Richard Roberts, "Listening for Silences," *History in Africa*, 17 (1990): 319–25.

64. CA, K 26, NEC Evidence, 2171, Vol. 4, testimony of Horace Blake Wallace, Ixopo Mag. and NC, Ixopo, 9 Sept. 1930. See also 6323–24, Vol. 7, testimony of Joint Council of Europeans and Natives, Durban, 4 Apr. 1931. For a discussion of the *amalaita* (street toughs) gangs of Durban, see Paul La Hausse, "'The Cows of Nongoloza': Youth, Crime and Amalaita Gangs in Durban, 1900–36," *Journal of Southern African Studies*, 16, no. 1 (Mar. 1990): 79–111.

65. See epigraph and n. 3 of this chapter.

66. NEC Evidence, 6710, Vol. 7, testimony of Chief Simon Gilbert Evans Majozi, Pietermaritzburg, 9 Apr. 1931. See also 6722e, testimony of Sikmeletu Nyongwana, Pietermaritzburg, 9 Apr. 1931, discussed in chapter 5.

67. See, e.g., "Stern Warning to Council of Zulu Chiefs," *Star*, 2 Feb. 1935; "A Great Indaba in the Thorn Country," *Star*, 11 Feb. 1935; "Growing Unrest in Eston Area," *Natal Mercury*, 11 May 1939; "30 Dead on Native Battlefield," *Natal Sunday Post*, 28 Mar. 1948. Cf. Jonathan Clegg, "*Ukubuyisa Isidumbu*—'Bringing Back the Body': A Study of the Ideology of Vengeance in the Msinga and Mpofana Rural Locations, 1882–1944," in *Working Papers in Southern African Studies*, vol. 2, ed. by Philip Bonner (Johannesburg: Ravan Press, 1981), 164–198. A recent study of a particular struggle has shown the micropolitics involved, suggesting that it is highly misleading to dismiss such disputes as "faction fights." Jabulani Sithole, "Tale of Two Boundaries: Land Disputes and the *Izimpi Zemibango* in the Umlazi Location of the Pinetown District, 1920–1936," *South African Historical Journal*, 37 (1997): 78–106.

68. Despite these recurring "wars," Chunu and Thembu identities are as constructed and fluid as other ethnic identities. See PAR, 1 EST 2/1/2/1, *Sitole v. Sitole*, Case 59, 1938, in which one litigant is reported to have changed allegiance from the Chunu to the Thembu. Thomas McClendon, "The Chunu-Thembu Blues: The Media and Historicizing Ethnicity in South Africa," paper presented at Berkeley-Stanford Joint Center for African Studies annual conference, 1994.

69. PAR, CNC 89A, 63/2/52, N1/9/2(47), Weenen NC to CNC, 26 Nov. 1934.

70. Ibid.

71. For an amplification of the connections of the urban and rural worlds through *amalaita* gangs, see La Hausse, "Cows of Nongoloza," 91–92 and n. 57. See also Bradford, *Taste of Freedom*, 46–47.

72. PAR, CNC 89A, 63/2/52, N1/9/2(47), H. O'Brien Despard to CNC, 18 Dec. 1934.

73. PAR, 1 WEN 3/3/1/1, 2/3/18, Weenen NC responses to NEC General Questionnaire, n.d. but apparently 1931.

74. PAR, 1 EST 3/1/2/7, 2/16/3A, Minutes of Quarterly Meeting of Natives, 3 Feb. 1938. It was not unusual for people in positions of leadership, such as farm *indunas* to claim the extra *lobola*, despite lack of official recognition of their position.

75. Natal's African fathers and chiefs were apparently not able to assert control over migrant youths through a system of cattle advances like that described by Beinart in *Political Economy of Pondoland*. In the five-district region I have studied, few went to work in the mines; most migrants worked as domestic servants or in small firms. They did not organize their work through labor recruiters; indeed, as we have seen, they resisted recruitment schemes.

76. Women were also migrating to the cities in increasing numbers, but theirs tended to be migration for long-term settlement rather than for short-term labor contracts. See Bozzoli, *Women of Phokeng*; Philip Bonner, "'Desirable or Undesirable Basotho women?' Liquor, Prostitution and the Migration of Basotho Women to the Rand, 1920–1945," in *Women and Gender in Southern Africa*, ed. by Walker, 221–50.

77. See chapter 3.

78. H. Maine, *Ancient Law*, 100, quoted in Chanock, "A Peculiar Sharpness," 69. See also Chanock, *Law, Custom and Social Order*, 71–84.

79. *Natal Code*, Chapter V, Section 25.

80. *Natal Code*, Chapter VI, Section 38.

81. Ibid., Section 35.

82. "[F]or the historian both these constructs [status and contract] are chimerical, and are part of a process of mutual definition by antithesis, and of an inherent censure of colonized societies. What should interest us is the *movement* which Maine mentions twice." Chanock, "A Peculiar Sharpness." 69.

83. *Natal Code*, Chapter X, Section 91. Note that the Code is silent on *lobola* for firstborn sons. Apparently the Code assumes that fathers will provide *lobola* for the first wife of the heir.

84. Stafford, *Native Law*, 90. The CNC similarly advised a disgruntled son that "in the ordinary course you have no right enforceable at law to demand from your father the *lobola* for your intended bride, though it is customary for a father to pay the *lobola* for the first wife taken by his son." PAR, CNC 18A, 14/6, 382, CNC to P. Ndhlovu, Durban, 4 Dec. 1935.

85. Cf. Glassman, *Feasts and Riot*.

86. PAR, 1 NHR 2/1/2/1, *Majozi v. Mude*, Case 18/1935. Many informants confirmed this ideal. Many claimed that their fathers had provided *lobola* for the first wife, but that they had provided their own *lobola* for the second and subsequent wives, if any. See, e.g., interview with Mgewu Mchunu, Mpofana, 28 Oct. 1992.

87. PAR, 1 HWK 2/1/2/1, Case 3/1943, *Zuma v. Ntombela*, testimony of Ndava Zuma. Official Witnesses officiated at marriages and hence were often called upon to testify about bridewealth arrangements.

88. Interview with Bettina Dladla.

89. Interview with Kotayi Mkhize, Weenen, 11 Mar. 1992.

90. *Zuma v. Ntombela*.

91. Brideservice is not a "normal" practice among Africans in Natal, and I have not encountered other direct evidence of it occurring there, but it is easy to see how it could emerge in the labor tenant situation. The NC cases in general suggest that transactions in cattle, around which marriage revolved, were much more complicated and open-ended than positivist descriptions of bridewealth would suggest. Cf. John

Comaroff and Simon Roberts, *Rules and Processes: The Cultural Logic of Dispute in an African Context* (Chicago and London: University of Chicago Press, 1981). See also McClendon, "Hiding Cattle," 43–58.

92. The standard *lobola* amount laid down by the Code was ten head of cattle payable to the father of the bride and an *nquthu* beast payable to her mother. Natal Code, Chapter X, Sections 87 and 96.

93. PAR, 1 NHR 2/1/2/1, Case 39/1936, *Ngema v. Ngema*. Like *Zuma v. Ntombela*, this case came to the NCC as an appeal from the chief's court. In this case the appeal was upheld.

94. *Ngema v. Ngema*, testimony of Fanyama Ngema.

95. The case also provides an interesting glimpse into how generational conflict may intersect with gender conflict. Cf. the case of Chief Vuta, discussed above, in which a dispute between the son and his father's wife led to a disinheritance case.

96. Ibid., testimony of Mahobe Ngema.

97. *Ngema v. Ngema*, judgment.

98. PAR, 1 EST 2/1/2/1, Case 153/1940, *Mfusi v. Mfusi*.

99. PAR, 1 WEN 2/1/2/2, Case 60/1943, *Majola v. Mcunu*.

100. Ibid., testimony of Sikopoli Mcunu. (The son, Zigebendu, was deceased by the time of the suit.)

101. PAR, 1 EST 2/1/2/1, *Vilagazi v. Vilagazi*, Case 89/1936.

102. Again the case displays a confluence of generational and gender issues. For instance, Mtateni notes that "My mother came to my father as a virgin when she was married and she cannot be brought down from the position as chief wife."

103. Ibid., testimony of Mlazalozi Vilagazi.

104. The NC dismissed ("absolution from the instance") Mlazalozi's claim without comment. Retired acting Chief Peni Mabaso testified for the defendant that Matshana had regarded Mtateni as his heir, and, more important, that as a commoner Matshana could not designate anyone other than his first wife as chief wife. The Natal Code concurs with this point.

105. For the last point, see also *Mazibuko v. Mazibuko*, where it occurs more obliquely.

106. For disinheritance, see *Mkwanana v. Mkwanasi* (Chief Vuta's case), above. For cattle claims between fathers and sons, see e.g. PAR, 1 EST 2/1/2/1, Case 16/1926, *Mabaso v. Mabaso* (son unsuccessfully seeks division of *umuzi* property during life of his father); 1 WEN 2/1/2/1, Case 6/1932, *Madondo v. Madondo* (father successfully seeks return of cattle and goats from his son).

5

COURTING TRADITION: LAW, SEXUALITY, AND THE CONTROL OF WOMEN, 1927–1944

[A] native female is deemed a perpetual minor in law and has no independent powers save as to her own person and as specially provided in this Code.[1]

It is a time-honoured custom that no women should leave their husbands or guardians, but now if they have any cause for complaint they get a divorce and go to the towns.[2]

The section of the Natal Code quoted here contrasts sharply with Chief Matole's complaint delivered at a conference of Natal chiefs in 1939. Although Matole's views were normatively in sync with the perspective of the Code, he observed that the existence of urban life and westernized courts gave women means to acquire "independent powers" and action. The customary law regime, erected and preserved to ensure ongoing hierarchical control by male elders, to some degree undermined that control. Nevertheless, as anxieties about loss of control permeated the consciousness of elders, farmers, and officials, the NC Courts proved ever more sympathetic to enforcing a uniform view of tradition and reasserting the control of husbands, fathers, and senior brothers. Intergenerational tensions were an important facet of the crisis of control that permeated social relations in rural South Africa from the late 1920s to the early 1940s, as reflected in the outcry over farm labor shortages and in the tensions over bridewealth discussed in the preceding chapters. Gender relations were even more central to the question of control in this period. Male anxiety about the control of women was linked to social tensions arising from industrialization, increased migrancy, and reduced resources available to labor tenants (as well as reserve dwellers). These tensions were reflected in rural households and therefore surfaced in litigation in Natal's NC Courts. This chapter will discuss several cases concerned with marriage, divorce, and *ukungena*. These cases provide insights into the nature of attempts by African men to assert control over women in a time of transition and social stress. They also show how women resisted control and challenged newly rigid views of custom and patriarchy promoted by the state and elder men in the segregation era. In addition, they provide openings to explore the ambiguous role of the state in mediating the resulting conflicts even while endorsing male power as part of the project of refurbishing traditionalism.[3]

Although wives in labor tenant homesteads did not work *isithupa*, they were in many ways the linchpin of the system. Scholars of southern Africa have long understood that male migrancy depended on the availability of female rural labor, to ensure continued access to land and domestic reproduction.[4] This was as true of labor tenant homesteads as of those in reserves. Young men and some of the young women worked *isithupa*, either on the same farm or on a farm or other business in a neighboring district. The young women returned to their homesteads, until marriage took them away, whereas men migrated to urban jobs in the "free" six months. As urban jobs became more plentiful, as rural homesteads became more cash dependent, and as farms offered less land to labor tenants, migrancy became more common and lasted longer into a man's life. One result was that migrant men became increasingly anxious about the potential waywardness of wives left behind. Migrants depended on their fathers and brothers, as well as the structures of the customary law regime, to control and discipline wives. Women, however, also used the NC Courts to seek freedom from oppressive marriages through the vehicle of divorce, as well as using to the forum provided by courts to produce their own versions of labor tenant histories and their own perspectives on conflicts of gender and generation.

The court records and oral testimonies I use below to examine gender relations in labor tenant homesteads do not always lend themselves to a strict chronology. Trials often refer to events many years earlier, and elderly nonliterate informants did not recall the events and processes of their youth in terms of calendar dates. I use these materials instead to point out the lines of conflict and the ways in which men and women used the courts and conflicts over tradition to maneuver in the context of household and interhousehold struggles in the interwar years. It is also evident that we cannot tell who is telling the "truth" in the cases, and I again want to emphasize that is not my purpose in examining them. Rather, my hope is to elucidate the issues, concerns, and motivations that animated the actors—and the way in which they conceptualized the proper roles of men, women, and juniors—as well as the role of the state and its representatives.

Before delving into the cases, the chapter will discuss the centrality of gender to the project of control through segregation. In the process, we will examine the ethnographic outlines of customary marriage and the intersection of custom with the customary law regime.

SEGREGATION AND THE CONTROL OF WOMEN

African chiefs and elder men testifying to the Natal Native Affairs Commission of 1906–1907, examining the causes of the Bambatha rebellion, expressed concern about losing control of women. They complained especially that the white courts gave women recourse that stymied men in their attempts to control, discipline, and manage women.[5] Like the complaints of elder men about the lack of respect shown by youths, complaints about the unruliness of women and their recourse to courts were perennial and widespread in the colonial era.[6] They tended to reach fever pitch, however, at times of crisis like that represented by the Bambatha rebellion and the general crisis of control bracketing the 1930s. An African witness before the NEC in Natal in 1931 strongly echoed this complaint about the role of courts. Voicing the concern over the loss of authority for those who held it "traditionally," Nyongwana complained that the courts undermined the authority of husbands and fathers. From his perspective as a court messenger, he believed that wives and daughters no longer brought their concerns to the head of the family but instead complained to the courts.

> In the olden days, the idea or law or custom amongst the Natives [was that] if a man marries a woman he marries the woman to feed him. . . . What do you find now? *The court is the husband of the wife; the court is the father of the daughter.* They run there for their clothing and food.[7]

This chorus reached a crescendo among Natal's chiefs in the late 1930s. *Amakhosi* were particularly concerned about African women leaving the countryside for the dangers and opportunities of urban centers. In 1936, the Port Shepstone chiefs unanimously passed a motion that called for higher damages for fathers in cases of seduction of their daughters. "Girls should be stopped from coming into towns and boys severely punished for interfering with them," and the granting of divorce must be restricted to "special deserving cases." They complained: "We are losing control of our wives and family [sic]."[8] At the 1939 Natal Chiefs' Conference, the Regent Mshiyeni expressed appreciation of the NAD's efforts to reinforce Zulu customs and traditions, but he complained that "these are now ignored in regard to the control of wives and daughters—fathers and husbands are helpless." Chief Matole encapsulated these fears in comments that combined complaints about female urbanization, the harsh treatment by white farmers, and the ease of divorce:

> It has grieved the people to lose their old laws and customs; the women are flocking to the towns and are being exploited and despoiled by foreign people, and the people cannot understand why the government does not do something about this. Some of these girls go to the towns to escape the harsh treatment they receive from European farmers. It is a time-honoured custom that no women should leave their husbands or guardians, but now if they have any cause for complaint they get a divorce and go to the towns.[9]

Another persistent worry was control of female sexuality.[10] In 1928, the Greytown magistrate noted that "unmarried Native girls" in his district were becoming engaged without the consent of their fathers. They had even "established a society of their own entitled 'MANJE' [now] or 'Free Love.'" An *induna* of the area insisted that this trend was the outcome of certain court decisions.[11] "Free love," the official's dubious translation of *manje*, apparently amounted to informal marriage, without benefit of the sanction of chiefs and fathers, and without more than partial payment of *lobola*. Some chiefs and NCs worried that fathers acquiesced in these arrangements, viewing their daughters "as a source of revenue and systematically bleed[ing] the so-called husband until he objects and dissolves the union."[12] In the 1930s, fears of unrestrained sexuality combined with anxieties surrounding female urbanization.[13] Nkantolo Mpembe of Loskop (Estcourt district) argued that women were "a source of trouble to their husbands and to the chiefs. They get into trouble and then they disappear." If the police were successful in tracing them to the big cities and brought them back, it was found that they were "infected with Venereal Disease."

Photo 5.1 "Native" policemen, Durban. (Supplied and reproduced by kind permission of the Campbell Collections of the University of Natal [D7.112].)

Therefore, he asserted, "Steps should be taken to restrict the movements of these women and no married woman should be allowed to leave for Johannesburg."[14]

In the interests of controlling female mobility as part of the segregation project, it was government policy (albeit ineffective) to severely restrict the immigration of women to the cities.[15] The NSCA, for instance, provided that women seeking employment in urban centers had to present written permission from their guardians—that is, fathers or husbands.[16] In 1936, the NAD issued instructions to the railway department designed to prevent women from traveling to towns without such permission.[17] By 1939, the government was expressing increased anxiety about female urbanization, and again it recommended "attack[ing] the influx at its source" through the cooperation of railway authorities. No other option appeared to be available. The direct application of pass laws to women was impossible because "Natives of all grades of society and shades of opinion would bitterly resent the application of the pass laws to their women."[18] Government officials frankly admitted that keeping women in the countryside was an indirect means of controlling men. "For so long as wives and families are kept in their kraals, husbands, brothers and sons will continue to return to them."[19]

As complaining African men saw, all these issues—divorce, sexuality, and mobility—were closely related. In her piece on the construction of Zulu ethnicity, Shula Marks analyzed the ideology and implementation of segregation in Natal in terms of attempts to foster the 'proper' conduct of women.[20]

> In the attempt to slow down the processes of African proletarianiza-tion, African women played a crucial role. For African men fears over the loss of control over women were deeply rooted in the role which women had played in precapitalist society as the producers of labour power both in their own right and as the bearers of children—future labour power.[21]

Marks argued that "the state and capital" shared this interest in the control of women for two reasons. First, women's agricultural production in rural areas lowered the cost of reproducing the urban workforce. Second, by aiding the hold of "traditional" patriarchal structures over women, the state could "control the return of the young men to the reserves and white farms which still needed their seasonal labor."[22] Marks went on to argue that these material interests lay behind the "alliance" of African men and the state that resulted in attempts to tighten the control of women in the segregation era. Her inquiry examined questions of culture and sexuality that were raised by the conservative *kholwa* elite in the 1920s and 1930s, focusing on the issue of "purity." In this chapter, I want to pursue this analysis into nonelite households, especially on farms and in other rural areas.

How were these anxieties about the proper conduct and control of women played out in rural African households of "ordinary" women and men, especially labor tenants? In the remainder of the chapter, I look at gender relations—especially tensions and conflict in those relations—in the context of the customary law regime. That regime, as we saw in chapters 2 and 4, sought to elevate and support patriarchal relations, but it also facilitated the undermining of those relations by giving women and juniors access to westernized courts. Moreover, the records of litigation in those courts provide a window onto aspects of relations between men and women in rural Natal in the segregation era.

MARRIAGE, DIVORCE, AND CONTROL OF
SEXUALITY IN THE NC COURTS

The "leading principles" of customary law, as conceived by colonial authorities in nineteenth and twentieth century Natal, are well illustrated by transcripts of trials held in the NC Courts in the segregation era.[23] The cases themselves make it even more clear than does the Natal Code that these leading principles were concerned primarily with the hierarchical control of bodies, especially female bodies and the children and cattle that they generated. This hierarchy of corporeal control was justified in terms of tradition and customary law. African women as litigants and witnesses in these cases, however, demonstrated understandings of tradition that were both more nuanced and more open to contestation.

Marriage among Africans in 1930s Natal was based on cultural practices derived from the precolonial era, but it was significantly affected by changes in the region's political economy in the nineteenth and early twentieth centuries. In the first chapter, I criticized the efforts of historians to describe "women's oppression" in precolonial Natal and Zululand on the basis of writings culled from a variety of sources in the late nineteenth and early twentieth centuries. The question of precolonial cultures and histories among Nguni-speaking peoples of southeastern Africa, and how these were transformed by the rise of militaristic polities in the late eighteenth and early nineteenth centuries followed by colonial invasions and impositions, awaits a great deal of further research.[24] However, the outlines of marriage practices in the region are known from the work of late nineteenth and early twentieth-century ethnographers, as well as from the changes deliberately introduced by Natal's colonial administration.[25] The following is an idealized account.

Marriage was effected among traditionalist Zulu speakers through the exchange of bridewealth and the movement of the bride (*umakoti*) from her father's homestead to that of her husband's father.[26] The Zulu kinship system was patrilineal, and marriage was patrilocal and exogamous; one could not marry anyone with the same *isibongo* as one's father or mother.[27] The journey of the *umakoti* was therefore both physical, in that the woman moved to her husband's family's homestead, and spiritual, in that she arrived as a member of a strange lineage but was progressively incorporated into her husband's lineage. At the end of her life she assumed the status of an ancestor in her husband's lineage.[28] The most significant aspect of the transfer of

bridewealth was that all children subsequently born to the woman became members of the husband's lineage. Gluckman, who pointed to
this feature as the basis of "stability" (rarity of divorce) in Zulu marriage, emphasized that it meant that biological paternity was unimpor-
tant in establishing a child's social paternity. Dead men, for instance,
could become fathers through the practice of *ukungena*; by similar
practices, an impotent man or even a woman could become a father.[29]

The colonial era in Natal introduced significant changes in marriage practices among Africans. Bryant suggests that in the mid-eigh-
teenth century *lobola* was paid in hoes, goats, or occasionally cattle.
By the time of Shaka, cattle became the standard medium, but "ordinary" people still exchanged only three or so head.[30] Krige states that
before the existence of the Natal Code, there was "no fixed amount,"
but the number "never was greater than four or five head of cattle."
In any case, these transfers were not completed at one moment prior
to the marriage, but continued during the life of the marriage as signs
of alliance and friendship between the two lineages.[31] The colonial
presence, resulting in the creation of wage labor and a money
economy, caused a significant inflation in *lobola* in the mid-nineteenth
century. The colonial government stepped in with marriage regulations
in 1869, setting maximum amounts for *lobola*; for commoners, the
amount was ten head of cattle, plus the *nquthu* beast provided to the
woman's mother. This quickly became the standard amount demanded
by fathers.[32] The colonial intervention in marriage practices was also
bent on liberating women by ending the practice of "forced" marriage,
especially to older polygynists; the law required that the marriage be
assented to by the woman, and that this be attested to by the presence
of an appointed Official Witness.[33]

The most important innovation resulting from colonial interventions,
however, was the legalization of marriage and divorce, making them
into public matters handled by judicial officers of the colonial state.[34]
Although other disputes could be brought to a chief's court and then
appealed to the NC, or could be brought to the NC directly, divorce
cases had to be initiated in the NC Court.[35] This suggests that the
drafters of the 1927 Native Administration Act viewed divorce as a
particularly important issue of hierarchical control, one that could not
be safely entrusted to the customary law regime's African functionaries. In precolonial times, marriage had been a private arrangement
between homesteads; neither its establishment nor its dissolution involved the intervention of judicial authorities. In practice, the separation of a husband and wife would be accompanied by the return of
the *lobola* cattle if it dissolved as a result of the woman's "adultery

or desertion."[36] By making divorce a legal institution that could occur only with the intervention of the NC court, the Natal Code formalized this practice, giving the wife's lineage a stake in the continuation of her marriage and an automatic role in divorce cases.[37] Divorce cases therefore involved strategizing, by the two lineages involved in the marriage, to control the *lobola* cattle.[38] Wives and their "guardians" (fathers or brothers) attempted to show that the breakdown in the marriage was attributable to the fault of the husband, so that (a) they could get divorced and (b) their lineage could retain the *lobola* cattle. Husbands (and their lineage allies) conversely attempted to show that the wife was at fault. If they succeeded, they would either (a) preserve the marriage and hence retain the wife for whom bridewealth had been transferred or promised, or (b) obtain the return of cattle with which a new wife could be married. The state, in the form of the NAD, was also involved by virtue of its administration of the legal system. The state was by no means a neutral actor, although it had contradictory impulses and aims that emerge in the cases.

Nearly all people I spoke with on the subject claimed that divorce was rare in the past, but most admitted that it happened occasionally.[39] One informant pointed out that marital breakdown did not always result in a formal divorce: "Maybe a wife would leave her husband and never come back or a husband leave his wife and never come back."[40] One woman offered the nostalgic and unlikely assessment that "No, we lived nicely before. There were no divorces; we led a real nice life."[41] The numbers of cases coming into the courts indicate that divorce was indeed not common, but it formed a substantial part of the NC court caseload. These cases are not put forward, then, as typical examples of relations among husbands, wives, and in-laws. Rather, they are examined as crisis points that may expose the fault lines of marriage and other aspects of gender relations in the relevant era. Most of these cases involve labor tenant litigants, but nonlabor tenant cases are included for their value in illustrating lines of tension and conflict in rural households in this period, and the ways in which the NC Court became a forum for African debates about the permissible boundaries of change.

Ngubane v. Mtshali: The Wayward Wife

A 1932 Lions River divorce case highlights the combined attempts of husbands, fathers, and the state to control the movements and sexuality of African women in the 1930s.[42] Because there were no reserves in the district, the litigants were no doubt farm tenants. Senzagabi

Ngubane sought a divorce from his wife Nomkosi Mtshali after an *induna* had failed to reconcile them and had found the wife at fault. Mtshali was "duly assisted" by her maternal uncle (*umalume*).[43] No attorneys were involved. Ngubane sought a divorce on the grounds of his wife's desertion and refusal to "render me conjugal rights." He complained that she had left five years earlier and was living with another man.[44] Mtshali, though not opposed to the divorce, faulted her husband for the breakdown of the marriage.

> I left Plaintiff because he ill-treated me and he would not have inter-course with me. I am his first wife, and I have had one child by Plain-tiff, which child died at birth. I have been pregnant three times by Plaintiff but two of my pregnancies ended in miscarriage.[45]

The head of Ngubane's *umuzi* testified that Mtshali was troublesome be-cause "she used to go about to beer drinks and she aggravated Plaintiff and me in her conduct." Cross-examined by Mtshali, the witness denied that her husband "was continually assaulting you," but admitted that on occasion her husband "did chastise you by beating you."[46]

The NC granted the divorce, with costs to be borne by the wife, and ordered that seven head of cattle be returned to the husband. The NC found that the wife was at fault because she left her husband and refused to return and "render Plaintiff conjugal rights." Furthermore, Mtshali's "conduct was troublesome to Plaintiff" because she "persisted in going to beer drinks" and was "keeping company with another man."[47] Spurred no doubt by the obligation to pay costs and return seven head of cattle (three head having been deducted for the three pregnancies), Mtshali's uncle hired an attorney to bring an appeal before the NAC. The higher court also blamed the "wayward" wife:

> It would seem that Appellant has a wayward nature and that she was in the habit of attending beer drinks and thus neglecting her domestic duties. This, coupled with her failure to bear children, is probably the cause of the estrangement between the parties.[48]

Thus Mtshali, apparently mistreated by her husband because of her fail-ure to produce children, was condemned for attending "beer drinks" and supposedly neglecting her wifely duties. The clear concern of the courts was with her unconstrained sexuality, which had not been successfully harnessed to the reproduction of the household.[49] Elderly male informants I spoke to also suggested that women's unrestrained sexuality was a ma-jor cause of divorce. "Boy" Ndlovu, for instance, specifically saw women's failure to obey, coupled especially with movements out of the *umuzi* into the sexually charged territory of the nighttime, as a major cause of divorce:

> [S]ometimes if the man says he doesn't want this to be done in the house, she then does it. This leads to anger, and then divorce. If I say that I don't want [my wife] to go all around and come back late at night, we quarrel because I don't know where you went to—that's it.[50]

Despite the husband's lack of interest in her, Mtshali's "traditional" wifely duty was to remain in her husband's *kraal*, engaging in domestic and agricultural labor. Her failure to do so subjected her to condemnation and divorce. On the other hand, this resulted in no obvious loss to her, since she had left her husband four or five years earlier and was reputed to be living with another man. The loss was to her guardian, who in the future would be concerned to more closely regulate the behavior of his female wards and to return them to the husbands from whom they had "strayed."

Dhlamini v. Dhlamini: The Milk Cow

Another Natal NC case, from Estcourt district in the late 1930s, shows a hardening of the concept of "custom" and "tradition" under the Natal Code, to the detriment of women's rights to control property, especially cattle. In *Dhlamini v. Dhlamini*, Bhixa, the defendant, appealed against the judgment of Chief Gilbert for eight head of cattle (plaintiff Nembe had claimed thirteen head).[51] Nembe was Bhixa's older brother from the same house, that of their father's third wife. Their father had died, and Nembe was claiming cattle that he said were "house" property. Bhixa claimed that the cattle were progeny of a milk cow (*inkomo yamasi*) given by their father to his wife, as he had done upon the marriage of each of his sons. Other witnesses disputed that such a gift was made, claiming that (as the plaintiff said), "If such a gift had been made all the sons and uncles would have been called to hear the announcement." Nembe admitted that "it is the custom to give two goats to the bride and it is also the custom to give a milk cow to the bride," but he reiterated, "This is always done in the presence of inmates of the kraal." Others, however, claimed that such a gift was not only customary but had been publicly made. A female witness stressed that such a beast belonged to the woman who received it, and it could not be used by the husband without her permission. Mamboza Sitole, the mother of the parties, supporting

Bhixa (with whom she had remained after her husband's death, despite the "custom" that she should live with her eldest son), stated:

> A beast was given to [Bhixa] by his father. This beast was a cow given
> to [Bhixa's] wife. The cow is still alive and he [Bhixa] can do as he
> likes but he would have to get the consent of his wife before selling it.
> The beast is the property of the woman and [Bhixa] could not sell it or
> have it attached for his debts. The bride's father does not make a
> present of a milk cow to his daughter, and it is our custom for the
> bride not to take the milk of the bridegroom's kraal, but she could take
> the milk of this particular cow.[52]

The NC, as in the "twin case" discussed in chapter 4, found the provisions of the Code more persuasive on the subject of "native custom" than the testimony of "natives" themselves. He confirmed the judgment of Chief Gilbert, finding that the gift of the milk cow had not been proved:

> Section 107 of the Natal Code . . . merely states that when a girl enters into a customary union her father may give her goods or cattle, no
> mention being made of a gift by the father of the bridegroom to the
> bride and *as this gift appears to be foreign to native custom,* the defendant under such circumstances would have to produce conclusive
> proof. [Emphasis added]

The NC found that the proof was lacking. The milk cow case reiterates the lesson of the twin case that the Code and the NCs held a rigid view of "custom" that sharply contrasted with (and often overrode) the contested and mutable sense of custom held by African litigants and witnesses. In addition, it provides a glimpse of a version of custom that women, in ongoing domestic struggle, presented as an alternative to the patriarchal views of African men and colonial officials.

Mkize v. Ngqalanga: Mobility and Mastery

This case, in which labor tenant Hlupizwe Ngqalanga's wife Nompepe Mkize failed to persuade the NC Court or the appeals court to grant her a divorce, illustrates the struggles and strategies over divorce and the return of *lobola* and demonstrates the material and spiritual concerns within labor tenant households.[53] In 1940, Mkize, the second wife of Ngqalanga, petitioned the Weenen NC Court for a divorce from her husband of eight years. She was supported in the action by her brother, her legal guardian, as required by the Natal Code. Both spouses were represented by lawyers.[54] After trial, the court granted the defendant husband "absolution from the instance" (dismissal). The NAC sent the case back to the NC Court on the grounds that the Code required an attempt at reconciliation of the parties by the woman's father or guardian.[55] The reconciliation was duly attempted but was not successful, and retrial of the case in 1941 resulted in a second dismissal, with costs to be paid by the plaintiff wife. The appeals court agreed this time that the grounds presented for divorce were inadequate.[56]

This long and fruitless path of litigation revolved around three principal quarrels, each of which concerned the husband's attempts to exert control over the wife and struggles against that control by the wife and "her people." In order to appreciate this, it is necessary to look at the text generated in the court in some detail. In the first incident, Mkize testified:

> The cause of the trouble was that defendant asked why I do not assist his other wife to brew beer. I told him that I had sent a child to fetch corn [sorghum] and bring it to my hut as I had a small child at the time. After I had told the defendant this it was time to go and draw water. I told him I couldn't do this, as the other children refused to look after my small baby. As a result of this, defendant took a stick and assaulted me.

Another time:

> We were invited to assist in thatching of a hut at my people's kraal. When I returned from the thatching of the hut my husband was not at home. When he arrived he asked me who told me to go, as he did not want me to go there. He then assaulted me. After he had assaulted me he told me to go back to my people. . . . My people took me back to defendant's kraal.

Following this incident there was a dispute over another trip to "her people" when she fetched some sorghum from her sister to give to a newly engaged woman. Ngqalanga accused his wife of taking away some oranges he had left in her hut. As a result of this argument, "[h]e took the key and locked the door," locking her out. She returned to her people and reported her presence to the Official Witness, who also instructed her to return to Ngqalanga. "My life on my return was not happy. [My husband] refused to eat food I cooked and would not come into my hut.

He would not sleep with me." These incidents culminated in accusations by Ngqalanga that Mkize would "not report to him if someone stabbed her in the stomach and bewitched him."[57] In addition, Ngqalanga insulted his wife by saying that if he went to her hut, "it would be like her father going in."[58] As a result, the *induna* ordered Ngqalanga to pay Mkize a fine of one beast.[59]

Mkize claimed that Ngqalanga had taken the first legal step by going to the *induna*, Majola Nqalanga. Majola, who lacked power to impose fines, said he was unable to reach a decision and referred the matter to the chief. This was perhaps fortunate for Mkize, as she noted that the *induna* was "my husband's brother."[60] The chief then referred the matter to another *induna*, who said that Ngqalanga must pay a fine of a beast for the above insult and for failing to "go into her hut." Yet another *induna*, Mayizekanye Canco, appeared in the case, the only one to testify. He testified that there was another source of conflict—a critical material one. Mkize had complained to him about the insufficiency of food provided for her during Ngqalanga's six-month work stint.

> Plaintiff came and reported to me that defendant went away leaving her with no food. . . . I told her to go and tell defendant's brothers. She did so. Defendant's brother went to [defendant's] kraal during his absence and took out one bag of mealies [maize] from one of [his] huts. Plaintiff refused to take this bag saying defendant would quarrel with her as he had told her a bag was to last her six months, and that they should wait until [he] came back.[61]

Ngqalanga's view of this incident was quite different: "This last quarrel arose out of two bags of mealies and I gave a bag each to my two wives. Plaintiff finished hers—she only had two children and the other wife has six children."

Women who were left behind on labor farms were faced with an increased workload, including the responsibility to plough and herd cattle (although these were ideally male activities). They were also left sometimes with inadequate food while the wage earners were away.[62] On the other hand, several women commented that the migration of men away to work during the six months "off" was positive in that the men earned good wages in Johannesburg, unlike on the farms. "We were happy because it meant that families will have more money as they were paid very low wages when working in the farms."[63] Females were responsible for domestic labor as well as for agriculture, but their work increasingly included responsibility for cattle and for ploughing (traditionally men's

Photo 5.2 Woman winnowing mealies near Empangeni in Zululand region of Natal province, 1933. (Supplied and reproduced by kind permission of the Campbell Collections of the University of Natal [D7.031].)

work, as it involved working with cattle) as boys went to school and young men went "out" to work. It was not desirable for girls to go out to work, as to do so implied poverty. "It was a shame for a girl to leave home and go and work somewhere else. She had to stay at home and help. We weren't that poor, as our fathers were working and had 'too much' stock."[64]

The testimony of Ngqalanga, the husband, was pivotal. Both the NC Court and the appeals court accepted it uncritically (and uncomprehendingly). His most important argument was that "*It is our cus-*

tom when a girl gets married and becomes a woman, she has to get her husband's permission to visit her people" (emphasis added). The NC endorsed this view in his Reasons for Judgment:

> In the first [incident] it being a Native Custom [sic] that the woman must obtain the consent of her husband when she wishes to visit her people. . . . In the second quarrel defendant had every right to know all about the corn, where it came from and where [she] was taking it.

Mkize implicitly endorsed this customary limitation on her movements. On cross-examination by her husband's attorney, she said: "I used to ask permission from defendant to go to my people; sometimes he allowed me to go and others he refused and I stayed. I did not go to my people if he refused to allow me to go."

The NC then went on to misinterpret the "poked-in-the-stomach" insult: "Defendant became angry and abused plaintiff by saying that 'If she was poked in the stomach with a stick she would not tell him,' (meaning presumably that if she became pregnant by another man she would not tell him)." The NC provided no grounds for this interpretation, which ignored the specific testimony of Mkize's brother that the remark concerned bewitchment.[65] It is clear that the husband was deeply concerned about his wife's visits to her people, and that one source of his concern was the possibility of witchcraft. This matter may be the key to the case, although Mkize did not make witchcraft accusations a ground for her suit.[66]

According to Austen's definition, witchcraft is "the use of preternatural power by one person to damage others," and its effectiveness is "held to be a direct function of the intimacy between witch and victim."[67] Since *amaZulu* wives were outsiders who became incorporated over time, they were especially dangerous from the point of view of a husband and his family. This was especially true of newer wives, who were not fully incorporated into the husband's lineage but who were in intimate daily contact with it. They thereby gained access to *insila* (body dirt), which they could use for witchcraft, and of course to food, which they could poison. The eruption of a dispute between husband and wife was viewed as evidence of the presence of witchcraft, and the wife herself was suspect.[68] According to Berglund, *ubuthakathi* (witchcraft) refers to both evil doing and the manipulation of *imithi* (medicines) by *abathakathi* (witches or sorcerers). Wives were dangerous both as potential witches, who were usually female and who engaged in an unconstrained and unnatural sexuality, and as potential bearers of *imithi* from enemies beyond the husband's family and neighbors.[69] It is easy to see why social changes that were causing male anxieties about the control of women might be expressed in the idiom of witchcraft accusations and counteraccusations; that is why men opposed making such accusations a ground for divorce (see chapter 4). Ngqalanga seems to have been concerned that he could not trust his wife as a result of her frequent trips to her people and her failure to accord him the proper degree of respect, a failure which itself was evidence of possible witchcraft.[70]

Did Ngqalanga think his wife Mkize was a witch? If so, why didn't he want to divorce her? Of course, trial records can give us only limited insight into the motivations of the actors, and historical context has to be supplied from other sources.[71] But what we know suggests that he was concerned that he might lose his wife and yet receive no compensatory return of cattle. He had to argue that her complaints were unjustified and that she was at fault in the quarrels, but he could not maintain an accusation of witchcraft in the white court—such a claim was beyond the colonial pale.[72] The result in this case—denial of divorce—was very unusual. I discuss the case here not to give the misleading impression that women seeking divorce were inevitable losers, but for the insight it offers into issues of control in the context of mid-twentieth-century labor tenancy. The case illustrates (a) the prevalence of assault in marriage—a recurring theme in divorce cases of the time;[73] (b) the tension over incorporation of the wife into the husband's lineage—involving anxieties over labor, loyalty, and witchcraft; (c) the active role of the woman in seeking her liberation from an untenable situation, first by repeatedly removing herself to "her people," and then by seeking a divorce; (d) the ambiguous role of the woman's lineage, which supported her application for divorce only after returning her several times to the husband; and (e) the ambiguous role of the state, which tinkered with the "customary" institution of marriage in ways designed to grant more freedom of choice to women, but which occasionally demonstrated its anxiety over the breakdown of patriarchal controls by criticizing women's disregard of "native custom" concerning limitations on their movements.[74] The state thereby displayed its contradictory support of liberal ideology and of the traditional order that underpinned segregation. This was a continuing point of tension in the state's administration of customary law.

Ngubane v. Langa: Anxieties and Assaults

Accusations of witchcraft and threats of violence featured even more starkly in another divorce case in Weenen the next year.[75] This nasty and violent struggle, which terminated the marriage in less than one year, also involved a dispute over the *umakoti* going back to "her people."[76] In this case it was the man who initiated proceedings, and he was successful in obtaining a divorce.[77] The husband was once again concerned to control the movements of his new wife in a polygynous household. He was especially concerned about her trips back to her father's *umuzi*, lest she "get medicine from them and kill him." His attempts to control her movements led him to take leave from his job in Johannesburg, confront her family, assault and threaten her, and, when all these methods had failed, divorce her. Tatawi Langa, the wife, appeared at first as a buffeted victim, trying to obey her husband's and in-laws' injunctions. Once husband Mahlatini Ngubane's demands and assaults began, however, Langa consistently resisted by running away, and finally repudiated her father's demand that she return to her husband (and thus save his *lobola* cattle from being repaid). There was also the suggestion of an underlying quarrel that was not revealed in the testimony in court. Perhaps Ngubane was concerned not just over possible witchcraft, which was serious enough, but also over the loss of his wife's labor in his *umuzi* while he was away in Johannesburg. Control of sexuality also appeared to be an issue, as the two parties disagreed over when and whether they had had sex and whether Ngubane had complained that his wife did not come into the marriage as a virgin.[78]

Ngubane had gone to Johannesburg two weeks after marrying Langa. Shortly thereafter, his wife returned to her people, causing Ngubane to return to Weenen in order to bring his wife back to his own *umuzi*. Langa's father persuaded Ngubane to go away, but the next day Ngubane, having threatened in front of her people to assault his wife, found Langa in the fields and took her back to his *umuzi*. There the threats of violence became more frightening:

> During the night Plaintiff and his brother ground some herbs and when his brother went out Plaintiff got some reins and fastened the door. After this Plaintiff took the cup with the ground herbs and told me to drink it.

He choked her and threatened to burn her, so she gave in and drank the medicine. The next day she ran away to return to her father's nearby home, but Ngubane again caught and choked her. Back at his own *umuzi*, Ngubane again threatened Langa, telling her, "Ntakonshana killed a girl and nothing was done to him, so he could kill me." He said he wanted her to "tell him I did not want him as he wanted to get his cattle back." In other words, if she could be blamed for the dissolution of the marriage, the *lobola* would be restored to him. Langa complained to the authorities, but in court she reported that neither the Official Witness nor the police "saw" the nail marks on her neck. Her father also continued to tell her to return to her husband.

The husband-plaintiff Ngubane's successive strategies of violence and legal action paid off. The divorce was granted, with costs, and the NC ordered that all ten head of *lobola* cattle (not including the *nquthu*) be returned to the plaintiff. The NC issued the standard order for Langa to "return to the kraal of her father . . . and to remain under his guardianship until remarriage."[79]

UKUNGENA, WIDOWS, AND CONTROL

Cases about *ukungena* (the levirate; literally, "entry"), shed further light on the control of women under "customary law." Under the practice of *ukungena*, the brother of a deceased man "entered" the hut of the widow in order to "raise up seed" for his dead brother. *Ukungena* was one of the practices that Gluckman associated with what he called the stability of Zulu marriage.[80] Mere death did not terminate the marriage, for in an important sense the marriage was more a relationship between two lineages than between two individuals. *Ukungena* was deemed especially important in cases where there were no living sons at the time of the husband's death. Through this practice, a surviving brother could provide his dead brother with an heir.

> By the *ngena* a junior takes the wife of his deceased elder in order to 'raise up seed' to the latter. . . . No cattle pass for *ukungena*, but one head of cattle belonging to the deceased's estate is customarily killed for the occasion. In addition, the raiser of seed is entitled to be paid one head of cattle for the *ukungena*.[81]

The court records reveal that there was considerable ambiguity in practice, however, leaving room for debate and dispute over inheritance and other rights and obligations stemming from an *ukungena* marriage.[82] The ambiguities, contrasting with the clear statement of rules by Krige, revolved around the nature and timing of rituals and announcements associated with *ukungena*. Ambiguity was heightened by anxieties concerned with control of women's labor and offspring. The spread of Christianity among some labor tenants further complicated the issues, as we see in the next case.

Radebe v. Mazibela: Syncretic Control

Sometime after the Anglo-Boer war, labor tenant George Mazibela *ngena*'d Martha, a widow in his father's *umuzi*, and eventually fathered three children by her.[83] As Christians, however, the members of the *umuzi* did not mark this event with the slaughter of a goat or any other formality. As a result of this lapse, George was branded an adulterer and thrown out of court when he sought compensation before the Lions River NC Court a generation later in 1937. The defendant, Aaron Radebe, was the eldest son, and therefore heir, of Martha and her deceased husband. George represented himself while Aaron was represented by a lawyer. George prevailed before an *induna*, but the NC court overturned the judgment of the *induna* and granted judgment with costs for Aaron.[84]

George testified that his father had ordered him to *ngena* the woman Martha after the death of her husband, a "brother" of George and a member of the *umuzi*. He was clear that the point of *ukungena* was to maintain control over the widow. "The idea of the *ukungena* was to prevent the woman leaving the kraal and getting married elsewhere."[85] He argued for compensation because "It is native custom that a man who *ngena*'s a woman is paid for his services and receives a beast for each child born." Aaron argued that there was no *ukungena* as there was "no celebration by any Official Witness. I say the three children are simply illegitimate children." He claimed not to know who the children's father was.[86] His supporting witnesses admitted that George was the father but denied that there was an *ukungena* union. As one of them stated, "It was simply an adultery."[87]

The issue of whether the union of George and Martha Mazibela constituted *ukungena* or adultery was complicated by the Christian beliefs of some of the parties. The coming of Christianity to southern Africa led in many cases to syncretic social practices. On mission stations, for instance, converts continued to exchange *lobola* despite engaging in Christian marriage.[88] In mixed communities of *amakholwa* and traditionalists, Africans found new ways of creating social bonds that defied the literalism and fixity of customary law. George's witnesses claimed that this syncretism allowed *ukungena* but precluded official celebration of the *ukungena* union, as Africans tried to steer a course between a rigid Christianity and a rigid understanding of custom.

> The parties are *kolwas* and they do not have any ceremony when *ukungena* takes place nor slaughter any beast. Even raw natives do not always slaughter a goat. . . . *We Kolwas still follow the practice of*

Photo 5.3   Married men in *umuzi,* curing a goat skin. (Courtesy of the Pietermaritzburg Archives Repository [Frame 22].)

> ukungena. *Our parsons are opposed to it but we continue the practice to preserve our families.*[89]

George's testimony was ambiguous on this point. He stated that "No goat was slaughtered as we were *kolwas.* The *Amakolwa* object to *ukungena* but I was not then a full member of the church."[90] George further testified that his elder brother would have been the proper one to *ngena* Martha, but he "was . . . a parson in the American Church and refused on that ground to *ukungena* the woman." The NC, relying on the principle that it was the plaintiff's burden to prove the existence of the *ukungena,* gave judgment for the defendant Aaron. He argued that "Defendant's rights as heir must . . . be protected and an *ukungena* union cannot be presumed."

The testimony of George and his supporters was unambiguous that *ukungena* was practiced, despite reservations imported from Christianity, "to prevent the woman leaving the kraal and getting married elsewhere." The case has the ironic element of showing a failure of the *ukungena* (or adulterous) strategy as a result of the complicated relationships in an *umuzi,* where a "brother" might turn out to be of another *isibongo.* The Mazibelas successfully kept Martha in the *umuzi.*

Her children (who would "belong to" her husband's heir whether they were products of *ukungena* or adultery), however, ended up being Radebes rather than Mabizelas, as Aaron had belatedly discovered his "true" *isibongo*. In this case *ukungena* enabled the Mabizelas to exert control over Martha's productive and reproductive labor but failed to ensure that her children remained in the circle of dependents. It lacks the element of female resistance, as Martha, the *ukungena* wife or adulterous partner of George, was dead at the time of the case. Even in this case however, female agency is evident—as participants in *ukungena* union or adultery, as opponents or supporters of such unions, and as witnesses in the NC Court. George's eventual loss of the case is not important to our analysis. What is important is the evidence of the ongoing significance of this precolonial social practice in a transitional era and the state's implicit and explicit endorsement of institutions for control of women.

Zondi v. Zondi: Property and Propriety

The Lions River NC Court faced more complicated facts in a 1944 case that again raised issues about the meaning of *ukungena* itself and concerned questions of legitimacy and inheritance.[91] The plaintiff Matshiki Zondi "claim[ed] to be the issue of an *ukungena* union between his mother, Mampunya Zondi, the widow of Stini Zondi, *ngena*'d by her husband's brother, Joli Zondi."[92] Matshiki thus claimed to be heir to the *ndhlunkulu* (main) house, meaning that he was the general heir. The defendant Mashingana Zondi was heir to the *ikhohlo* [left-hand] house of Sitini Zondi and claimed that Matshiki was an illegitimate child (and thus subject to Mashingana), rather than the child of an *ukungena* union.[93] Plaintiff claimed fifteen head of cattle and 22 pounds that derived from his house but had been used for the benefit of the defendant's house. Both parties were represented by counsel. The plaintiff apparently abandoned the case in midstream, leading the NC to rule for the defendant.

The first witness was Mampunya Zondi, the mother of the plaintiff. She explained the circumstances of her *ukungena* union with Joli and the birth of the plaintiff:

> I am the widow of the late Sitini Zondi. . . . Joli Zondi, in arranging kraal matters, decided that he would *ngena* me as there was no male heir to my house. . . . As a result of the *ukungena* union the Plaintiff [Matshiki] was born to me and so he is the heir of my house and general heir to the kraal of the late Sitini, my husband.

Due to the objections of Joli's chief wife, Sikeyu, however, the *ukungena* was not arranged immediately, which strengthened the case of those who said it never occurred. Mampunya testified that she returned for a time to her people, where she bore a son to another man. After Sikeyu's death, Joli brought Mampunya back to his *umuzi* on Shaw's farm and established her as an *ukungena* wife. She remained on the farm until she and her children were evicted the year before the case began, forcing her to settle in the neighboring district of New Hanover.

The difficulty, as in the previous case, resulted from the lack of a formal announcement or ceremony to mark the commencement of the *ukungena* union, leading to an ambiguity that was exacerbated by her subsequent informal union with another man. The problem surfaced when Mampunya and her children were evicted, as there was a dispute about which cattle belonged to her, a dispute that hinged on whether Matshiki was an *ukungena* child or the child of the informal union. "It was then that we were surprised to hear Joli state that the Plaintiff was not his son."[94] The witnesses also debated the timing of her relationship with another man on Shaw's farm, Mandolwane Madhlala, whom the defendant and his allies claimed was the father of the plaintiff. They argued that although Mampunya had returned to Joli's *kraal*, she had never been an *ukungena* wife. Mampunya claimed that Mandolwane "took up with me" when the Plaintiff was already "quite a big herd boy." She said that by then Joli was no longer "coming into me," that is, exercising his *ngena* rights, as she was past childbearing.[95]

The main issue, as in the Mazibela case, was the control of widowed women's sexuality and fertility. Here, the *umnumzane* had clearly failed to effectively control the widow. Whether or not Joli *ngena*'d Mampunya, it is clear that the *ukungena* was at least delayed when she left the *umuzi* for some period of time and had a child by another man. It is also clear that the delay was the result of the choice of a woman. Either Mampunya had declined to be *ngena*'d, or the chief wife had declined to allow the *ukungena* to go forward. Then, both while she was away from Joli's *umuzi* and at some point after her return, Mampunya took lovers who did not furnish *lobola*.

The case was not just about the abstract control of women, however, but involved a dispute over property under the woman's control. The material issue giving rise to the case was the ownership of the cattle. The paternity of the plaintiff became an issue because he and his mother were evicted from the farm, requiring a separation of the cattle in Joli's *umuzi*. Mampunya had taken the stock with her when she was evicted, and Matshiki was apparently suing to retain control of that cattle or to gain control of cattle that Mashingana had withheld for his own use, probably for *lobola*. This of course complicates the notion of gender relations, as it suggests the possibility of alliances between mothers, lovers, and sons against other interested parties.

DANGERS OF THE CITY

Two final cases point up the tension between the efforts of African men and state officials to control the sexuality and mobility of women amid the growing movement of women from country to city and their pursuit of unsanctioned sexual unions. Like the last case, these cases also complicate the notion of gender relations by showing cross-cutting alliances among women, their brothers, and their fathers, who sometimes supported their sisters' and daughters' efforts to escape the control of husbands. In these conflicts, the legal and administrative organs of the state tended to side with husbands, emphasizing their authority over wives.

Mbhele v. Mazibuko: Her Proper Place

This case also involved a man asserting the "permanence" of marriage and his rights over his brother's widow, but it did not concern a claim of an *ukungena* union. In 1933, Nonkovini Mbhele brought a claim in the Estcourt NC Court for the custody of five children of Nobatini Mazibuko, the widow of his brother. After his brother's death Mbhele went to Johannesburg for work. The widow Mazibuko wrote to him there saying she had left the *umuzi* (taking her three children) after a quarrel with his mother. He ordered her to return but she refused. She gave birth to twins while away, and Mbhele claimed, "These children belong to me as the defendant is not divorced."[96] Mazibuko claimed that she had been driven from the *umuzi* and that the plaintiff had sanctioned this on his return. He had done nothing to support the children after she had left. The NC, however, was more interested in the origins of her illegitimate children. Mazibuko, who said that the father was a man she met in Durban, admitted, "I got nobody's permission to go to Durban. . . . I left my children with my father."[97] This testimony ensured an unfavorable ruling from the NC. In awarding custody of the three elder children to the plaintiff, the NC noted, "I might add that in making this order I did so hoping the defendant would return and live at the Plaintiff's kraal which is her proper place of abode until she remarries."[98] An appeal was dismissed with costs. The courts thus discounted the evidence that the woman had been driven away and intervened in an attempt to influence her to return to her "proper place," where she could be properly supervised, as her father was clearly failing to keep her under control.

Mcunu v. Nzuza: Deserting Farms, Deserting Husbands

The image of uncontrollable women escaping to the dangerous environs of the city also surfaced in a 1941 divorce case involving labor tenants in Estcourt.[99] Dingindawu Mcunu, a tenant of T. Lotter's farm, sought a divorce from his wife, Ida Nzuza (duly assisted by Releba Nzuza), a resident of Henderson's farm.[100] He claimed that she had deserted five days after the marriage. She counterclaimed for divorce on the grounds of desertion and refusal to render conjugal rights. Both were represented by counsel.

Dingindawu explained that his wife had left a few days after the wedding, taking his passes. He searched unsuccessfully for her in Durban and Johannesburg. The cross-examining attorney asked a series of questions designed to show that the wife's "desertion" was a conspiracy between the couple to avoid farm service. Mcunu denied this. "I did not tell her that she had to go to Durban and that I would follow her and that I did not want to work on the farm. . . . I am unable to account for the woman taking my passes." [101] But Nzuza affirmed the existence of such a plan:

> I went to Durban because I was told by the Plaintiff to do so because he did not want to work for Mr. Henderson on the farm. Plaintiff said he would follow me. . . . The Plaintiff had often mentioned before the marriage that we should go to Durban. . . . it was arranged that we should meet at the hostel on the Monday.

She claimed that Mcunu duly met her but then returned to his *umuzi* to fetch his things, leaving her in the care of Sgcili Mfeni at the hostel of a Durban dairy. Mcunu did not return. After a month Mfeni contacted Nzuza's brother Sijembe who wrote to Mcunu but received no reply. Sijembe supported her (from his work at the Durban dairy) at his place in Mapumulo, where she went to live. She did not return to her father's place at Van Rooyen's farm in Mooi River even though she admitted, "I know our custom that if a woman is deserted she should return to the kraal of her father."[102] The NC ruled for the husband, Mcunu, granting the divorce with costs and ordering the return of seven head of *lobola* cattle. He ordered Nzuza to reside at her father's *umuzi* "until such time as she is remarried." The child was to remain with Mcunu.[103] Once again, the court proved itself the ally of husbands seeking to control or discipline unruly wives, and the ally of "tradition" in ordering that the wife return to her father. This part of the order was unlikely to be enforceable, however.

As in some of the other cases, it is impossible to determine what "really" happened. While the woman's story of a conspiracy with her husband to escape to Durban is plausible, there is no obvious explanation for his failure to return. However, it is clear that at least one of them, and perhaps both, plotted to emigrate from the country to the city. Although most informants denied that women left the farms as young men were doing from the late 1920s through the 1940s, some admitted that it was common.[104] One man in particular told me, "Women also left the farms, went back home to other farms and cities. Married couples also left in droves."[105] The mobility of women, however, was threatening to the male rural establishment of elders, husbands, farmers, and officials. The NC Courts, which sometimes acted to protect women from the arbitrary acts of men, more often sought to put the lid on the behavior of straying women.

CONCLUSION

Litigation under the Natal Code provides a view of the domestic struggles of labor tenants (and reserve dwellers) that can illuminate the changing meaning and nature of rural gender relations in an era of transition. The transition to a segregated capitalist order was achieved in part by preserving African patriarchal structures in the countryside, but also by hardening those structures in the face of opposition by women and juniors. Officials deemed such a system necessary to constrain social change while at the same time ensuring adequate supplies of compliant workers to both booming industries and struggling white farmers. The colonial customary law regime in Natal, constructed out of an alliance of African elder men and colonizers, saw control of women's productive and reproductive labor as the foundation of social order. Segregation and retribalization gave new urgency to the old ideologies surrounding control of women's bodies. It was essential both for men and for the settler state that women remain on the land and participate in reproduction of the homestead. Just as labor tenant fathers depended on the *isithupa* labor of their sons (primarily) to secure and retain access to land for grazing and crops, male tenant migrants depended on the domestic labor and social reproduction provided by wives. Wayward wives, then, posed a danger to the security and control of labor tenant (and reserve) migrants. Husbands therefore looked to customary law authorities (NCs and *amakhosi*) to restrain wives. As the customary law regime turned to the hardened view of custom indicated by the twins case in chapter 4, the courts tended to be friendly environments for men seeking tightened control of women.

Looking at the cases brought by Africans under this regime, however, shows that the picture was never so simple. To be sure, there was an intensified state ideology of segregation and tribalism, and this is reflected in the rigid views taken by NCs and the appeals court in some cases from the 1930s and 1940s. Even in those cases, however, it is clear that Africans had a very different conception of custom and of customary law from that reflected in the Natal Code. Africans, especially subalterns such as women and juniors, took advantage of the space provided by a westernized adjudication of "customary law" to continuously challenge and contest the nature and meaning of custom. Women thus were active agents, not only through drastic actions such as seeking divorce and fleeing to the city, and everyday forms of resistance such as returning to their "own people," but also through appearing as witnesses and litigants in the NC Courts. The settler colonial project to control African women through institutions such as "customary law" was therefore contradictory and only partly successful. The intensification of that project in the segregation era in many ways reflects the determination of African women and juniors to shape their own destinies and to challenge patriarchal views of custom.

NOTES

1. *Natal Code*, section 27(2).

2. PAR, Chief Native Commissioner (CNC) 110A, 94/19, N1/15/5, Chiefs' Conference, Pietermaritzburg, 31 Jul. 1939, comments of Chief Matole.

3. For comprehensive examinations of women and the law in South Africa, see T.W. Bennett, *A Sourcebook of African Customary Law for Southern Africa* (Cape Town: Juta, 1991); Simons, *African Women: Their Legal Status in South Africa* (London: C. Hurst, 1968).

4. See discussion in chapter 1.

5. See M. Rowlands, "The Zulu Family in Transition: A Study of Some of the Social and Moral Problems of African Adaptation to White Colonial Society As Revealed in the Evidence Led before the Colony of Natal Native Affairs Commission of 1906–7," (B.A. honors thesis, University of Natal, Pietermaritzburg, 1973). Adam Ashforth has shown how commissions of inquiry in South Africa constructed the "native" as a certain type of problem to be dealt with through government policies such as segregation. Ashforth, *The Politics of Official Discourse*. In much the same

way, African male witnesses to these commissions constructed women and youth as problems that they solicited the state's aid in solving.

6. See, e.g., Alan R. Booth, "'European Courts Protect Women and Witches': Colonial Law Courts As Redistributors of Power in Swaziland 1920–1950," *Journal of Southern African Studies*, 18, no. 2 (Jun. 1992): 253–75.

7. SAIRR, AD 1438, NEC Evidence, 6722e, testimony of Nyongwana (emphasis added). African witnesses had made similar complaints fifty years earlier. Natal, *Report of the Natal Native Commission, 1881–82*, para. 14.

8. PAR, CNC 18A, 14/1, N1/12/3, Chiefs' Quarterly Meeting, Port Shepstone, 1936.

9. PAR, CNC 110A, 94/19, N1/15/5, Chiefs' Conference, Pietermaritzburg, 31 Jul. 1939. Divorce was not always easy to obtain in the era of heightened respect for authority, tradition and patriarchy, as we shall see in the case records reviewed below.

10. Cf. Jeater, *Marriage, Perversion and Power*.

11. PAR, CNC 20A, 14/1, N1/12/3, Greytown Mag. to CNC, 23 Apr. 1928.

12. PAR, CNC 108A, 94/2, N1/15/6, Port Shepstone NC to CNC, 12 Aug. 1929; CNC 18A, 14/1, 2/6/3, Ixopo NC to CNC, 1 Sept. 1936.

13. While I am focusing on social relations in the Natal countryside, these processes were reflected across southern and Central Africa in the 1930s. See, e.g., Jeater, *Marriage, Perversion and Power*; Marcia Wright, *Strategies of Slaves and Women: Life Stories from East/Central Africa* (New York: Lilian Barber Press, 1993); Schmidt, *Peasants, Traders and Wives*; Chanock, *Law, Custom and Social Order*.

14. PAR, 1 EST 3/1/2/7, Minutes of Quarterly Meeting of Natives, Location No. 1, 23 Apr. 1936.

15. Cherryl Walker, "Women and Gender in Southern Africa to 1945: An Overview," and Philip Bonner, "'Desirable or undesirable Basotho women?'" both in *Women and Gender*, ed. Walker, 1–33 and 221–50.

16. For discussion of the NSCA, see chapter 3.

17. PAR, 1 EST 3/1/2/7, 2/16, 3A, Minutes of Quarterly Meeting of Natives at Estcourt, 3 Sept. 1936.

18. Central Archives (CA), NTS 7725, 166/333, Johannesburg NC to Director of Native Labour, 27 Jun. 1939. In fact, the state did not succeed in applying pass laws to African women until the late 1950s, and even then the state had to overcome strong organized resistance. See Julia Wells, *We Now Demand! The History of Women's Resistance to Pass Laws in South Africa*, (Johannesburg, Witwatersrand University Press, 1993).

19. "Black Paradise Feared on Rand: Expert Sees Johannesburg as Home of 75 Percent of Union's Natives," *Sunday Express*, 28 May 1939, quoting an anonymous government official. This policy was not the inevitable outcome of capitalist production in Africa. In the Copperbelt of Northern Rhodesia, the mines adopted a policy of attracting a settled workforce by allocating plots to married workers. There were, however, ongoing struggles over what constituted a "real" marriage and rural African fathers sought to end the practice of informal urban marriage in order to assert continued control over daughters and the brideservice of sons-in-law. See George Chauncey, Jr., "The Locus of Reproduction: Women's

Labour in the Zambian Copperbelt, 1927–1953," *Journal of Southern African Studies*, 7, no. 2 (Apr. 1981): 135–64; Jane Parpart, "Sexuality and Power on the Zambian Copperbelt: 1926–1964," in *Patriarchy and Class*, ed. by Sharon Stichter and Jane Parpart (Boulder: Westview Press, 1988), 115–38; Jane Parpart, "The Household and the Mine Shaft: Gender and Class Struggles on the Zambian Copperbelt, 1926–64, *Journal of Southern African Studies*, 13, no. 1 (Oct. 1986): 36–56.

20. Marks, "Patriotism, Patriarchy and Purity." Marks also ties this ideology to the creation of Zulu ethnic consciousness in the 1920s and 1930s.

21. Ibid., 226.

22. Ibid.

23. The first principle named in the 1878 Code was the "subjection of the female sex." See chapter 1.

24. Carolyn Hamilton and John Wright have initiated work in this direction. See, e.g., John Wright and Carolyn Hamilton, "The Making of the Amalala: Ethnicity, Ideology and Relations of Subordination in a Precolonial Context," *South African Historical Journal*, 22 (Nov. 1990): 3–23; Carolyn Hamilton, "Ideology, Oral Tradition and the Struggle for Power in the Early Zulu State" (M.A. thesis, University of the Witwatersrand, 1985); John Wright, "The Dynamics of Power and Conflict in the Thukela-Mzimkhulu Region in the Late 18th and Early 19th Centuries: A Critical Reconstruction" (Ph.D. dissertation, University of the Witwatersrand, 1989).

25. See Bryant, *The Zulu People*; Krige, *The Social System of the Zulus*. Gluckman published an influential structural-functionalist study of Zulu marriage practices, based on fieldwork in Zululand in the mid-1930s. Max Gluckman, "Kinship and Marriage among the Lozi of Northern Rhodesia and the Zulu of Natal," in *African Systems of Kinship and Marriage*, ed. by A.R. Radcliffe-Brown and Daryll Forde, (London: Oxford University Press, 1950), 166–206.

26. For convenience, I will refer in this account to Zulu speakers as "Zulus," although that is, of course, a term with variable referents and connotations over time.

27. Zulu marriage patterns therefore differ significantly from the patrilineal but endogamous system among Tswana described by Comaroff and Roberts, *Rules and Processes*.

28. Harriet Sibisi Ngubane, "Marriage, Affinity and the Ancestral Realm: Zulu Marriage in Female Perspective," in *Essays on African Marriage in Southern Africa*, ed. by Eileen Jensen Krige and John L. Comaroff (Cape Town: Juta, 1981), 84–95.

29. Gluckman, "Kinship and Marriage," 182–85. For a critique of Gluckman's theory of stable marriage, see James L. Gibbs, Jr., "Marital Instability among the Kpelle: Towards a Theory of Epainogamy," *American Anthropologist*, 65, no. 3 (Jun. 1963): 552–73. Gibbs, also working from a structural-functionalist paradigm, argued that a wide range of interdependent features contribute to the stability or instability of marriage systems.

30. Bryant, *Zulu People*, 590–91.

31. Krige, *Social System*, 120–22.

32. Lambert, "The Undermining of the Homestead Economy," 58–59. See also *Natal Code*, Section 87. Fifteen cattle could be transferred as *lobola* for the daugh-

ters of headmen (*izinduna*) or Official Witnesses. There was no limit for the daughters of chiefs. The marriage regulations of 1869 required that the entire amount be transferred prior to formalization of the marriage. Ibid. In the 1920s–1940s, ten head was still the standard *lobola* amount, but marriages were often established with some or all of the *lobola* still owing, and these debts were often the subject of litigation. McClendon, "'Hiding Cattle."

33. Bennett, *African Customary Law*, 176. Cf. Jeater, *Marriage, Perversion and Power*. See also discussion of marriage laws in chapter 1.

34. The Natal Code provided for divorce in Section 76:

(1) An action for divorce in respect of a customary union may be maintained by either partner on any of the following grounds:

(a) Adultery on the part of the other partner.

(b) Continued refusal on the part of the other partner to render conjugal rights.

(c) Wilful [sic] desertion on the part of the other partner.

(d) Continued gross misconduct on the part of the other partner.

(e) The other partner is undergoing a term of imprisonment of not less than five years.

(f) That conditions are such as to render the continuous living together of the partners insupportable or dangerous.

(2) The wife of a customary union may in addition maintain a suit for divorce from her husband by reason of:

(a) gross cruelty or ill-treatment on the part of the husband;

(b) accusations of witchcraft or other serious allegations made against her by the husband.

35. Divorce of Christian or civil marriages (as opposed to customary unions) were heard in the regional Native Divorce Court, which, however, could not rule on subsidiary issues such as bridewealth and custody of children. Native Administration Act of 1927.

36. John Lambert, "Africans in Natal," 42, citing *The James Stuart Archive*, 3, ed. by J.B. Wright and C. de B. Webb, (Pietermaritzburg: University of Natal Press, 1982), 133.

37. "The dissolution of an [sic] customary union by divorce, except when decreed at the suit of a wife by reason of the wrongful acts, misdeeds or omissions of the husband, must be accompanied by the return of at least one beast or its equivalent by the father or protector of the woman to the husband." *Natal Code*, Section 81, quoted in Stafford, *Native Law*, 81.

38. There is some dispute whether "lineage" is a meaningful category in the context of southern Africa. See Kuper, *Wives for Cattle*, 43–58. I am using it here merely as a shorthand for the wife's natal homestead, which could be a confusing expression in matters dealing with the province of Natal.

39. See, e.g., interview with Bettina Dladla. Gluckman states that divorce in Zululand was very rare in the 1930s. Gluckman, "Kinship and Marriage," 180–81.

40. Interview with Paulina Nzuza, Nottingham Road, 3 Mar. 1992; see also interview with Khumalo, Weenen, 13 Aug. 1992.

41. Interview with MaMazane Mchunu, Mpofana, 28 Oct. 1992.

42. PAR, 1 HWK 2/1/2/1, Case 9/1932, *Ngubane v. Mtshali.*

43. Nomkosi was "illegitimate" and hence her legal guardian was her maternal uncle.

44. *Ngubane v. Mtshali*, testimony of Senzakabi Ngubane.

45. Ibid., testimony of Nomkosi Ntshali. She was concerned to mention this in order to prove that she was not sterile. On a level of litigation strategy, the three pregnancies insulated at least three of the lobola cattle from being returned.

46. Ibid., testimony of Gilimu Ngubane.

47. Ibid., judgment.

48. Ibid., Native Appeals Court Case 18/1 of 1932. The NAC dismissed the appeal with costs.

49. Cf. Schmidt, *Peasants, Traders, and Wives*, 7–8.

50. Interview with Boy Ndlovu. Interview with Mzumeni Myaka contains similar comments.

51. PAR, 1 EST 2/1/2/1, Case 53/1939, *Dhlamini v. Dhlamini.*

52. An informant confirmed that a cow given to a woman by, in this case, her father, belonged to her along with the increase. Interview with Mchunu women, Mchunu-1, Weenen, 13 Aug. 1992.

53. PAR, 1 WEN 2/1/2/1, *Mkize v. Ngqalanga*, Case 31/1940. Technically, she petitioned for dissolution of customary union, since only civil and Christian unions were recognized as "marriage" terminable by "divorce" under the 1927 Native Administration Act. Bennett, *African Customary Law*, 204. Customary marriage is now recognized as "marriage" as a result of post-apartheid legislation, The Recognition of Customary Marriages Act, no. 120 of 1998.

54. See chapter 1 for a discussion of the prevalence of lawyers in the NC Court records.

55. *Natal Code*, Section 78.

56. The bill of costs due from the wife to the husband's attorney was seven pounds, twelve shillings, and six pence, equivalent to the value of at least two cows or fifteen months of rural wages earned by a woman; it is likely that she owed a similar amount to her own attorney. Litigation in the NC Courts was an expensive prospect for those who lost, and therefore a risky undertaking. It is likely that the wife would have been assisted by "her people" to pay the costs; it is also likely that such large bills of costs resulted in the creation of a debt to the litigant's attorney or perhaps the farm owner. For evidence of labor tenant debts, see chapter 2.

57. *Mkize v. Ngqalanga*, testimony of Velemsuti Mkize.

58. This was the gravest insult that could be directed at a woman, suggesting sexual relations between herself and her father-in-law. Krige, *Social System*, 31. In this instance, the insult appears to imply sexual relations between the woman and her own father, but this may result from the ambiguity of the *isiZulu* word *baba*, which is generally used to refer to elder or respected males.

59. *Mkize v. Ngqalanga*, testimony of Hlupizwe Ngqalanga.

60. Ngqalanga denied this, stating that they merely shared the same *isibongo*. This dispute reflects the ambiguity of the concept of "brother," which has a broad

set of possible referents in southern African cultures and languages compared to standard English usage. See Kuper, *Wives for Cattle*; Krige, *Social System*. The dispute also reflects the possibility of confusion and manipulation in courtroom translation.

61. *Mkize v. Ngqalanga*, testimony of Mayizekanye Canco.

62. Interviews with MaMajozi Sithole and Bachithile Mchunu, Mpofana, 28 Oct. 1992.

63. Interview with Nunu Thusi, Waaihoek, 12 Aug. 1992.

64. Interview with Nomgqhigqho Mbata (source of this quote) and Nozimpi Sithole, Mkolombe, Weenen, 12 Mar. 1992.

65. Furthermore, medicines (*imithi*) are commonly administered to the body with a sharp instrument, such as a porcupine quill. Nelson Ntshangase, personal communication, Pietermaritzburg, 1992.

66. Men in Weenen had opposed this ground of divorce when it was introduced, as they feared it would "be the cause of endless divorces . . . as soon as a woman wanted a divorce she would state that her husband had accused her of witchcraft. PAR, CNC 18A, 2/5/3, Weenen NC to CNC, 11 Nov. 1932.

67. Ralph Austen, "The Moral Economy of Witchcraft: An Essay in Comparative History," in *Modernity and Its Malcontents: Ritual and Power in Postcolonial Africa*, ed. by Jean Comaroff and John Comaroff (Chicago: University of Chicago Press, 1993), 90.

68. My comments on witchcraft arise from my understanding of Zulu marriage patterns, outlined above, combined with the specific ethnography in Axel-Ivar Berglund, *Zulu Thought-Patterns and Symbolism* (Bloomington: Indiana University Press, 1989). A classic text on witchcraft that informs Berglund is E.E. Evans-Pritchard, *Witchcraft, Oracles, and Magic among the Azande* (Oxford: Clarendon Press, 1976).

69. Berglund, *Zulu Thought-Patterns*, 266–68, 304. The presence of "faction fighting" exacerbated these tensions. The Weenen area has been periodically wracked by so-called "faction fighting" since the late nineteenth century. See Clegg, "'*Ukubuyisa Isidumbu*,'" 184–98. When a man has a wife who comes from an *isigodi* with which his *isigodi* is fighting, he is concerned about the timing and frequency of his wife's visits to "her people" lest she be used to carry harmful *umuthi* (medicine) to his homestead. One of my informants in a neighboring district forbade his second wife to return to his home from her visit to her family for the duration of a "war" in 1992 for exactly this reason. S. Zulu, personal communication, 1992. For discussion of "faction fights" and "wars" in rural Natal, see chapter 4.

70. Berglund, *Zulu Thought-Patterns*, 271.

71. Richard Roberts, "Text and testimony." See discussion in chapter 1.

72. Chanock, *Law, Custom*, 85–102; Timothy Lane, "'Pernicious Practice': Witchcraft Eradication and History in Northern Province, South Africa, c.1880–1930," Ph.D. dissertation, Stanford University: 1999, 157–211.

73. Many tenants also experienced violence in the form of farmers' discipline. One informant stressed beatings by white farmers as a cause of both young men and young women leaving the farm. Interview with Mfuthunza Chonco, Nottingham Road, 21 May 1992. Cf. Charles Van Onselen, "The Social and Eco-

nomic Underpinning of Paternalism and Violence on the Maize Farms of the South-Western Transvaal, 1900–1950," *Journal of Historical Sociology*, 5, no. 2 (Jun. 1992): 127–60.

74. The case, incidentally, illustrates the prevalence of polygynous marriage in this time and region. Interviews confirmed that polygyny was common at the time and indeed remains common in the thornveld. Litigants never explicitly cited the taking of another wife, or disputes between wives, as causes of divorce. Cf. Parpart, "Sexuality and Power," 128. I asked several female informants about their attitudes concerning polygyny but received only guarded responses that tended to assert that the institution was traditional and could not be questioned. "I was fine [after my husband took a second wife], and was still loyal, as my father had told me." Interview with Domby Phungula. Another informant put it this way: "I couldn't do anything, because he loved her." Interview with Nocokololo Masoga. She noted that she got along very well with her co-wife. However, the husband eventually left the farm and went to the location with the second wife, leaving Masoga and her daughter on the farm. When the daughter married, Masoga had to leave the farm. Ibid. Finally, an anonymous female informant stated, "It's a nice thing because people from long ago practised it—we were born whilst it was there—and they practised it while they were having nothing." Interview with Mchunu women, comments of Mchunu-1.

75. PAR, 1 WEN 2/1/2/1, *Ngubane v. Langa*, Case 23/1941.

76. There were similar tensions in this period in western Tanzania over the issue of wives returning "home" while their husbands were absent on migrant labor. See Margot Lovett, "On Power and Powerlessness: Marriage and Political Metaphor in Colonial Western Tanzania," in *International Journal of African Historical Studies*, 27, no. 2 (1994): 292–93.

77. Although the case says nothing directly about labor tenancy, it revolves around the husband's journey to Johannesburg, reminding us that labor tenancy was a form of migrant labor and that farm work was only half of the migration cycle for male tenants.

78. Ngubane's payment of an *nquthu* beast, along with the ten *lobola* cattle, signaled Langa's presumptive virginity prior to his relationship with her. Issues of control of sexuality were congruent with fears about witchcraft, although sorcery, the use of medicine for evil purposes, was a separate issue. See Berglund, *Zulu Thought-Patterns*, 268.

79. *Ngubane v. Langa*, judgment.

80. Gluckman, "Kinship and Marriage."

81. Krige, *Social System*, 182. *Ukungena* was also covered by the Natal Code: Section 1 provides in relevant part:

(s) 'Ukungena' means a union with a widow undertaken on behalf of her deceased husband by his full or half brother or other paternal male relative for the purpose (i) in the event of her having no male issue by the deceased husband of raising an heir to inherit the property or property rights attaching to the house of such widow or (ii) in the event of her having such male issue of increasing the nominal offspring of the deceased.

Section 71 states:

The essentials of ukungena are:

(a) that the union be contracted for one or other of the purposes specified in the definition of ukungena under section one;

(b) that the union be entered into with the free consent of the woman;

(c) that it be a family arrangement, entered into with the approval of the family head. . . .

(d) that no lobola be paid in respect of the union.

72. The offspring of an ukungena rank as if they were in fact children of the deceased husband.

73. An ukungena may at any time be dissolved by either party.

82. Cf. Comaroff and Roberts, *Rules and Processes.*

83. PAR, 1 HWK 2/1/2/1, Case 6/1937, *Radebe v. Mazibela.*

84. Litigants in nondivorce cases could bring their cases either to a chief (or *induna*) or to the NC Court. The losing party in the chief's court had the right to appeal to the NC. Those who did so sometimes complained of bias on the part of the *induna*. Interview with Mfuthunza Chonco.

85. *Radebe v. Mazibela*, testimony of George Mazibela. I note that this is not one of the purposes recognized by the statute, but it was supported by another witness and was not disputed by any of the witnesses or even by the NC.

86. Ibid., testimony of Aaron Radebe. Aaron had adopted the *isibongo* Radebe after he learned that his father was a Radebe, not a Mazibela, despite being a member of the Mazibela *umuzi.*

87. *Radebe v. Mazibela*, testimony of Nanana Kunene.

88. See Sheila Meintjes, "Family and Gender in the Christian Community at Edendale, Natal, in Colonial Times," in *Women and Gender*, ed. by Walker, 140–43.

89. *Radebe v. Mazibela*, testimony of Buleki Zaca (emphasis added).

90. Ibid., testimony of George Mazibela. The *isiZulu* word for Christian is now standardized as *kholwa.*

91. PAR, 1 HWK 2/1/2/1, Case 16/1944, *Zondi v. Zondi.*

92. Ibid., opening statement of Mr. Howard.

93. For the houses in a Zulu *umuzi* see Krige, *Social System*, 39–43, 177–82.

94. *Zondi v. Zondi*, testimony of Mampunya Zondi.

95. Ibid.

96. PAR, 1 EST 2/1/2/1, *Mbhele v. Mazibuko*, Case 62/1933, testimony of Nonkovini Mbhele. This case was among residents of Location No. 2, Estcourt, and did not involve labor tenants. The common factor of male migrancy, however, gave rise to similar issues over the control of women in the reserves.

97. Ibid., testimony of Nobatini Mazibuko.

98. The illegitimate twins were allowed to remain with their mother during their infancy, as was common.

99. PAR, 1 EST 2/1/2/1, *Mcunu v. Nzuza*, Case 120/1941.

100. These were adjoining farms in Mooi River in the Estcourt district. Ibid., testimony of Dingindawu Mcunu.

101. Ibid.

102. Ibid., testimony of Ida Nzuza

103. The bill of costs to plaintiff's attorney was a staggering ten pounds, nine-teen shillings, and six pence. Ibid., judgment.

104. For a typical denial that women left the farms, see interviews with Paulina Nzuza and Boy Ndlovu.

105. Interviews with John Dladla and Sukengani Ndlovu, Nottingham Road 18 May 1992.

6

CONCLUSION

African tenants on white-owned farms in Central Natal experienced profound transformations as a result of changing economic, political, and social forces in the second quarter of the twentieth century. The social organization of African communities in this region, combined with the competing interests involved in labor tenant arrangements and the accelerating industrialization of the South African economy, helped ensure that rural Africans' understanding of these changes divided partly along lines of gender and generation. At the same time, the South African state attempted to control social change unleashed by widespread economic and cultural transformations through the vehicle of a customary law regime administered by the NAD. That regime attempted to restrain change by reinforcing and harnessing traditional hierarchies. Ironically, the trial courts charged with hearing customary law cases became venues for debates over custom and challenges to tradition even as they attempted to enforce a newly rigid and hierarchical version of "native custom."

By the 1940s, labor tenancy persisted in a form remarkably similar to what had emerged in the late nineteenth century, but it was under considerable strain as a result of growing tensions within labor tenant families. From the late 1920s through the early 1940s, nearly all former rent tenants were transformed into labor tenants, greatly reducing their independence from landlords. In addition, the expansion of production on white farms led, albeit unevenly, to a reduction in tenants' access to land for cultivation and especially for grazing. This loss of privileges combined with the existence of new economic and social opportunities in South Africa's rapidly expanding urban areas to exacerbate the intrafamilial tensions that were inherent to the system. The central point of friction was that *abanumzane* gained access to land on white farms by supplying the labor of their sons and daughters and relied on the labor of wives to maintain the homestead while men were absent at work on farms, and in the "off" months, in cities.

This tiered contract increased the sensitivity of *abanumzane* to the independence displayed by tenants' daughters, sons, and wives as they migrated to urban jobs, failed to return after their "off" months, left unsatisfactory marriages, or refused to enter into *ukungena* arrangements. At the same time, white farmer-landlords were increasingly vocal about the hemorrhage of labor to urban areas, and they asked for increasingly draconian regulations while often, ironically, declining to enforce them because of their own need for flexible labor supplies. Farmers were also divided between "progressives" committed to efficient, modern styles of management and production and the bulk of undercapitalized farmers, who managed only through the flexibility offered by the six-month system.

At the same time, the state and conservative alliances of business and "traditional" leaders were attempting, through the broad policy of segregation, to deflect the threat posed by the growth of an urban proletariat and eruptions of rural radicalism. They hoped to contain social upheaval by imposing a vision of orderly and hierarchical tradition on the African countryside. One arm of this policy was the Unionwide recognition of customary law. Like the institution of labor tenancy, the customary law regime in Natal in the segregation era retained the form it had assumed in the nineteenth century, but it operated in the changed circumstances of radically altered social and economic conditions. Litigation in the NC Courts from this era reflects the state's attempt to enforce a hardened and inflexible concept of custom. Simultaneously, it shows the continuing attempt of African litigants to redefine custom and to use the colonial institution of the NC Courts to seek ends not imagined by colonizers or functionaries of the settler state.

My explorations in this book have only made a beginning toward understanding the social history of labor tenancy and the operation of the customary law regime in Natal and other regions of South Africa. We need to know much more about the precolonial intersections of land, labor, gender, and generation in order to understand more fully their operation in the colonial situation. Considerable further research is also needed on the construction of the customary law regime in the nineteenth century. For the twentieth century, our understanding will be enhanced by studies that are able to gain from lengthy periods of participant-observation fieldwork, in which my efforts were limited by the constraints of war and suspicion in the dying days of apartheid South Africa. It will also widen our perspective to have other studies that make extensive in-depth use of NC Court records to generate more nuanced understandings of South Africa's social histories. Despite these qualifications, this book has made some important advances in our understanding of labor tenancy and customary law in the segregation era. Most significant, it has shown that gender and generational dynamics were at the heart of this history. In addition, it has shown that despite the tragic destruction of most NC Court records, the surviving records offer valuable insights—not available in such detail from any other contemporary source—into the complex lives of labor tenants and other rural Africans. They show, furthermore, that despite the array of forces that sought to confine and define tenant lives, African women and men continued to create their own histories, though not, as Marx reminds us, in conditions of their own choosing.

Although South Africa changed dramatically in the first half of the twentieth century, labor tenancy remained the most important system of agricultural labor in the Natal interior. Tenants complained about poor wages and conditions, and commercial farmers decried the system's inefficiency, but labor tenancy continued to offer redeeming advantages to both tenants and farmers. Indeed, the migration of rural youth threatened the system much more seriously than did its supposed inefficiency; the system was remarkably successful in supplying a reliable and flexible source of cheap skilled labor. The six-month system endured through the first half of the apartheid era with relatively little change, as the National Party's rise to power in 1948 resulted in sharply strengthened enforcement of pass systems, enabling farmers to gain tighter control over tenant laborers. The system therefore persisted until mechanization enabled farmers and the state to combine to expel "surplus" tenants beginning in the late 1960s. Many of these former tenants are now seeking to return to land that they say belongs to them by virtue of generations of work and residence. From "the time of GG," labor tenancy was a changed system; usually requiring tenants to work full time rather than *isithupa*.

The apartheid years brought a renewed commitment to the customary law regime, formalizing the settler state's alliance with the chiefly class while adding new layers of bureaucracy in newly created "homeland" governments. From the early 1950s, the Nationalists began to implement legislation giving increasing power to "Bantu Authorities," leading to the homeland system of the 1970s. The ideologues of apartheid had limited success with this plan. It brought four of the ten homeland governments to "independence" (never recognized beyond South Africa), but the youth revolt of 1976 that coincided with the year of Transkei's independence heralded apartheid's eventual demise. In the then Natal province, the Kwazulu homeland government at first walked a fine line between doing the bidding of Pretoria and spearheading cultural resistance through its ruling Inkatha Freedom Party (IFP), which adopted the symbols of the exiled ANC. Under apartheid's bizarre jurisdictional divisions, Natal was carved into a jigsaw puzzle of "homeland" and "white" areas. The war that raged in Natal from the mid-1980s until 1994, superficially pitting adherents of the ANC (and its aboveground ally, the United Democratic Front [UDF]) against followers of the IFP, had many dimensions. Some of these involved ideological disagreements; others reflected differences of class and level of integration into urban political economies. One dimension was a struggle of those disadvantaged by traditional-cum-apartheid hierarchies against those seeking to maintain, strengthen, and enforce those structures in the face of social and political upheaval.[1] It was the very intensity of the struggle of the late 1980s and early 1990s in this region that led me to focus on the question of gender and generational divides among labor tenant families in the precursive era of segregation.

Divisions of gender and generation, as well as the more concrete issues of customary law and tenant labor, have continued to be important issues in the new South Africa, following the negotiated end of apartheid and dawn of democratic government in 1994. Leaving aside the postwar traumas of appalling levels of rape, murder, and mayhem, continued unemployment, and the tragic devastation of AIDS, the political compromise that produced South Africa's permanent constitution in 1996 has left open some of the central issues raised by this study. These include land tenure and the place of indigenous traditions in a liberal state—issues that are very widespread in postcolonial Africa.[2] The government has attempted to deal with issues of land and farm labor through a variety of legislative and bureaucratic measures encompassing restitution of land that was taken under apartheid regulations, distribution of some rural land to aspirant peasant farmers, and providing for the secure tenure of labor tenants.[3] Although the government has enacted legislation providing for labor tenant security, some commentators have doubted whether it will succeed in reforming farm labor any more than the failed efforts of previous eras.[4] In carrying out reforms, the government has been severely limited by the Constitution's recognition of private property and by revenue constraints, as well as by the prevailing neoliberal climate of world politics that restrains state spending and intervention in favor of capitalist enterprise and free trade. South African news articles in recent years indicated concern over the failure of South African land reform efforts to spend their full budgets, while the political turmoil over land invasions on Zimbabwe's white-owned farms led to a renewed sense of urgency over the land question in South Africa.

The question of customary law poses an even more central conceptual and practical contradiction in post-apartheid South Africa. The Constitution aspires to a rights-centered democracy, with a sweeping guarantee of equality, but it also seeks to respect indigenous and minority cultural practices. Central to the constitution's Bill of Rights is the Equality Clause, which contains specific prohibitions against unfair discrimination on the grounds of race, gender, or culture, among a long list of other attributes. There is a stark potential conflict between the Equality Clause, however, and the Constitution's recognition of customary law. The Constitution requires, in an ambiguous phrase that only a lawyer could create or love, "[t]he courts must apply customary law when that law is applicable."[5] In addition, it provides that everyone has the right to "participate in the cultural life of their choice," and it recognizes "traditional leaders."[6] It is not clear how South African courts will ultimately reconcile the enlightened conceptions of the constitution with the patriarchal outlook of its colonial tradition of customary law and chiefly governance. Customary law, as a product of colonial exploitations and appropriations of premodern norms, is based on inequalities, especially inequalities of gender. The codifiers of customary law in Natal, we should recall, declared that the most basic principle of that law was "the subjugation of women." While this was demonstrably a distortion, that characterization gave shape to the customary law that South Africans have inherited. This is not simply a legal issue; it is a political issue that reflects South Africa's tangled historical legacy of a dual legal system and multiple levels of discrimination alongside changing notions of universal principles.

How then should South Africans approach the question of customary law in the context of a new constitutional dispensation that guarantees equality to all citizens? Is customary law simply a relic of segregation and apartheid that should be thrown out, baby with bathwater? How can notions of democracy and equality be reconciled with an incorporated legal system based on hierarchy and "decentralized despotism"? My historical investigations suggest that courts and law commissions should be open to a wider range of voices in deciding principles and issues of customary law. A first step in reforming customary law is to recognize its colonial heritage and listen to alternative versions of the customary.

NOTES

1. See Catherine Campbell, "Learning to Kill? Masculinity, the Family and Violence in Natal," *Journal of Southern African Studies*, 18, no. 3 (Sept. 1992): 614–28.
2. Mamdani, *Citizen and Subject*.

3. E.g., Land Reform (Labour Tenants) Act, No. 3 of 1996; and Extension of Security of Tenure Act, No. 62 of 1997.

4. Gavin Williams, "Transforming Labour Tenants," in *Land, Labour and Livelihoods in Rural South Africa. Vol. 2, Kwazulu/ Natal and Northern Province*, ed. by M. Lipton et al. (Durban: Indicator Press, 1996), 215–38.

5. Constitution of the Republic of South Africa, 1996, Section 211 (3).

6. Ibid., Sections 30–31 and Chapter 12.

BIBLIOGRAPHY

GOVERNMENT ARCHIVES

Central Archives Depot (CA), Pretoria

Native Economic Commission (NEC)
Native Farm Labor Committee (NFLC)
Department of Native Affairs (NTS)
Department of Justice (JUS)
Governor-General (URU)

Pietermaritzburg Archives Repository (PAR)

Chief Native Commissioner
Estcourt Magistrate and Native Commissioner
Lions River Magistrate and Native Commissioner
New Hanover Magistrate and Native Commissioner
Umvoti Magistrate and Native Commissioner
Weenen Magistrate and Native Commissioner

OFFICIAL PUBLICATIONS

Annual Departmental Reports (Abridged), Department of Agriculture. U.G. 1922–U.G. 1927.
Cape of Good Hope. *Commission on Native Laws and Customs*. 1883.
Census of Population, 5th May, 1936: Preliminary Report.
Farming in South Africa, annual reports of the Secretary for Agriculture, 1927–1950.
Industrial and Agricultural Requirements Commission. *Third Interim Report*. U.G. 40-1941.
Interim Report of the Drought Investigation Commission. U.G. 20-1922.

Natal Code of Native Law. Johannesburg: University of Witwatersrand Press, 1945.

Natal Parks Board. *Visitors' Guide, Weenen Nature Reserve.* n.d.

Ordinances and Laws of Natal, 2, 1870–1878.

Ordinances and Laws of Natal, 5, 1890–1898.

Population Census, 1951.

Proceedings and Report of the Commission Appointed to Inquire into the Past and Present State of the Kafirs in the District of Natal. Natal Colony: 1853.

Report on the Agricultural and Pastoral Production of the Union of South Africa, Agricultural Census. U.G. 1922–U.G. 1950.

Report of the Land and Agricultural Bank of South Africa. U.G. 1921–U.G. 1951.

Report of the Commissioners for Locating Natives in this District. Natal: 1847.

Report of the Desert Encroachment Committee. U.G. 59-1951.

Report of the Marketing Act Commission (1947). U.G. 48-1949.

Report of the Natal Native Commission, 1881–82. Natal Colony: 1882.

Report of the National Marketing Council on Marketing Boards 1949 to 1950. U.G. 44-1951.

Report of the Native Affairs Commission for the Year 1921. U.G. 15-1922.

Report of the Native Affairs Department. U.G. 1927–U.G. 1953.

Report of the Native Economic Commission 1930–32. U.G. 22-1932.

Report of the Native Farm Labour Committee 1937–1939.

Report on Distribution of Food. U.G. 31-1946.

Report on the Sixth Census of Population of the Union of South Africa, 5th May, 1936. Age and Marital Condition of the Bantu Population.

Sixth Census. 5th May, 1936, Vol. 9, Natives (Bantu) and Other Non-European Races. U.G. 12-1942.

Social and Economic Planning Council. *First Annual Report for the Year Ended 30th September 1945.* U.G. 38-1945.

Social and Economic Planning Council. *The Economic and Social Conditions of the Racial Groups in South Africa. Report No. 13.* U.G. 53-1948.

Third Census of the Population of the Union of South Africa. U.G. 15-1923.

Third Interim Report of the Industrial and Agricultural Requirements Commission. U.G. 40-1941.

Union Statistics for Fifty Years 1910–1960. Pretoria: Union of South Africa, 1960.

Yearly Report of the Central Board of the Land and Agricultural Bank of South Africa. U.G. 1926–U.G. 1927.

CASES CITED

Dhlamini v. Dhlamini. PAR, 1 EST 2/1/2/1, Case 53/1939.

Koza v. Mapumulo. PAR, 1 EST 2/1/2/1/, Case 106/1943.

Langa v. Mbongwa. PAR, 1 WEN 2/1/2/2, Case 53/1949.

Luvona v. Luvona. PAR, 1 HWK 2/1/2/1, Case 8/1920.

Mabaso v. Mabaso. PAR, 1 EST 2/1/2/1, Case 16/1926.

Madhlala v. Tshangase. PAR, 1 HWK 2/1/2/1, unnumbered case, 1932.

Madondo v. Madondo. PAR, 1 WEN 2/1/2/1, Case 6/1932.

Majola v. Mcunu. PAR, 1 WEN 2/1/2/2, Case 60/1943.
Majozi v. Mude. PAR, 1 NHR 2/1/2/1, Case 18/1935.
Makatini v. Makatini. PAR, 1 IIWK 2/1/2/1, Case 12/1940.
Mazibuko v. Mazibuko. PAR, 1 EST 2/1/2/1, Case 60/1929.
Mbhele v. Mazibuko. PAR, 1 EST 2/1/2/1, Case 62/1933.
Mcunu v. Nzuza. PAR, 1 EST 2/1/2/1, Case 120/1941.
Mfusi v. Mfusi. PAR, 1 EST 2/1/2/1, Case 153/1940.
Mkize v Mcunu. PAR, 1 WEN 2/1/2/1, Case 23/1942.
Mkize v. Mkize. PAR, 1 WEN 2/1/2/1, Case 20/1942.
Mkize v. Ngqalanga. PAR, 1 WEN 2/1/2/1, Case 31/1940.
Mkwanana v. Mkwanasi. PAR, 1 EST 2/1/2/1, Case 28/1928.
Nene v. Ndhlovu. PAR, 1 EST 2/1/2/1, Case 31/1942.
Nene v. Ngqulungu. PAR, 1 WEN 2/1/2/1, Case 18/1936.
Ngcobo v. Zondi. PAR, 1 HWK 2/1/2/2, Case 4/1950.
Ngema v. Ngema. PAR, 1 NHR 2/1/2/1, Case 39/1936.
Ngubane v. Langa. PAR, 1 WEN 2/1/2/1, Case 23/1941.
Ngubane v. Mtshali. PAR, 1 HWK 2/1/2/1, Case 9/1932.
Nsutshu v. Sokela. PAR, 1 HWK 2/1/2/1, Case 22/1930.
Radebe v. Mazibela. PAR, 1 HWK 2/1/2/1, Case 6/1937.
Sitole v. Dhlamini. PAR, 1 EST 2/1/2/2, Case 76/1943.
Sitole v. Sitole. PAR, 1 EST 2/1/2/1, Case 59/1938.
Vilagazi v. Vilagazi. PAR, 1 EST 2/1/2/1, Case 89/1936.
Zondi v. Zondi. PAR, 1 HWK 2/1/2/1, Case 16/1944.
Zuma v. Ndhlovu. PAR, 1 HWK 2/1/2/1, Case 5/1939.
Zuma v. Ntombela. PAR, 1 HWK 2/1/2/1, Case 3/1943.
Zuma v. Sitole. PAR, 1 HWK 2/1/2/1, Case 9/1947.
Zuma v. Zuma. PAR, 1 HWK 2/1/2/1, Case 25/1945.

PRIVATE PAPERS

Faye, C. PAR.
Gold, Henry Callaway. Killie Campbell Africana Library.
Lugg, Henry C. PAR.
Marwick, J.S. Killie Campbell Africana Library.
Natal Agricultural Union Minutes and Resolutions. Natal Agricultural Union.
Nicholls, George Heaton. Killie Campbell Africana Library.
Parkinson, A. H. PAR.
Scofield, J. PAR.
South African Institute of Race Relations. University of the Witwatersrand. Historical Documents.

INTERVIEWS

Chonco, Mfuthunza. Nottingham Road, 21 May 1992.
Dladla, Bettina MaNene. Nottingham Road, 1 Mar. 1992.
Dladla, John. Nottingham Road, 27 Feb. 1992.
Dladla, Mashiya. Keate's Drift, 10 Aug. 1994.

Dladla, Nokwabiwa. Mpofana, 28 Oct. 1992.
Hall, Don. Willow Grange, 18 Feb. 1992.
Haw, John. Willow Grange, 18 Feb. 1992.
Khumalo. Weenen, 13 Aug. 1992.
Masoga, Nocokololo. Mpofana, 29 Oct. 1992.
Mbata, Nomgqhigqho. Weenen, 12 Mar. 1992.
Mchunu, Bachithile. Mpofana, 28 Oct. 1992.
Mchunu, MaMazane. Mpofana, 28 Oct. 1992.
Mchunu, Mgewu. Mpofana, 28 Oct. 1992.
Mchunu, Shupu. Mpofana, 29 Oct. 1992.
Mchunu women. Weenen, 13 Aug. 1992.
Mkhize, Kotayi. Weenen, 11 Mar. 1992.
Myaka, Mzumeni. Keate's Drift, 26 Oct. 1992.
Ndlovu, Boy. Nottingham Road, 18 May 1992.
Ndlovu, Sukengani. Nottingham Road, 18 May 1992.
Ntshaba. Mpofana, 27 Oct. 1992.
Nzuza, Paulina. Nottingham Road, 3 Mar. 1992.
Phungula, Domby MaButhelezi. Nottingham Road, 20 May 1992.
Sithole, MaMajozi. Mpofana, 28 Oct. 1992.
Sithole, Nozimpi. Weenen, 12 Mar. 1992.
Symons, Godfrey. Willow Grange, 18 Feb. 1992.
Thusi, Nunu. Waaihoek, 12 Aug. 1992.
Zamisa, Disemba. Willow Grange, 18 Feb. 1992.

NEWSPAPERS

Cape Times
Ilanga Lase Natal
Natal Mercury
Natal Sunday Post
Natal Witness
Rand Daily Mail
Star
Sunday Express
Sunday Times

PUBLISHED SOURCES (NONGOVERNMENTAL)

Alexander, G.D. "Administration of Agriculture." *Natal Mercury*, 15 Mar. 1938.
Anderson, David. "Depression, Dust Bowl, Demography and Drought: The Colonial
    State and Soil Conservation in East Africa during the 1930s." *African Affairs*,
    83, no. 332 (Jul. 1984): 321–44.
Ashforth, Adam. *The Politics of Official Discourse in Twentieth-Century South Af-
    rica*. Oxford: Clarendon Press, 1990.
Austen, Ralph. "The Moral Economy of Witchcraft: An Essay in Comparative His-
    tory." In *Modernity and Its Malcontents: Ritual and Power in Postcolonial*

Africa, edited by Jean Comaroff and John L. Comaroff. Chicago: University of Chicago Press, 1993.

Ballard, Charles. "Traders, Trekkers and Colonists." In *Natal and Zululand from Earliest Times to 1910: A New History*, edited by Andrew Duminy and Bill Guest, 116–45. Pietermaritzburg: University of Natal Press, 1989.

Beinart, William. "Soil Erosion, Conservationism and Ideas about Development: A Southern African Exploration, 1900–1960." *Journal of Southern African Studies*, 11, no. 1 (Oct. 1984): 52–83.

————. *The Political Economy of Pondoland 1860–1930*. Johannesburg: Ravan Press, 1982.

Beinart, William and Colin Bundy. *Hidden Struggles in Rural South Africa: Politics and Popular Movements in the Transkei and Eastern Cape 1890–1930*. Johannesburg: Ravan Press, 1987.

Beinart, William and Peter Delius. "Introduction." In *Putting a Plough to the Ground: Accumulation and Dispossession in Rural South Africa 1850–1930*, edited by William Beinart, et al., 1–55. Johannesburg: Ravan Press, 1986.

Beinart, William, Peter Delius and Stanley Trapido, eds. *Putting a Plough to the Ground: Accumulation and Dispossession in Rural South Africa 1850–1930*. Johannesburg: Ravan Press, 1986.

Bennett, T.W. *A Sourcebook of African Customary Law for Southern Africa*. Cape Town: Juta, 1991.

Berger, Iris. "'Beasts of Burden' Revisited: Interpretations of Women and Gender in Southern African Societies." In *Paths toward the Past: African Historical Essays in Honor of Jan Vansina*, edited by Robert Harms, et al. Atlanta: African Studies Association Press, 1994.

Berglund, Axel-Ivar. *Zulu Thought-Patterns and Symbolism*. Bloomington: Indiana University Press, 1989.

Berman, Bruce and John Lonsdale. *Unhappy Valley: Conflict in Kenya and Africa. Book One: State and Class*. London: James Currey, 1992.

Berry, Sara. *No Condition Is Permanent: The Social Dynamics of Agrarian Change in Sub-Saharan Africa*. Madison: University of Wisconsin Press, 1993.

————. *Fathers Work for Their Sons: Accumulation, Mobility, and Class Formation in an Extended Yoruba Community*. Berkeley and Los Angeles: University of California Press, 1985.

Blackburn, Douglas. *Leaven: A Black and White Story*. Pietermaritzburg: University of Natal Press, 1991.

Bonner, Philip. "'Desirable or Undesirable Basotho Women?' Liquor, Prostitution and the Migration of Basotho Women to the Rand, 1920–1945." In *Women and Gender in Southern Africa to 1945*, edited by Cherryl Walker, 221–50. Cape Town: David Philip, 1991.

Booth, Alan R. "'European Courts Protect Women and Witches': Colonial Law Courts As Redistributors of Power in Swaziland 1920–1950." *Journal of Southern African Studies*, 18, no. 2 (Jun. 1992): 253–75.

Boserup, Ester. *Woman's Role in Economic Development*. New York: St. Martin's Press, 1970.

Bozzoli, Belinda with the assistance of Mmantho Nkotsoe. *Women of Phokeng: Consciousness, Life Strategy and Migrancy in South Africa, 1900–1983*. Johannesburg: Ravan Press, 1991.

Bozzoli, Belinda. "Marxism, Feminism and Southern African Studies." *Journal of Southern African Studies*, 9, no. 2 (1983): 139–71.

Bozzoli, Belinda and Peter Delius. "Radical History and South African Society." In *History from South Africa*, edited by Belinda Bozzoli and Peter Delius, special issue of *Radical History Review*, 46/7 (Winter 1990): 13–46.

Bradford, Helen. "Women, Gender and Colonialism: Rethinking the History of the British Cape Colony and Its Frontier Zones, c.1806–70" *Journal of African History*, 37, no. 3 (1996): 351–70.

———. "Highways, Byways and Culs-de-Sacs: The Transition to Agrarian Capitalism in Revisionist South African History." In *History from South Africa*, edited by Belinda Bozzoli and Peter Delius, special issue of *Radical History Review*, 46/7 (Winter 1990): 59–88.

———. "Getting Away with Murder: 'Mealie Kings,' the State and Foreigners in the Eastern Transvaal, c.1918–1950." In *Apartheid's Genesis 1935–1962*, edited by Philip Bonner, Peter Delius and Deborah Posel, 96–125. Johannesburg: Ravan Press, 1993.

———. *A Taste of Freedom: The ICU in Rural South Africa 1924–1930*. New Haven: Yale University Press, 1987.

Bryant, A.T. *The Zulu People As They Were before the White Man Came*. Pietermaritzburg: Shuter and Shooter, 1949.

Bundy, Colin. "The Emergence and Decline of a South African Peasantry." *African Affairs*, 71 (1972): 360–88.

———. *The Rise and Fall of the South African Peasantry*. London: Heinemann, 1979.

Burman, Sandra. "Fighting a Two-Pronged Attack: The Changing Legal Status of Women in Cape-Ruled Basutoland, 1872–1884." In *Women and Gender in Southern Africa to 1945*, edited by Cherryl Walker, 48–75. Cape Town: David Philip, 1990.

Campbell, Catherine. "Learning to Kill? Masculinity, the Family and Violence in Natal." *Journal of Southern African Studies*, 18, no. 3 (Sept. 1992): 614–28.

Carton, Benedict. *"Blood from Your Children:" The Colonial Origins of Generational Conflict in South Africa*. Charlottesville: University of Virginia Press, 2000.

———. "'The New Generation . . . Jeer at Me, Saying We Are All Equal Now': Impotent African Patriarchs, Unruly African Sons in South Africa." In *The Politics of Age and Gerontocracy in Africa,* edited by M. Aguilar. Trenton: Africa World Press, 1998.

Cell, John. *The Highest Stage of White Supremacy: The Origins of Segregation in South Africa and the American South*. Cambridge, UK: Cambridge University Press, 1982.

Chanock, Martin. *The Making of South African Legal Culture 1902–1936: Fear, Favour, and Prejudice*. Cambridge, UK: Cambridge University Press, 2001.

———. "A Peculiar Sharpness: An Essay on Property in the History of Customary Law in Colonial Africa." *Journal of African History*, 32, no. 1 (1991): 65–88.

———. "Law, State and Culture: Thinking about 'Customary Law' after Apartheid." In *Acta Juridica: 1991*, 53–70. Cape Town: Juta, 1991.

————. "Writing South African Legal History: A Prospectus." *Journal of African History*, 30, no. 2 (1989): 265–88.

————. *Law, Custom and Social Order: The Colonial Experience in Malawi and Zambia*. Cambridge, UK: Cambridge University Press, 1985.

————. "Making Customary Law: Men, Women and Courts in Colonial Northern Rhodesia." In *African Women and the Law: Historical Perspectives*, edited by Margaret Jean Hay and Marcia Wright, 53–67. Boston: Boston University Papers on Africa, VII, 1982.

Chauncey, George Jr. "The Locus of Reproduction: Women's Labour in the Zambian Copperbelt, 1927–1953." *Journal of Southern African Studies*, 7, no. 2 (Apr. 1981): 135–64.

Clark, Nancy. "The Limits of Industrialisation under Apartheid." In *Apartheid's Genesis 1935–62*, edited by Philip Bonner, Peter Delius and Deborah Posel, 65–95. Johannesburg: Ravan Press, 1993.

Clegg, Jonathan. *"Ukubuyisa Isidumbu*—'Bringing Back the Body': A Study of the Ideology of Vengeance in the Msinga and Mpofana Rural Locations, 1882–1944." In *Working Papers in Southern African Studies*. Vol. 2, edited by Philip Bonner, 164–98. Johannesburg: Ravan Press, 1981.

Clifford, James. *The Predicament of Culture: Twentieth Century Ethnography, Literature and Art*. Cambridge, MA: Harvard University Press, 1988.

Cohen, David William. "A Case for the Basoga: Lloyd Fallers and the Construction of an African Legal System." In *Law in Colonial Africa*, edited by Kristin Mann and Richard Roberts, 239–54 (Portsmouth: Heinemann, 1991).

Comaroff, Jean. *Body of Power, Spirit of Resistance: The Culture and History of a South African People*. Chicago: University of Chicago Press, 1985.

Comaroff, Jean and John L. Comaroff. *Ethnography and the Historical Imagination*. Boulder: Westview Press, 1992.

Comaroff, John and Simon Roberts. *Rules and Processes: The Cultural Logic of Dispute in an African Context*. Chicago: University of Chicago Press, 1981.

Cooper, Frederick and Ann Stoler. "Introduction: Tensions of Empire: Colonial Control and Visions of Rule." *American Ethnologist*, 16 (1989): 609–21.

Cooper, Frederick, et al. *Confronting Historical Paradigms: Peasants, Labor, and the Capitalist World System in Africa and Latin America*. Madison: University of Wisconsin Press, 1993.

Cope, Nicholas. *To Bind the Nation: Solomon kaDinuzulu and Zulu Nationalism 1913–1933*. Pietermaritzburg: University of Natal Press, 1993.

————. "The Zulu Petit Bourgeoisie and Zulu Nationalism in the 1920s: Origins of Inkatha." *Journal of Southern African Studies*, 16, no. 3 (1990): 431–51.

Dangarembga, Tsitsi. *Nervous Conditions: A Novel*. Seattle: Seal Press, 1996.

Delius, Peter. *The Land Belongs to Us: The Pedi Polity, the Boers and the British in the Nineteenth-Century Transvaal*. Berkeley and Los Angeles: University of California Press, 1984.

————. "Migrant Labour and the Pedi, 1840–80." In *Economy and Society in Pre-Industrial South Africa*, edited by Shula Marks and Anthony Atmore, 293–312. New York: Longman, 1980.

Dent, G.R. and C.L.S. Nyembezi, *Scholar's Zulu Dictionary*. Pietermaritzburg: Shuter and Shooter, 1969.

Dinesen, Isak. *Out of Africa*. New York: Vintage International, 1989.

Dubow, Saul. *Scientific Rascism in Modern South Africa*. Cambridge: Cambridge University Press, 1995.

———. *Racial Segregation and the Origins of Apartheid in South Africa, 1919–36*. Houndmills, UK: Macmillan, 1989.

Edwards, Terry. *Seasons of Change: 100 Years of the Natal Agricultural Union*. Pietermaritzburg: Natal Agricultural Union, 1991.

Engels, Frederick. *The Origin of the Family, Private Property and the State*, edited by E. Leacock. New York: International, 1972.

Etherington, Norman. "The 'Shepstone System' in the Colony of Natal and beyond the Borders." In *Natal and Zululand from Earliest Times to 1910: A New History*, edited by Andrew Duminy and Bill Guest, 170–92. Pietermaritzburg: University of Natal Press, 1989.

———. *Preachers, Peasants and Politics in Southeast Africa: African Christian Communities in Natal, Pondoland and Zululand*. London: Royal Historical Society, 1978.

Evans-Pritchard, E.E. *Witchcraft, Oracles, and Magic among the Azande*. Oxford: Clarendon Press, 1976.

Fair, T.J.D. *The Distribution of Population in Natal*. Vol. 3 of *Natal Regional Survey*. Cape Town: Oxford University Press, 1955.

Foner, Eric. *Nothing but Freedom: Emancipation and Its Legacy*. Baton Rouge: Louisiana State University Press, 1984.

Fredrickson, George. *White Supremacy: A Comparative Study in American and South African History*. Oxford: Oxford University Press, 1981.

Freund, Bill. *Insiders and Outsiders: The Indian Working Class of Durban, 1910–1990*. Portsmouth: Heinemann, 1995.

Geiger, Susan. *TANU Women: Gender and Culture in the Making of Tanganyikan Nationalism, 1955–65*. Portsmouth: Heinemann, 1997.

Gibbs, James L., Jr. "Marital Instability among the Kpelle: Towards a Theory of Epainogamy." *American Anthropologist*, 65, no. 3 (Jun. 1963): 552–73.

Glassman, Jonathon. *Feasts and Riot: Revelry, Rebellion, and Popular Consciousness on the Swahili Coast, 1856–1888*. Portsmouth: Heinemann, 1995.

Gluckman, Max. "Kinship and Marriage among the Lozi of Northern Rhodesia and the Zulu of Natal." In *African Systems of Kinship and Marriage*, edited by A.R. Radcliffe-Brown and Daryll Forde, 166–206. London: Oxford University Press, 1950.

Guest, Bill. "Colonists, Confederation and Constitutional Change." In *Natal and Zululand from Earliest Times to 1910: A New History*, edited by Andrew Duminy and Bill Guest, 146–69. Pietermaritzburg: University of Natal Press, 1989.

———. "Towards responsible government, 1879–93." In *Natal and Zululand from Earliest Times to 1910: A New History*, edited by Andrew Duminy and Bill Guest, 233–48. Pietermaritzburg: University of Natal Press, 1989.

Guy, Jeff. "Gender Oppression in Southern Africa's Precapitalist Societies." In *Women and Gender in Southern Africa to 1945*, edited by Cherryl Walker, 33–47. Cape Town: David Philip, 1990.

———. "The Destruction and Reconstruction of Zulu Society." In *Industrialisation and Social Change in South Africa: African Class Formation, Culture and*

Consciousness 1870–1930, edited by Shula Marks and Richard Rathbone, 167–94. London: Longman, 1979.

Guyer, Jane and Pauline Peters, eds. Introduction to *Conceptualizing the Household: Issues of Theory and Policy in Africa*. Special issue of *Development and Change*, 18 (1987): 197–214.

Hamilton, Carolyn. *Terrific Majesty: The Powers of Shaka Zulu and the Limits of Historical Invention*. Cambridge, MA: Harvard University Press, 1998.

Harries, Patrick. *Work, Culture and Identity: Migrant Laborers in Mozambique and South Africa, c.1860–1910*. Portsmouth: Heinemann, 1994.

Harris, V.S. *Land, Labour and Ideology: Government Land Policy and the Relations between Africans and Whites on the Land in Northern Natal 1910–1936*. Pretoria: Archives Yearbook 1, 1991.

Hart, Gillian. "Imagined Unities: Constructions of 'The Household' in Economic Theory." In *Understanding Economic Process*, edited by Sutti Ortiz and Susan Lees, 111–29. Lanham, MD: University Press of America, 1992.

———. "Engendering Everyday Resistance: Gender, Patronage and Production Politics in Rural Malaysia." *Journal of Peasant Studies*, 19, no. 1 (1991): 93–121.

Hay, Margaret Jean and Marcia Wright, eds. *African Women and the Law: Historical Perspectives*. Boston: Boston University Papers on Africa, 7, 1982.

Henige, David. *The Chronology of Oral Tradition: Quest for a Chimera*. Oxford: Clarendon Press, 1974.

Henn, Jeanne Koopman. "The Material Basis of Sexism: A Mode of Production Analysis." In *Patriarchy and Class*, edited by Sharon B. Stichter and Jane L. Parpart. Boulder: Westview Press, 1988.

Hurwitz, N. *Agriculture in Natal 1860–1950*. Vol. 12 of *Natal Regional Survey*. Cape Town: Oxford University Press, 1957.

Jeater, Diana. *Marriage, Perversion and Power: The Construction of Moral Discourse in Southern Rhodesia 1894–1930*. Oxford: Clarendon Press, 1993.

Jeeves, Alan and Jonathan Crush. *White Farms, Black Labor: The State and Agrarian Change in Southern Africa, 1910–50*. Portsmouth: Heinemann, 1997.

Kanogo, Tabitha. *Squatters and the Roots of Mau Mau*. London: James Currey, 1987.

Keegan, Timothy J. *Facing the Storm: Portraits of Black Lives in Rural South Africa*. Cape Town: David Philip, 1988.

———. *Rural Transformations in Industrializing South Africa: The Southern Highveld to 1914*. Johannesburg: Ravan Press, 1986.

Kidder, Robert. "Western Law in India: External Law and Local Response." In *Social System and Legal Process*, edited by Harry M. Johnson. San Francisco: Jossey-Bass, 1978.

Krige, Eileen J. *The Social System of the Zulus*. Pietermaritzburg: Shuter & Shooter, 1950.

Krikler, Jeremy. *Revolution from Above, Rebellion from Below*. Oxford: Clarendon Press, 1993.

Kuper, Adam. *Wives for Cattle: Bridewealth and Marriage in Southern Africa*. London: Routledge & Kegan Paul, 1982.

Lacey, Marian. *Working for Boroko: The Origins of a Coercive Labour System in South Africa*. Johannesburg: Ravan Press, 1981.

Ladurie, Emmanuel Le Roy. *Montaillou: The Promised Land of Error*. New York: Vintage Books, 1979.

La Hausse, Paul. "Oral History and South African Historians." In *History from South Africa*, edited by Belinda Bozzoli and Peter Delius, special issue of *Radical History Review*, 46/7 (Winter 1990): 346–56.

———. "'The Cows of Nongoloza': Youth, Crime and Amalaita Gangs in Durban, 1900–36." *Journal of Southern African Studies*, 16, no. 1 (Mar. 1990): 79–111.

Lambert, John. *Betrayed Trust: Africans and the State in Colonial Natal*. Scottsville: University of Natal Press, 1995.

———. "The Undermining of the Homestead Economy in Colonial Natal." *South African Historical Journal*, 23 (1990): 54–73.

———. "From Independence to Rebellion: African Society in Crisis, c.1880–1910." In *Natal and Zululand from Earliest Times to 1910: A New History*, edited by Andrew Duminy and Bill Guest, 373–401. Pietermaritzburg: University of Natal Press, 1989.

Lovett, Margot. "On Power and Powerlessness: Marriage and Political Metaphor in Colonial Western Tanzania." *International Journal of African Historical Studies*, 27, no. 2 (1994): 272–302.

Loudon, J.B. *White Farmers and Black Labour-Tenants: A Study of a Farming Community in the South African Province of Natal*. Cambridge, UK: African Studies Center, 1970.

Mamdani, Mahmood. *Citizen and Subject: Contemporary Africa and the Legacy of Late Colonialism*. Princeton: Princeton University Press, 1996.

Mann, Kristin and Richard Roberts, eds. *Law in Colonial Africa*. Portsmouth: Heinemann, 1991.

Marais, J.S. "Editorial: Activities of the Food Control Organization." *Farming in South Africa*, 27, no. 201 (Dec. 1942): 753–55.

Marks, Shula. "Patriotism, Patriarchy and Purity: Natal and the Politics of Zulu Ethnic Consciousness." In *The Creation of Tribalism in Southern Africa*, edited by Leroy Vail, 215–40. Berkeley: University of California Press, 1989.

———. *The Ambiguities of Dependence in South Africa: Class, Nationalism, and the State in Twentieth Century Natal*. Baltimore: Johns Hopkins University Press, 1986.

———. *Reluctant Rebellion: The 1906–08 disturbances in Natal*. Oxford: Clarendon Press, 1970.

Mason, John. "Hendrik Albertus and His Ex-Slave Mey: A Drama in Three Acts." *Journal of African History*, 31, no. 3 (1990): 423–46.

McClendon, Thomas. "'Hiding Cattle on the White Man's Farm': Cattle Loans and Commercial Farms in Natal, 1930–1950." *African Economic History*, 25 (1997): 43–58.

———. "'A Dangerous Doctrine': Twins, Ethnography, and Inheritance in Colonial Africa." *Journal of Legal Pluralism*, 39 (1997): 121–40.

———. "Tradition and Domestic Struggle in the Courtroom: Customary Law and the Control of Women in Segregation-Era Natal," *International Journal of African Historical Studies*, 28, no. 3 (1995): 527–61.

McKittrick, Meredith. *To Dwell Secure: Generation, Christianity, and Colonialism in Ovamboland.* Portsmouth: Heinemann, 2002.

Meillassoux, Claude. "The 'Economy' in Agricultural Self-Sustaining Societies: A Preliminary Analysis." In *Relations of Production: Marxist Approaches to Economic Anthropology,* edited by David Seddon, 127–57. London: Frank Cass, 1978.

———. "From Production to Reproduction: A Marxist Approach to Economic Anthropology." *Economy and Society,* 1, no. 1 (1972): 93–105.

Meintjes, Sheila. "Family and Gender in the Christian Community at Edendale, Natal, in Colonial Times." In *Women and Gender in Southern Africa to 1945,* ed. by Cherryl Walker. Cape Town: David Philip, 1990.

Merry, Sally Engle. "Law and Colonialism." *Law and Society Review,* 25, no. 4 (1991): 889–922.

Miles, Miranda and Jonathan Crush. "Personal Narratives As Interactive Texts: Collecting and Interpreting Migrant Life-Histories." *The Professional Geographer,* 45 (Feb. 1993): 84–94.

Miller, Joseph, ed. *The African Past Speaks: Essays on Oral Tradition and History.* Folkstone, UK: 1980.

Mirza, Sarah and Margaret Strobel, eds. *Three Swahili Women: Life Histories from Mombassa, Kenya.* Bloomington: Indiana University Press, 1989.

Moore, Donald and Richard Roberts. "Listening for Silences." *History in Africa,* 17 (1990): 319–25.

Moore, Sally Falk. *Social Facts and Fabrications: "Customary" law on Kilimanjaro, 1880–1980.* Cambridge, UK: Cambridge University Press, 1986.

Murray, Colin. *Black Mountain: Land, Class and Power in the Eastern Orange Free State 1880s–1980s.* Johannesburg: Witwatersrand University Press for the International African Institute, 1992.

———. *Families Divided: The Impact of Migrant Labour in Lesotho.* Cambridge, UK: Cambridge University Press, 1981.

Ngubane, Harriet Sibisi. "Marriage, Affinity and the Ancestral Realm: Zulu Marriage in Female Perspective." In *Essays on African Marriage in Southern Africa,* edited by Eileen Jensen Krige and John L. Comaroff, 84–95. Cape Town: Juta, 1981.

Oboler, Regina Smith. *Women, Power, and Economic Change: The Nandi of Kenya.* Stanford: Stanford University Press, 1985.

Palmer, Robin and Neil Parsons, eds. *The Roots of Rural Poverty in Central and Southern Africa.* Berkeley and Los Angeles: University of California Press, 1977.

Parpart, Jane. "Sexuality and Power on the Zambian Copperbelt: 1926–1964." In *Patriarchy and Class: African Women in the Home and the Workforce,* edited by Sharon Stichter and Jane Parpart, 115–38. Boulder: Westview Press, 1988.

———. "The Household and the Mine Shaft: Gender and Class Struggles on the Zambian Copperbelt, 1926–64." *Journal of Southern African Studies,* 13, no. 1 (Oct. 1986): 36–56.

Parpart, Jane L. and Kathleen Staudt, eds. *Women and the State in Africa.* Boulder: Lynne Rienner, 1989.

Platzky, Laurine and Cherryl Walker. *The Surplus People: Forced Removals in South Africa*. Johannesburg: Ravan Press, 1985.

Ranger, Terence. "The Invention of Tradition Revisited." In *Legitimacy and the State in Africa: Essays in Honour of A.H.M. Kirk-Greene*, edited by Terence Ranger and Olufemi Vaughan, 62–111. Houndmills, UK: Macmillan, 1993.

———. "The Invention of Tradition in Colonial Africa." In *The Invention of Tradition*, edited by Eric Hobsbawm and Terrence Ranger, 211–62. Cambridge, UK: Cambridge University Press, 1983.

Roberts, Richard. "Text and Testimony in the *Tribunal de Premiere Instance*, Dakar, during the Early Twentieth Century." *Journal of African History*, 31, no. 3 (1990): 447–63.

———. "Women's Work and Women's Property: Household Social Relations in the Maraka Textile Industry of the Nineteenth Century." *Comparative Studies in Society and History*, 26, no. 2 (1984): 229–50.

Robertson, Claire and Iris Berger, eds. *Women and Class in Africa*. New York: Africana, 1986.

Ross, Robert. *Cape of Torments: Slavery and Resistance in South Africa*. London: Routledge and Kegan Paul, 1983.

"Rural Tenants and Land Rights." *AFRA News*, 29 (Aug./Sept. 1994): 13.

Schirmer, Stefan. "Land, Legislation and Labor Tenants: Resistance in Lydenburg, 1938." In *White Farms, Black Labor: The State and Agrarian Change in Southern Africa, 1910–50*, edited by Alan Jeeves and Jonathan Crush, 46–60. Portsmouth: Heinemann, 1997.

———. "Reactions to the State: The Impact of Farm Labour Policies in the Mid-Eastern Transvaal, 1955–1960." *South African Historical Journal*, 30 (May 1994): 61–84.

Schmidt, Elizabeth. *Peasants, Traders, and Wives: Shona Women in the History of Zimbabwe, 1870–1939*. Portsmouth: Heinemann, 1992.

———. "Negotiated Spaces and Contested Terrain: Men, Women and the Law in Colonial Zimbabwe, 1890–1939." *Journal of Southern African Studies*, 16, no. 4 (Dec. 1990): 622–48.

Scott, James. *Domination and the Arts of Resistance: Hidden Transcripts*. New Haven: Yale University Press, 1992.

———. *Weapons of the Weak: Everyday Forms of Peasant Resistance*. New Haven: Yale University Press, 1985.

Scully, Pamela. *Liberating the Family? Gender and British Slave Emancipation in the Rural Western Cape, South Africa, 1823–1853*. Portsmouth: Heinemann, 1997.

———. "Rape, Race and Colonial Culture: The Sexual Politics of Identity in the Nineteenth Century Cape Colony, South Africa." *American Historical Review*, 100, no. 2 (Apr. 1995): 335–59.

Simkins, Charles. "African Population, Employment and Incomes on Farms Outside the Reserves." Paper no. 25, 2nd Carnegie Inquiry into Poverty and Development in Southern Africa. Cape Town: University of Cape Town, 1984.

Simons, H.J. *African Women: Their Legal Status in South Africa*. London: C. Hurst, 1968.

Sithole, Jabulani. "Tale of Two Boundaries: Land Disputes and the *Izimpi Zemibango* in the Umlazi Location of the Pinetown District, 1920–1936." *South African Historical Journal*, 37 (1997): 78–106.

Slater, Henry. "Land, Labour and Capitalism: The Natal Land and Colonisation Company, 1860–1948." *Journal of African History*, 16, no. 2 (1975): 257–83.

Smith, R.H. "Native Farm Labour in Natal." *South African Journal of Economics*, 9 (1941): 154–75.

Stafford, W.G. *Native Law As Practised in Natal*. Johannesburg: Witwatersrand University Press, 1935.

Stern, Steve J. *The Secret History of Gender: Women, Men, and Power in Late Colonial Mexico*. Chapel Hill: University of North Carolina Press, 1995.

Stichter, Sharon B. and Jane L. Parpart, eds. *Patriarchy and Class*. Boulder: Westview Press, 1988.

Sundkler, Bengt. *Bantu Prophets in South Africa*, 2nd ed. London: Oxford University Press, 1961.

Taylor, William. *Drinking, Homicide and Rebellion in Colonial Mexican Villages*. Stanford: Stanford University Press, 1979.

Thompson, Leonard. *A History of South Africa*, 2nd ed. New Haven: Yale University Press, 1995.

Transvaal Rural Action Committee (TRAC). *A toehold on the land*. Johannesburg: TRAC, 1988.

Van Onselen, Charles. *The Seed Is Mine: The Life of Kas Maine, A South African Sharecropper, 1894–1985*. New York: Hill and Wang, 1996.

————. "The Reconstruction of a Rural Life from Oral Testimony: Critical Notes on the Methodology Employed in the Study of a Black South African Sharecropper." *Journal of Peasant Studies*, 20, no. 3 (Apr. 1993): 494–514.

————. "The Social and Economic Underpinning of Paternalism and Violence on the Maize Farms of the South-Western Transvaal, 1900–1950." *Journal of Historical Sociology*, 5, no. 2 (Jun. 1992): 127–60.

————. "Race and Class in the South African Countryside: Cultural Osmosis and Social Relations in the Sharecropping Economy of the South-Western Transvaal, 1900–1950." *American Historical Review*, 95, no. 1 (Feb. 1990): 99–123.

————. *Chibaro: African Mine Labour in Southern Rhodesia 1900–1933*. London: Pluto Press, 1976.

Vansina, Jan. *Oral Tradition As History*. Madison: University of Wisconsin Press, 1985.

————. *Oral Tradition: A Study in Historical Methodology*, translated by H.M. Wright. London: Routledge and Kegan Paul, 1965.

Walker, Cherryl. "Women and Gender in Southern Africa to 1945: An Overview." In *Women and Gender in Southern Africa to 1945*, 1–32. Cape Town: David Philip, 1990.

————. "Gender and the Development of the Migrant Labour System c.1850–1930." In *Women and Gender in Southern Africa to 1945*, 168–96. Cape Town: David Philip, 1990.

Watts, Michael. "Living under Contract: Work, Production Politics, and the Manufacture of Discontent in a Peasant Society." In *Reworking Modernity:*

Capitalisms and Symbolic Discontent, edited by Alan Predd and Michael Watts, 65–105. New Brunswick, NJ: Rutgers University Press, 1992.

Wells, Julia. *We Now Demand! The History of Women's Resistance to Pass Laws in South Africa*. Johannesburg, Witwatersrand University Press, 1993.

Welsh, David. *The Roots of Segregation: Native Policy in Colonial Natal, 1845–1910*. Cape Town: Oxford University Press, 1971.

White, Luise. *The Comforts of Home: Prostitution in Colonial Nairobi*. Chicago: University of Chicago Press, 1990.

Williams, Gavin. "Transforming Labour Tenants." In *Land, Labour and Livelihoods in Rural South Africa: Vol. 2, Kwazulu/ Natal and Northern Province*, edited by M. Lipton and F. Ellis, 215–38. Durban: Indicator Press, 1996.

Wolpe, H. "Capitalism and Cheap Labour-Power in South Africa: From Segregation to Apartheid." *Economy and Society*, 1 (1972): 425–56.

Worger, William H. *South Africa's City of Diamonds: Mine Workers and Monopoly Capitalism in Kimberley, 1867–1895*. New Haven: Yale University Press, 1987.

Wright, John. "Control of Women's Labour in the Zulu Kingdom." In *Before and after Shaka: Papers in Nguni History*, edited by J.B. Peires, 82–99. Grahamstown, South Africa: Institute of Social and Economic Research, 1981.

Wright, John and Carolyn Hamilton. "The Making of the Amalala: Ethnicity, Ideology and Relations of Subordination in a Precolonial Context." *South African Historical Journal*, 22 (Nov. 1990): 3–23.

———. "Traditions and Transformations: The Phongolo-Mzimkhulu Region in the Late Eighteenth and Early Nineteenth Centuries." In *Natal and Zululand from Earliest Times to 1910: A New History*, edited by Andrew Duminy and Bill Guest, 49–82. Pietermaritzburg: University of Natal Press, 1989.

Wright, J.B. and C. de B. Webb, eds. *The James Stuart Archive*, vol. 3. Pietermaritzburg: University of Natal Press, 1982.

Wright, Marcia. *Strategies of Slaves and Women: Life Stories from East/Central Africa*. New York: Lilian Barber Press, 1993.

———. "Justice Women and the Social Order in Abercorn, Northeastern Rhodesia, 1897–1903." In *African Women and the Law: Historical Perspectives*. Edited by Margaret Jean Hay and Marcia Wright, 33–50. Vol. 7 of *Boston University Papers on Africa*. Boston: Boston University, 1982.

THESES AND UNPUBLISHED PAPERS

Edley, David W.M. "Population, Poverty and Politics: A Study of Some Aspects of the Depression in Greater Durban." M.A. thesis, University of Natal, Durban, 1983.

Etherington, Norman. "South Africa's Bantustans: A Legacy of African Resistance to Colonial Rule." Paper presented at the African Studies Association annual meeting, Chicago, 1998.

Guy, Jeff. "An Accommodation of Patriarchs: Theophilus Shepstone and the Foundations of the System of Native Administration in Natal." Paper presented at Conference on Masculinities in Southern Africa, University of Natal, Durban, July, 1997.

Hamilton, Carolyn. "Ideology, Oral Tradition and the Struggle for Power in the Early Zulu State." M.A. thesis, University of the Witwatersrand, 1985.

Lambert, John. "Africans on White-Owned Farms in the Mist Belt of Natal, c.1850–1906." Paper no. 4 presented at Workshop on Regionalism and Restructuring in Natal, University of Natal, Durban, 28–31 Jan., 1988.

———. "Africans in Natal, 1880–1899: Continuity, Change and Crisis in a Rural Society." Ph.D. dissertation, University of South Africa, 1986.

Lane, Timothy. "'Pernicious Practice': Witchcraft Eradication and History in Northern Province, South Africa, c.1880–1930." Ph.D. dissertation, Stanford University, 1999.

———. "'A Reasonable Amount of Harmony': Conflict, Witchcraft Accusation, and Violence in Rural Households, 1910–1920." Paper presented at Symposium on Law, Colonialism and Human Rights in Africa, 8 May 1999.

Mazower, Benjamin L. "Agriculture, Farm Labour and the State in the Natal Mid lands, 1940–60." M.A. thesis, University of Cape Town, 1991.

McClendon, Thomas. "The Chunu-Thembu Blues: The Media and Historicizing Ethnicity in South Africa." Paper presented at Berkeley-Stanford Joint Center for African Studies annual conference, Apr. 1994.

Miescher, Stephan. "Gender, Personhood, and Legal Consciousness in Colonial Ghana." Paper presented at Symposium on Law, Colonialism, and Human Rights in Africa, Stanford University, 8 May 1999.

Moore, Donald S. "Contesting Terrain in Zimbabwe's Eastern Highlands. The Cultural Politics of Place, Identity, and Resource Struggles." Ph.D. dissertation, Stanford University, 1995.

Posel, Deborah. "Traditions of Power and the Power of Tradition: The State and African Customary Marriage in South Africa." Paper presented at History Workshop, University of the Witwatersrand, 13–15 Jul. 1994.

Redding, Sean. "The Making of a South African Town: Social and Economic Change in Umtata, 1870–1950." Ph.D. dissertation, Yale University, 1987.

Rowlands, M. "The Zulu Family in Transition: A Study of Some of the Social and Moral Problems of African Adaptation to White Colonial Society as Revealed in the Evidence Led before the Colony of Natal Native Affairs Commission of 1906–7." B.A. honors thesis, University of Natal, Pietermaritzburg, 1973.

Streak, Judith. "Perceptions and Conflict: White Farmers, Labour Shortages, Tenancy and Labour Control in Northern and Mid-Natal during the Late 1930s." B.A. honors thesis, University of Natal, Pietermaritzburg, 1990.

Worger, William. "Law at the Margins of Empire." Paper presented at African Studies Association Annual Meeting, San Francisco, November, 1996.

Wright, John. "The Dynamics of Power and Conflict in the Thukela-Mzimkhulu Region in the Late 18th and Early 19th Centuries: A Critical Reconstruction." Ph.D. dissertation, University of the Witwatersrand, 1989.

INDEX

About the Author

THOMAS V. McCLENDON is Assistant Professor of History at South-western University, Georgetown, Texas.